The Path of Divine Love "Neter Merri"

"Give thyself to GOD, keep thou thyself daily for God; and let tomorrow be as today."

"Seekest thou God, thou seekest or the Beautiful. One is the Path that leadeth unto It Devotion joined with Wisdom."

"Have devotion of purpose"

"O behold with thine eye God's plans. Devote thyself to adore God's name. It is God who giveth Souls to millions of forms, and God magnifyeth whosoever magnifyeth God."

O ye gods who are in heaven.
O ye gods who are on the earth.
O ye gods who are in the Netherworld).
O ye gods who are in the abyss.
O ye gods who are in the service of the deep.
We follow the Lord, the Lord of Love.

—Ancient Egyptian Proverbs

Fifth Edition - Expanded

Neter Merri

PO.Box 570459
Miami, Florida, 33257
(305) 378-6253 Fax: (305) 378-6253

First U.S. edition 1996

© 1997 Second Edition By Muata Ashby
© 2000 Third Edition By Muata Ashby
© 2002 Fourth Edition By Muata Ashby
© 2003 Fourth Edition By Muata Ashby
© 2006 Fifth Edition By Muata Ashby

All rights reserved. No part of this book may be used or reproduced in any manner whatsoever without written permission (address above) except in the case of brief quotations embodied in critical articles and reviews. All inquiries may be addressed to the address above.

Ashby, Muata
The Mystic Path of Divine Love -ISBN 1-884564-11-9

Library of Congress Cataloging in Publication Data

1 Yoga 2 Egyptian Philosophy, 3 Eastern Philosophy, 4 Esoterism, 5 Meditation, 6 Self Help.

Cruzian Mystic Books

Also by Muata Ashby

Egyptian Yoga: The Philosophy of Enlightenment
Initiation Into Egyptian Yoga: The Secrets of Sheti
Egyptian Proverbs: Tempt Tchaas,
Mystical Wisdom Teachings and Meditations
The Egyptian Yoga Exercise Workout Book
Mysticism of Ushet Rekhat: Worship of the Divine Mother

For more listings see the back section.

Sema
Institute of Yoga

Sema (☥) is an Ancient Egyptian word and symbol meaning union. The Sema Institute is dedicated to the propagation of the universal teachings of spiritual evolution which relate to the union of humanity and the union of all things within the universe. It is a non-denominational organization which recognizes the unifying principles in all spiritual and religious systems of evolution throughout the world. Our primary goals are to provide the wisdom of ancient spiritual teachings in books, courses and other forms of communication. Secondly, to provide expert instruction and training in the various yogic disciplines including Ancient Egyptian Philosophy, Christian Gnosticism, Indian Philosophy and modern science. Thirdly, to promote world peace and Universal Love.

A primary focus of our tradition is to identify and acknowledge the yogic principles within all religions and to relate them to each other in order to promote their deeper understanding as well as to show the essential unity of purpose and the unity of all living beings and nature within the whole of existence.

The Institute is open to all who believe in the principles of peace, non-violence and spiritual emancipation regardless of sex, race, or creed.

About the author and editor:
Dr. Muata Abhaya Ashby

About The Author

Reginald Muata Ashby holds a Doctor of Philosophy Degree in Religion, and a Doctor of Divinity Degree in Holistic Healing. He is also a Pastoral Counselor and Teacher of Yoga Philosophy and Discipline. Dr. Ashby is an adjunct faculty member of the American Institute of Holistic Theology and an ordained Minister. Dr. Ashby has studied advanced Jnana, Bhakti and Kundalini Yogas under the guidance of Swami Jyotirmayananda, a world renowned Yoga Master. He has studied the mystical teachings of Ancient Egypt for many years and is the creator of the Egyptian Yoga concept. He is also the founder of the Sema Institute, an organization dedicated to the propagation of the teachings of Yoga and mystical spirituality.

Karen Clarke-Ashby, "Vijaya-Asha", is the wife and spiritual partner of Muata. She is an independent researcher, practitioner and teacher of Yoga, a Doctor in the Sciences and a Pastoral Counselor, author of Yoga Mystic Metaphors, the editor of Egyptian Proverbs and Egyptian Yoga by Muata.☥

Sema Institute
P.O. Box 570459, Miami, Fla. 33257 (305) 378-6253, Fax (305) 378-6253
©2002

TABLE OF CONTENTS

FIFTH EDITION - EXPANDED	1
Author's Foreword	8
EARLY BEGINNINGS: THE FIRST RELIGION	11
A Long History	11
Where Was Shetaut Neter Practiced in Ancient Times?	13
The Land of Ancient Egypt-Nile Valley	14
The Term Kamit and the Origins of the Ancient Egyptians	15
The Term Kamit and the Origins of the Ancient Egyptians	16
Ancient Origins	16
The Hieroglyphic Text for the Name Qamit	17
When Was Neterian Religion Practiced?	18
OLD KINGDOM PERIOD	19
MIDDLE KINGDOM PERIOD	19
NEW KINGDOM PERIOD	20
WHO WERE THE ANCIENT EGYPTIANS AND WHAT IS YOGA PHILOSOPHY?	21
Ancient Kemetic Terms and Ancient Greek Terms	24
WHY IS IT NECESSARY TO STUDY RELIGION?	25
THE FUNDAMENTAL PRINCIPLES OF NETERIAN RELIGION AND THE DISCIPLINE OF DIVINE LOVE	**26**
"The practice of the Shedy disciplines leads to knowing oneself and the Divine. This is called being True of Speech"	27
Neterian Great Truths	28
Summary of The Great Truths and the Shedy Paths to their Realization	30
The Spiritual Culture and the Purpose of Life: Shetaut Neter	31
SHETAUT NETER	31
WHO IS NETER IN KAMITAN RELIGION?	32
Sacred Scriptures of Shetaut Neter	33
NETER AND THE NETERU	34
THE NETERU	34
The Neteru and Their Temples	35
The Neteru and Their Interrelationships	37
Listening to the Teachings	38
The Anunian Tradition	39
The Theban Tradition	41
The Theban Tradition	41
The Goddess Tradition	42
The Aton Tradition	44
Akhnaton, Nefertiti and Daughters	44
THE GENERAL PRINCIPLES OF SHETAUT NETER	45
The Forces of Entropy	46
The Great Awakening of Neterian Religion	48
WHO WERE THE ANCIENT EGYPTIANS AND WHAT IS YOGA PHILOSOPHY?	49
WHAT IS YOGA PHILOSOPHY AND SPIRITUAL PRACTICE	51

INTRODUCTION TO EGYPTIAN YOGA ... 54

What is Egyptian Yoga? ... 57
The Sema Tawi of Wisdom ... 63
The Sema Tawi of Right Action ... 65
The Sema Tawi of Divine Love ... 66
The Sema Tawi of Meditation ... 68
The Yogic Postures in Ancient Egypt ... 71
The Sema Tawi of Tantrism ... 75

PART I: THE TEACHINGS WHICH LEAD TO THE UNFOLDMENT OF DIVINE LOVE ... 81

INTRODUCTION TO NETER MERRI ... 82
NETER AND THE NETERU ... 85
Ritualism Versus True Spiritual Work Which Leads To Real Transformation ... 88

PART II SEMA (YOGA) OF DEVOTION: BECOMING ONE WITH THE DIVINE ... 102

"THAT PERSON (THE ASPIRANT) IS BELOVED BY THE LORD." PMH, CH 4 ... 105
PURIFICATION OF THE HEART ... 106
THE OPENING OF THE WAY ... 109
THE ETERNAL WITNESS ... 110
Continuous meditation on the divine: the key to spiritual realization ... 113
The Movement Toward Divine Love ... 125
A COMPENDIUM OF THE AUSARIAN RESURRECTION MYTH ... 127
"placing the face to the ground" ... 138
Prostration is a sign of humility and reverence accorded to the Divine and exalted personalities. It is the act of reverencing the Divine image and what it represents. This allows the ego to be sublimated and the flow of divine grace showers over the aspirant, leading him/her to spiritual enlightenment. ... 138
The Supreme Offering ... 147
The Practice of Devotional Meditation ... 149
Waking up from the Dream of Ignorance and Awakening to the Wisdom of the Self ... 154
Incorporating the Rituals and Mystical Teachings Into Your Life ... 156
The Power of Divine Love ... 160
THE LOTUS IN KEMETIC (ANCIENT EGYPTIAN MYSTICAL PHILOSOPHY ... 162
Nefertem and the Mysticism of the Memphite Trinity ... 163
FORMS FOR THE WORSHIP OF THE DIVINE ... 166

THE DAILY PROGRAM OF THE PATH FO DIVINE LOVE	179
(UASH NETER)	179
Ritual of the Divine Embrace	*188*
Basic Daily Practice of Divine Worship (Uash) and Spiritual Disciplines (outline)	*192*
Recitations (Readings) for Ushet In The Morning	*195*
Recitations (Readings) for Ushet At Noontime	*199*
Recitations (Readings) for Ushet at Sunset	*201*
PERT M HERU CHAPTER 8(23)	202
INDEX	211
OTHER BOOKS FROM C M BOOKS	215
MUSIC BASED ON THE PRT M HRU AND OTHER KEMETIC TEXTS	221

Author's Foreword

In order to gain a feel for the special subject of this volume it will be necessary to gain a basic knowledge of who the originators of the philosophy of Devotion were. Beginning with the Ancient Egyptians who created the vast temples and pyramids as offerings to the Divine to the extensive literature of the Hymns to the Divine, the discipline of Divine Love, is one of the most powerful means for spiritual development. Further, in order to understand the path of Devotion it the Divine it is necessary to have a context. Devotion to God, the Path of Divine Love, is integral to all the spiritual traditions of Kamit and it is a necessary element for the success of any spiritual advancement. Therefore, we will begin with the essential elements of Ancient Egyptian History, The Spiritual Traditions of Ancient Kamit and Sema Tawi, Yoga Philosophy. Further on in the text we will present a summary of the Ancient Egyptian Myth of Asar (Osiris), which is the best example of Myth and its relation to Devotion on the Spiritual Path and the spiritual practices of Ancient Egypt.

Why is Devotion to the Divine so important?

"Seekest thou God, thou seekest for the Beautiful. One is the Path that leadeth unto It:

Devotion joined with Knowledge."

-Ancient Proverb of Shetaut Neter

Devotion to God allows the depth of the teaching to be revealed. Approaching the teaching intellectually will only promote a superficial understanding and therefore a limited attainment. Intellectual study allows the teaching to be thought about but this thinking process can become circular if the depth of the teaching is not approached. Devotion-Divine Love towards God allows the depth of the teaching to be approached. In essence the teaching must be felt as well as known. Intellectual knowledge must be augmented by feeling the teaching. The feeling aspect of the soul, when tapped into, does not allow the intellectual aspect to become deluded. In fact, it will plague the intellect with insecurities, torment the intellect with doubts until the right path is pursued this is the deeper conscience of a person-whose source is their own soul. This cannot occur of the divine feeling is dulled due to delusion and worldly desire. Devotional exercises and rituals allow the intellectual teaching to be experience as well as thought.

"O behold with thine eye God's plans. Devote thyself to adore God's name. It is God who giveth Souls to millions of forms, and God magnifyeth whosoever magnifieth God."

-Ancient Proverb of Shetaut Neter

Super-conscious state – in order for the process of spiritual evolution to occur there must be experience of the superconscious state of mind. The mind must experience going beyond the bounds of its own constrictive concepts and desires and the world of time and space. Otherwise, the teaching and the feeling of the spiritual process will remain short of the highest attainment no matter how pious the person may be or how elevated the mind and personality may appear to be. All the disciplines lead to a meditative experience in which time and space are transcended and all-encompassing, eternal existence and unlimited expanded consciousness is discovered. First in small measure and eventually in full splendor. Even a short glimpse which is merely a preview, unlocks lifetimes of mental fetterings and sparks the true awakening if the final phase of the march towards spiritual awakening.

Meditation is the key to opening the mind to the experience of superconsciousness and this can only be achieved when the mind and personality has been cleansed of delusion, passion, attachment for worldly objects and desires. This purity leads to spiritual strength and spiritual strength is the key factor needed to attain entry into the superconscious state. In order to attain the highest meditative state, concentration and extended practice of mental focus is required. Without mental purity, and peace concentration is impossible and the superconscious state will elude even the cleverest intellect.

Spiritual Strength – In order to succeed on the spiritual path an aspirant needs spiritual strength. Spiritual strength is the strength that emerges when the mind is freed of ignorance, delusion and passion. The ignorant, deluded and passionate mind is fettered by its conscious and subtle desires and misconceptions. The conscious desires lead to worldly pursuits but this process, being unfulfilled, leaves residues of unfulfilled desire and also produces new subtle desires for other pursuits (if this desire did not work, maybe another will-etc. For Example: the deluded mind may reason thus- If a blue car did not make me happy, maybe a red one will) and these all become lodged in the unconscious level of mind. This constitutes a continued fettering of the mind in the present and in the future. These fetter the minds power because each subtle desire locks a portion of will power with itself in the unconscious level of mind. So even a person who appears to be free of desires may harbor these in the unconscious mind and thereby be weak willed. Such a person cannot resist worldly desires, nor can they sit still for meditation because thoughts constantly emerge to disturb the mind and even if thought do not seem to be emerging at some particular time there are energy disturbances throughout the body and there is illusory discomfort and the person claims they cannot succeed in meditation. So mental restlessness due to subtle desires, or energies must be resolved (cleansed and transcended by the mind) in order to succeed on the spiritual path. This is done by

        a-practice of devotion to god
        b- practice of right action
        c- practice of dispassion and detachment for the world
        d- practice of attachment to the teaching
        e- repeated effort in the above (a-d) until there is ultimate success

Desires are of three types: Heavenly (Maatian), Worldly (Un-Maatian) and mixed. Those who seek success on the spiritual path must turn away from the worldly to the mixed and then from the mixed to the Divine. When Maatian (principles of right action based on truth) actions are practiced the personality becomes purified, the mind becomes unburdened from vises and egoistic tendencies. Then the personality is capable of understanding and experiencing the higher consciousness talked about in the teachings. Therefore, desire the for worldly attainments but be replaced with desire for spiritual attainments in the form of increasing Divine Love, increasing dispassion and increasing peace and desire to study the teachings and be in the company of those who espouse it. Thus, spiritual evolution entails turning away from worldly desire and towards desire to attain spiritual awakening. Therefore, desire is not the problem, what is the problem is what is desired. The right desire leads to freedom and enlightenment. The wrong desire leads to ignorance, delusion, fettered bondage to the world and its accompanying virtually boundless source of human suffering, unfulfillment and sorrow.

<u>Success on the Path of Devine Love:</u> In order to succeed on the spiritual path it is necessary to begin with Devotion to God with Bes – a concrete form. Devotion to God in the abstract nt per, is for the advanced practice of higher initiates. Therefore an aspirant should choose a form that captivates the interest of the aspirant, and then that form is to be worshipped, studied and offerings should be made to that form to propitiate Divine Grace. Then there will be an opening to the higher possibilities of the teaching.

Early Beginnings: The First Religion

Shetaut Neter is the Ancient Egyptian Religion and Philosophy. Ancient Egypt was the first and most ancient civilization to create a religious system that was complete with all three stages of religion, as well as an advanced spiritual philosophy of righteousness, called Maat Philosophy, that also had secular dimensions. Several temple systems were developed in Kamit; they were all related. The pre-Judaic/Islamic religions that the later Jewish and Muslim religions drew from in order to create their religions developed out of these, ironically enough, only to later repudiate the source from whence they originated. In any case, the Great Sphinx remains the oldest known religious monument in history that denotes high culture and civilization as well. Ancient Egypt and Nubia produced the oldest religious systems and their contact with the rest of the world led to the proliferation of advanced religion and spiritual philosophy. People who were practicing simple animism, shamanism, nature based religions and witchcraft were elevated to the level of not only understanding the nature of the Supreme Being, but also attaining salvation from the miseries of life through the effective discovery of that Transcendental being, not as an untouchable aloof Spirit, but as the very essence of all that exists.

NETERIANISM 10.000 B.C.E. – 2001 A.C.E.

A Long History

For a period spanning over 10,000 years the Neterian religion served the society of ancient Kamit. It is hard to comprehend the vastness of time that is encompassed by Ancient Egyptian culture, religion and philosophy. Yet the evidence is there to be seen by all. It has been collected and presented in the book African Origins of Civilization, Religion and Yoga Philosophy. That volume will serve as the historical record for the Neterian religion and as record of its legacy to all humanity. It serves as the basis or foundation for the work contained in all the other books in this series that have been created to elucidate on the teachings and traditions as well as disciplines of the varied Neterian religious traditions.

The book African Origins of Civilization, Religion and Yoga Philosophy, and the other volumes on the specific traditions detail the philosophies and disciplines that should be practiced by those who want to follow the path of Hm or Hmt, to be practitioners of the Shetaut Neter religion and builders of the Neterian faith worldwide.

The Path of Divine Love

Where Was Shetaut Neter Practiced in Ancient Times?

Below left: A map of North East Africa showing the location of the land of Ta-Meri **or** Kamit, **also known as Ancient Egypt and South of it is located the land which in modern times is called Sudan.**

Egypt IS In Africa and Ancient Egyptian Religion and Philosophy are African Religion and African Philosophy

The Land of Ancient Egypt-Nile Valley

The cities wherein the major theologies of Neterianism developed were:

A. Sais (temple of Net),

B. Anu (Heliopolis- temple of Ra),

C. Men-nefer or Hetkaptah (Memphis, temple of Ptah),

D. Sakkara (Pyramid Texts),

E. Akhet-Aton (City of Akhenaton, temple of Aton),

F. Abdu (temple of Asar),

G. Denderah (temple of Hetheru),

H. Waset (Thebes, temple of Amun),

I. Edfu (temple of Heru),

J. Philae (temple of Aset). The cities wherein the theology of the Trinity of Asar-Aset-Heru was developed were Anu, Abydos, Philae, Edfu, Denderah and Edfu.

The Path of Divine Love

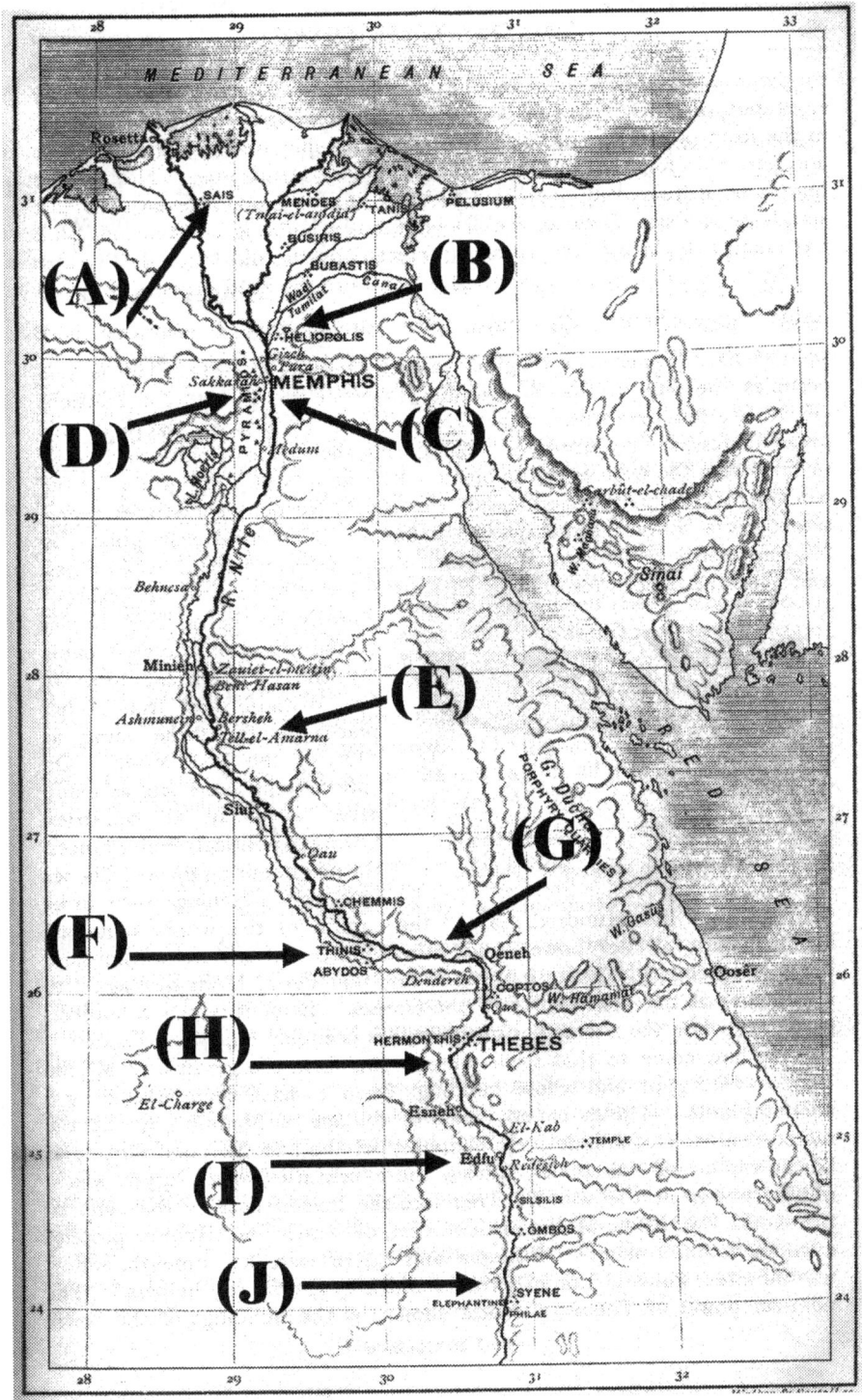

The Term Kamit and the Origins of the Ancient Egyptians

Ancient Origins

The Ancient Egyptians recorded that they were originally a colony of Ethiopians from the south who came to the north east part of Africa. The term "Ethiopian," "Nubian," and "Kushite" all relate to the same peoples who lived south of Egypt. In modern times, the land which was once known as Nubia ("Land of Gold"), is currently known as the Sudan, and the land even further south and east towards the coast of east Africa is referred to as Ethiopia (see map above).

Recent research has shown that the modern Nubian word kiji means "fertile land, dark gray mud, silt, or black land." Since the sound of this word is close to the Ancient Egyptian name Kish or Kush, referring to the land south of Egypt, it is believed that the name Kush also meant "the land of dark silt" or "the black land." Kush was the Ancient Egyptian name for Nubia. Nubia, the black land, is the Sudan of today. Sudan is an Arabic translation of sûd which is the plural form of aswad, which means "black," and ân which means "of the." So, Sudan means "of the blacks." In the modern Nubian language, nugud means "black." Also, nuger, nugur, and nubi mean "black" as well. All of this indicates that the words Kush, Nubia, and Sudan all mean the same thing — the "black land" and/or the "land of the blacks."[1] As we will see, the differences between the term Kush and the term Kam (Qamit - name for Ancient Egypt in the Ancient Egyptian language) relate more to the same meaning but different geographical locations.

As we have seen, the terms "Ethiopia," "Nubia," "Kush" and "Sudan" all refer to "black land" and/or the "land of the blacks." In the same manner we find that the name of Egypt which was used by the Ancient Egyptians also means "black land" and/or the "land of the blacks." The hieroglyphs below reveal the Ancient Egyptian meaning of the words related to the name of their land. It is clear that the meaning of the word Qamit is equivalent to the word Kush as far as they relate to "black land" and that they also refer to a differentiation in geographical location, i.e. Kush is the "black land of the south" and Qamit is the "black land of the north." Both terms denote the primary quality that defines Africa, "black" or "Blackness" (referring to the land and its people). The quality of blackness and the consonantal sound of K or Q as well as the reference to the land are all aspects of commonality between the Ancient Kushitic and Kamitan terms.

---

[1] "Nubia," Microsoft® Encarta® Africana. © 1999 Microsoft Corporation. All rights reserved.

The Path of Divine Love

The Hieroglyphic Text for the Name Qamit

Qamit - Ancient Egypt

Qamit - blackness – black

Qamit - literature of Ancient Egypt – scriptures

Qamiu or variant -

Ancient Egyptians-people of the black land.

When Was Neterian Religion Practiced?

c. 65,000 B.C.E. Paleolithic – Nekhen (Hierakonpolis)
c. 10,000 B.C.E. Neolithic – period

PREDYNASTIC PERIOD

c. 10,500 B.C.E.-7,000 B.C.E. Creation of the Great Sphinx Modern archeological accepted dates – Sphinx means Hor-m-akhet or Heru (Heru) in the horizon. This means that the King is one with the Spirit, Ra as an enlightened person possessing an animal aspect (lion) and illuminated intellect. Anunian Theology – Ra - Serpent Power Spirituality

c. 10,000 B.C.E.-5,500 B.C.E. The Sky GOD- Realm of Light-Day – NETER Androgynous – All-encompassing –Absolute, Nameless Being, later identified with Ra-Herakhti (Sphinx)

>7,000 B.C.E. Kemetic Myth and Theology present in architecture

OLD KINGDOM PERIOD

5500+ B.C.E. to 600 A.C.E. Amun -Ra - Ptah (Heru) – Amenit - Rai – Sekhmet (male and female Trinity-Complementary Opposites)

5500+ B.C.E. Memphite Theology – Ptah

5500+ B.C.E. Hermopolitan Theology- Djehuti

5500+ B.C.E. The Asarian Resurrection Theology - Asar

5500+B.C.E. The Goddess Principle- Theology, Aset-Hetheru-Net-Mut-Sekhmet-Buto

5500 B.C.E. (Dynasty 1) Beginning of the Dynastic Period (Unification of Upper and Lower Egypt)

5000 B.C.E. (5th Dynasty) Pyramid Texts - Egyptian Book of Coming Forth By Day - 42 Precepts of MAAT and codification of the Pre-Dynastic theologies (Pre-Dynastic period: 10,000 B.C.E.-5,500 B.C.E.) Coming Forth By Day (Book of the Dead)

4241 B.C.E. The Pharaonic (royal) calendar based on the Sothic system (star Sirius) was in use.

MIDDLE KINGDOM PERIOD

3000 B.C.E. WISDOM TEXTS-Precepts of Ptahotep, Instructions of Any, Instructions of Amenemope, Etc.

2040 B.C.E.-1786 B.C.E. COFFIN TEXTS Coming Forth By Day (Book of the Dead)

1800 B.C.E.-Theban Theology - Amun

NEW KINGDOM PERIOD

1570 B.C.E.-Books of Coming Forth By Day (Book of the Dead)

1353 B.C.E. Atonism- Non-dualist Pre-Dynastic Philosophy was redefined by Akhenaton.

712-657 B.C.E. The Nubian Dynasty

657 B.C.E. - 450 A.C.E. This is the last period of Ancient Egyptian culture which saw several invasions by foreigners from Asia Minor (Assyrians, Persians) and Europe (Greeks and Romans) and finally the closing of the temples, murdering of priests and priestesses, the forced conversion to the foreign religions and destruction of Neterian holy sites by Christians and Muslims. The teaching went dormant at this time until the 20th century A.C.E.

Who Were the Ancient Egyptians and What is Yoga Philosophy?

The Ancient Egyptian religion (Shetaut Neter), language and symbols provide the first "historical" record of Yoga Philosophy and Religious literature. Egyptian Yoga is what has been commonly referred to by Egyptologists as Egyptian "Religion" or "Mythology", but to think of it as just another set of stories or allegories about a long lost civilization is to completely miss the greatest secret of human existence. Yoga, in all of its forms and disciplines of spiritual development, was practiced in Egypt earlier than anywhere else in history. This unique perspective from the highest philosophical system which developed in Africa over seven thousand years ago provides a new way to look at life, religion, the discipline of psychology and the way to spiritual development leading to spiritual Enlightenment. Egyptian mythology, when understood as a system of Yoga (union of the individual soul with the Universal Soul or Supreme Consciousness), gives every individual insight into their own divine nature and also a deeper insight into all religions and Yoga systems.

Diodorus Siculus (Greek Historian) writes in the time of Augustus (first century B.C.):

"Now the Ethiopians, as historians relate, were the first of all men and the proofs of this statement, they say, are manifest. For that they did not come into their land as immigrants from abroad but were the natives of it and so justly bear the name of autochthones **(sprung from the soil itself)**, is, they maintain, conceded by practically all men..."

"They also say that the Egyptians are colonists sent out by the Ethiopians, Asar having been the leader of the colony. For, speaking generally, what is now Egypt, they maintain, was not land, but sea, when in the beginning the universe was being formed; afterwards, however, as the Nile during the times of its inundation carried down the mud from Ethiopia, land was gradually built up from the deposit...And the larger parts of the customs of the Egyptians are, they hold, Ethiopian, the colonists still preserving their ancient manners. For instance, the belief that their kings are Gods, the very special attention which they pay to their burials, and many other matters of a similar nature, are Ethiopian practices, while the shapes of their statues and the forms of their letters are Ethiopian; for of the two kinds of writing which the Egyptians have, that which is known as popular **(demotic)** is learned by everyone, while that which is called sacred **(hieratic)**, is understood only by the priests of the Egyptians, who learnt it from their Fathers as one of the things which are not divulged, but among the Ethiopians, everyone uses these forms of letters. Furthermore, the orders of the priests, they maintain, have much the same position among both peoples; for all are clean who are engaged in the service of the gods, keeping themselves shaven, like the Ethiopian priests, and having the same dress and form of staff, which is shaped like a plough and is carried by their kings who wear high felt hats which end in a knob in the top and are circled by the serpents which they call asps; and this symbol appears to carry the thought that it will be the lot who shall dare to attack the king to encounter death-carrying stings. Many other things are told by them concerning their own antiquity and the colony which they sent out that became the Egyptians, but about this there is no special need of our writing anything."

The Ancient Egyptian texts state:
"Our people originated at the base of the mountain of the Moon,
at the origin of the Nile river."

"KMT"
"Egypt", "Burnt", "Land of Blackness","Land of the Burnt People."

KMT (Ancient Egypt) is situated close to Lake Victoria in present day Africa. This is the same location where the earliest human remains have been found, in the land currently known as Ethiopia-Tanzania. Recent genetic technology as reported in the new encyclopedias and leading news publications has revealed that all peoples of the world originated in Africa and migrated to other parts of the world prior to the last Ice Age 40,000 years ago. Therefore, as of this time, genetic testing has revealed that all humans are alike. The earliest bone fossils which have been found in many parts of the world were those of the African Grimaldi type. During the Ice Age, it was not possible to communicate or to migrate. Those trapped in specific locations were subject to the regional forces of weather and climate. Less warmer climates required less body pigment, thereby producing lighter pigmented people who now differed from their dark-skinned ancestors. After the Ice Age when travel was possible, these light-skinned people who had lived in the northern, colder regions of harsh weather during the Ice Age period moved back to the warmer climates of their ancestors, and mixed with the people there who had remained dark-skinned, thereby producing the Semitic colored people. "Semite" means mixture of skin color shades.

Therefore, there is only one human race who, due to different climatic and regional exposure, changed to a point where there seemed to be different "types" of people. Differences were noted with respect to skin color, hair texture, customs, languages, and with respect to the essential nature (psychological and emotional makeup) due to the experiences each group had to face and overcome in order to survive.

From a philosophical standpoint, the question as to the origin of humanity is redundant when it is understood that <u>ALL</u> come from one origin which some choose to call the "Big Bang" and others "The Supreme Being."

> **"Thou makest the color of the skin of one race to be different from that of another, but however many may be the varieties of mankind, it is thou that makes them all to live."**
> —Ancient Egyptian Proverb from The Hymns of Amun

> **"Souls, Heru, son, are of the self-same nature, since they came from the same place where the Creator modeled them; nor male nor female are they. Sex is a thing of bodies not of Souls."**
> —Ancient Egyptian Proverb from The teachings of Aset to Heru

Historical evidence proves that Ethiopia-Nubia already had Kingdoms at least 300 years before the first Kingdom-Pharaoh of Egypt.

"Ancient Egypt was a colony of Nubia - Ethiopia. ...Asar having been the leader of the colony..."

"And upon his return to Greece, they gathered around and asked, "tell us about this great land of the Blacks called Ethiopia." And Herodotus said, "There are two great Ethiopian nations, one in Sind (India) and the other in Egypt."

Recorded by Egyptian high priest Manetho **(300 B.C.)**
also Recorded by Diodorus **(Greek historian 100 B.C.)**

The pyramids themselves however, cannot be dated, but indications are that they existed far back in antiquity. The Pyramid Texts (hieroglyphics inscribed on pyramid walls) and Coffin Texts (hieroglyphics inscribed on coffins) speak authoritatively on the constitution of the human spirit, the vital Life Force along the human spinal cord (known in India as "Kundalini"), the immortality of the soul, reincarnation and the law of Cause and Effect (known in India as the Law of Karma).

Below., Egyptian man and woman-(tomb of Payry) 18th Dynasty displaying the naturalistic style (as people really appeared in ancient times).

Ancient Kemetic Terms and Ancient Greek Terms

In keeping with the spirit of the culture of Kemetic Spirituality, in this volume we will use the Kemetic names for the divinities through which we will bring forth the Philosophy of the Prt M Hru. Therefore, the Greek name Osiris will be converted back to the Kemetic (Ancient Egyptian) Asar (Ausar), the Greek Isis to Aset (Auset), the Greek Nephthys to Nebthet, Anubis to Anpu or Apuat, Hathor to Hetheru, Thoth or Hermes to Djehuti, etc. (see the table below) Further, the term Ancient Egypt will be used interchangeably with "Kemit" ("Kamit"), or "Ta-Meri," as these are the terms used by the Ancient Egyptians to refer to their land and culture.

Kemetic (Ancient Egyptian) Names	Greek Names
Amun	Zeus
Ra	Helios
Ptah	Hephastos
Nut	Rhea
Geb	Kronos
Net	Athena
Khonsu	Heracles
Set	Ares or Typhon
Bast	Artemis
Uadjit	Leto
Asar (Ausar)	Osiris or Hades
Aset (Auset)	Isis or Demeter
Nebthet	Nephthys
Anpu or Apuat	Anubis
Hetheru	Hathor (Aphrodite)
Heru	Horus or Apollo
Djehuti	Thoth or Hermes
Maat	Astraea or Themis

Why is it Necessary to study Religion?

In order to fully understand the process of Kamitan Devotion it is necessary to have a basic understanding of Kamitan religion, as the two aspects of Ancient Egyptian-African culture are related. Devotional Love for the Divine in varied forms is integral to all the traditions of Kamit and it is essential to understand that Devotion is the Key to success on the spiritual path but devotion to what? An aspirant cannot devote to a philosophical teaching alone. In the beginning there must be a connection, to the higher principle of the spirit and this begins with devotion to the Divine with form and specific attributes that allow the mind to become interested, then devoted to that principle as represented in the divine form. The forms are not realities but principles which are accessible to the mind and as understanding increases the worship is to move to the abstract and transcendental form. Then that principle is discovered and united in the self and thereby an aspirant experiences the Divine.

The religion of Ancient Kamit incorporated several traditions, each of which enjoined a variation on the practice of divine worship and meditation based on the particular divinity of that tradition. However, it was always recognized that all the divinities are in reality aspects of the transcendental divinity which has neither shape nor form nor name. So just as in other African religions (see the book African Origins by Muata Ashby) the religion of Ancient Egypt (Shetaut Neter) is composed of an advanced system by which human beings can discover the transcendental divine.

Therefore, this first section of this book will present an overview of Shetaut Neter or Neterian religion (Neterianism) of ancient Egypt-Africa and also the Sema disciplines or what is in modern times refered to as "Yoga" that was practiced in ancient times and can be practiced today in order to advance on the path of Kamita Spirituality (spiritual traditions of Ancient Egypt-Africa).

The Fundamental Principles of Neterian Religion and the Discipline of Divine Love

In order to understand the Path of Divine Love of ancient Kamit (Africa) it is necessary to understand that the path of "Neter Merri" (Divine Love) is actually an aspect or part of Ancient Egyptian religion (Shetaut Neter). Notice principle #3 closely. See the book The Book of Shetaut Neter by Muata Ashby for more on the fundamental principles of Neterianism (Ancient Egyptian religion – Shetaut Neter).

The term "Neterianism" is derived from the name "Shetaut Neter." Shetaut Neter means the "Hidden Divinity." It is the ancient philosophy and mythic spiritual culture that gave rise to the Ancient Egyptian civilization. Those who follow the spiritual path of Shetaut Neter are therefore referred to as "Neterians." The fundamental principles common to all denominations of Neterian Religion may be summed up as follows.

Summary of Ancient Egyptian Religion

NETERIANISM
(The Oldest Known Religion in History)

The term "Neterianism" is derived from the name "Shetaut Neter." Shetaut Neter means the "Hidden Divinity." It is the ancient philosophy and mythic spiritual culture that gave rise to the Ancient Egyptian civilization. Those who follow the spiritual path of Shetaut Neter are therefore referred to as "Neterians." The fundamental principles common to all denominations of Ancient Egyptian Religion may be summed up in four "Great Truths" that are common to all the traditions of Ancient Egyptian Religion.

The Path of Divine Love

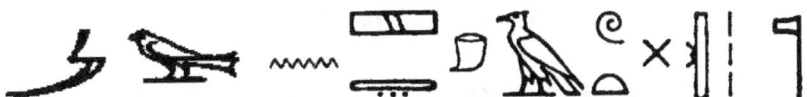

Maa Ur n Shetaut Neter
"Great Truths of The Shetaut Neter Religion"

I

Pa Neter ua ua Neberdjer m Neteru
"The Neter, the Supreme Being, is One and alone and as Neberdjer, manifesting everywhere and in all things in the form of Gods and Goddesses."

II

an-Maat swy Saui Set s-Khemn
"Lack of righteousness brings fetters to the personality and these fetters cause ignorance of the Divine."

III

s-Uashu s-Nafu n saiu Set
"Devotion to the Divine leads to freedom from the fetters of Set."

IIII

ari Shedy Rekh ab m Maakheru
"The practice of the Shedy disciplines leads to knowing oneself and the Divine. This is called being True of Speech"

Neter Merri

Neterian Great Truths

1. ***"Pa Neter ua ua Neberdjer m Neteru"*** -"The Neter, the Supreme Being, is One and alone and as Neberdjer, manifesting everywhere and in all things in the form of Gods and Goddesses."

Neberdjer means "all-encompassing divinity," the all-inclusive, all-embracing Spirit which pervades all and who is the ultimate essence of all. This first truth unifies all the expressions of Kamitan religion.

2. ***"an-Maat swy Saui Set s-Khemn"*** - "Lack of righteousness brings fetters to the personality and these fetters lead to ignorance of the Divine."

When a human being acts in ways that contradict the natural order of nature, negative qualities of the mind will develop within that person's personality. These are the afflictions of Set. Set is the neteru of egoism and selfishness. The afflictions of Set include: anger, hatred, greed, lust, jealousy, envy, gluttony, dishonesty, hypocrisy, etc. So to be free from the fetters of set one must be free from the afflictions of Set.

3. ***"s-Uashu s-Nafu n saiu Set"*** -"Devotion to the Divine leads to freedom from the fetters of Set."

To be liberated (Nafu - freedom - to breath) from the afflictions of Set, one must be devoted to the Divine. Being devoted to the Divine means living by Maat. Maat is a way of life that is purifying to the heart and beneficial for society as it promotes virtue and order. Living by Maat means practicing Shedy (spiritual practices and disciplines).

Uashu means devotion and the classic pose of adoring the Divine is called "Dua," standing or sitting with upraised hands facing outwards towards the image of the divinity.

4. ***"ari Shedy Rekh ab m Maakheru"*** - "The practice of the Shedy disciplines leads to knowing oneself and the Divine. This is called being True of Speech."

Doing Shedy means to study profoundly, to penetrate the mysteries (Shetaut) and discover the nature of the Divine. There have been several practices designed by the sages of Ancient Kamit to facilitate the process of self-knowledge. These are the religious (Shetaut) traditions and the Sema (Smai) Tawi (yogic) disciplines related to them that augment the spiritual practices.

All the traditions relate the teachings of the sages by means of myths related to particular gods or goddesses. It is understood that all of these neteru are related, like brothers and sisters, having all emanated from the same source, the same Supremely Divine parent, who is neither male nor female, but encompasses the totality of the two.

The Path of Divine Love

The Great Truths of Neterianism are realized by means of Four Spiritual Disciplines in Three Steps

The four disciples are: Rekh Shedy (Wisdom), Ari Shedy (Righteous Action and Selfless Service), Uashu (Ushet) Shedy (Devotion) and Uaa Shedy (Meditation)

The Three Steps are: Listening, Ritual, and Meditation

SEDJM REKH SHEDY

LISTEN

- <u>Sedjm REKH Shedy</u> - **Listening** to the WISDOM of the Neterian Traditions
    - Shetaut Asar — Teachings of the Asarian Tradition
    - Shetaut Anu — Teachings of the Ra Tradition
    - Shetaut Menefer — Teachings of the Ptah Tradition
    - Shetaut Waset — Teachings of the Amun Tradition
    - Shetaut Netrit — Teachings of the Goddess Tradition
    - Shetaut Aton — Teachings of the Aton Tradition

ARI SHEDY

RITUAL

- <u>Ari Maat Shedy</u> – **Righteous Actions** – Purifies the GROSS impurities of the Heart
    - Maat Shedy — True Study of the Ways of hidden nature of Neter
    - Maat Aakhu — True Deeds that lead to glory
    - Maat Aru — True Ritual

UASHU (USHET) SHEDY

- <u>Ushet Shedy</u> – **Devotion to the Divine** – Purifies the EMOTIONAL impurities of the Heart
    - Shmai — Divine Music
    - Sema Paut — Meditation in motion
    - Neter Arit — Divine Offerings – Selfless-Service – virtue -

UAA SHEDY

MEDITATE

- <u>Uaa m Neter Shedy</u> - 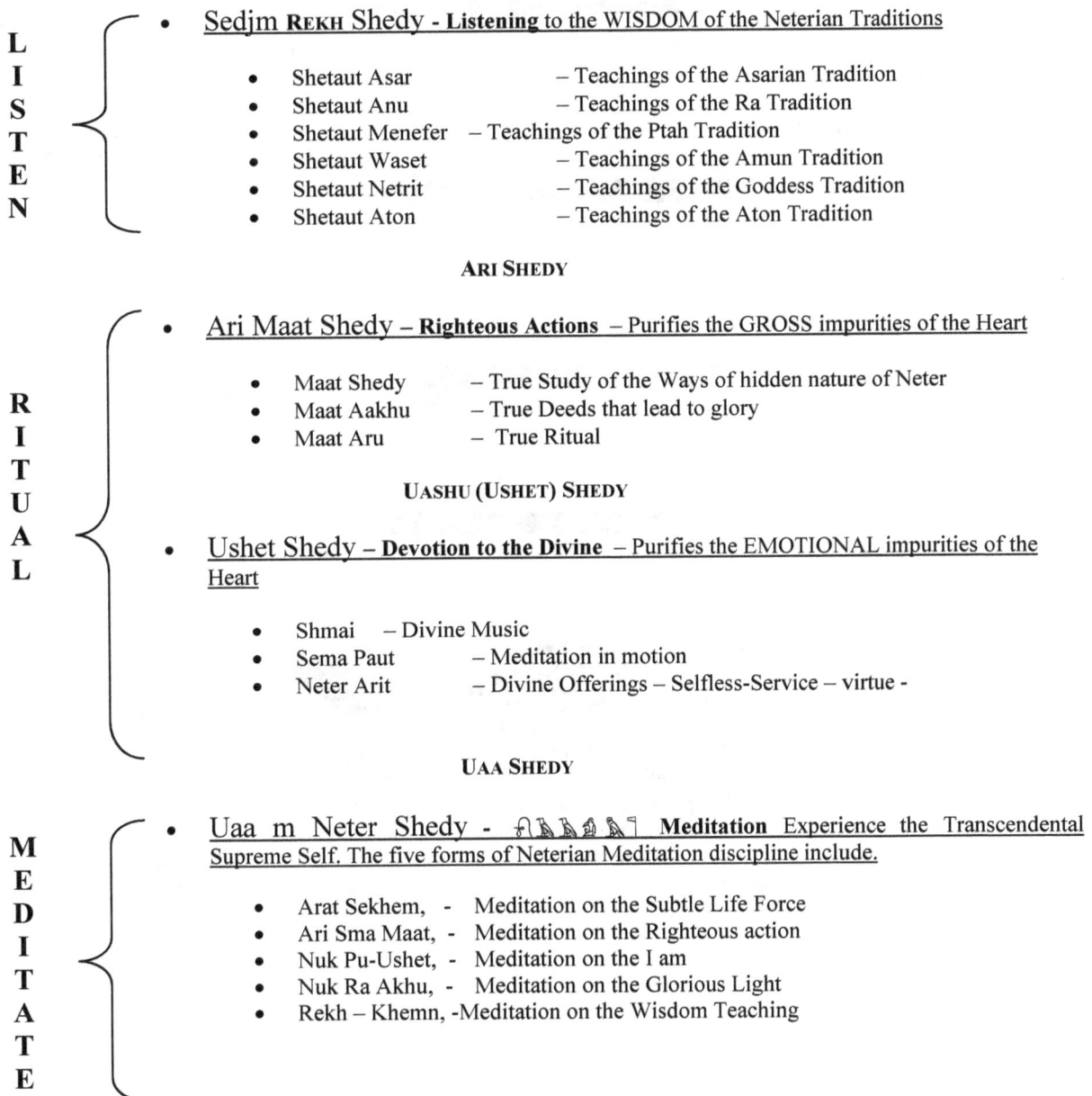 **Meditation** Experience the Transcendental Supreme Self. The five forms of Neterian Meditation discipline include.
    - Arat Sekhem, - Meditation on the Subtle Life Force
    - Ari Sma Maat, - Meditation on the Righteous action
    - Nuk Pu-Ushet, - Meditation on the I am
    - Nuk Ra Akhu, - Meditation on the Glorious Light
    - Rekh – Khemn, -Meditation on the Wisdom Teaching

Neter Merri

Summary of The Great Truths and the Shedy Paths to their Realization

Great Truths 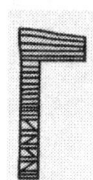 Shedy Disciplines

I
God is One and in all things manifesting through the Neteru

I
Listen to the Wisdom Teachings (Become Wise)
Learn the mysteries as taught by an authentic teacher which allows this profound statement to be understood.

II
Unrighteousness brings fetters and these cause ignorance of truth (#1)

II
Acting (Living) by Truth
Apply the Philosophy of right action to become virtuous and purify the heart

III
Devotion to God allows the personality to free itself from the fetters

III
Devotion to the Divine
Worship, ritual and divine love allows the personality purified by truth to eradicate the subtle ignorance that binds it to mortal existence.

IIII
The Shedy disciplines are the greatest form of worship of the Divine

IIII
Meditation
Allows the whole person to go beyond the world of time and space and the gross and subtle ignorance of mortal human existence to discover that which transcends time and space.

Great Awakening
Occurs when all of the Great Truths have been realized by perfection of the Shedy disciplines to realize their true nature and actually experience oneness with the transcendental Supreme Being.

The Path of Divine Love

The Spiritual Culture and the Purpose of Life: Shetaut Neter

"Men and women are to become God-like through a life of virtue and the cultivation of the spirit through scientific knowledge, practice and bodily discipline."

-Ancient Egyptian Proverb

The highest forms of Joy, Peace and Contentment are obtained when the meaning of life is discovered. When the human being is in harmony with life, then it is possible to reflect and meditate upon the human condition and realize the limitations of worldly pursuits. When there is peace and harmony in life, a human being can practice any of the varied disciplines designated as Shetaut Neter to promote {his/her} evolution towards the ultimate goal of life, which Spiritual Enlightenment. Spiritual Enlightenment is the awakening of a human being to the awareness of the Transcendental essence which binds the universe and which is eternal and immutable. In this discovery is also the sobering and ecstatic realization that the human being is one with that Transcendental essence. With this realization comes great joy, peace and power to experience the fullness of life and to realize the purpose of life during the time on earth. The lotus is a symbol of Shetaut Neter, meaning the turning towards the light of truth, peace and transcendental harmony.

Shetaut Neter

We have established that the Ancient Egyptians were African peoples who lived in the north-eastern quadrant of the continent of Africa. They were descendants of the Nubians, who had themselves originated from farther south into the heart of Africa at the Great Lakes region, the sources of the Nile River. They created a vast civilization and culture earlier than any other society in known history and organized a nation that was based on the concepts of balance and order as well as spiritual enlightenment. These ancient African people called their land Kamit, and soon after developing a well-ordered society, they began to realize that the world is full of wonders, but also that life is fleeting, and that there must be something more to human existence. They developed spiritual systems that were designed to allow human beings to understand the nature of this secret being who is the essence of all Creation. They called this spiritual system "Shtaut Ntr (Shetaut Neter)."

Shetaut means secret.

Neter means Divinity.

Who is Neter in Kamitan Religion?

The symbol of Neter was described by an Ancient Kamitan priest as:
"That which is placed in the coffin"

The term Ntr, or Ntjr, comes from the Ancient Egyptian hieroglyphic language which did not record its vowels. However, the term survives in the Coptic language as "Nutar." The same Coptic meaning (divine force or sustaining power) applies in the present as it did in ancient times. It is a symbol composed of a wooden staff that was wrapped with strips of fabric, like a mummy. The strips alternate in color with yellow, green and blue. The mummy in Kamitan spirituality is understood to be the dead but resurrected Divinity. So the Nutar (Ntr) is actually every human being who does not really die, but goes to live on in a different form. Further, the resurrected spirit of every human being is that same Divinity. Phonetically, the term Nutar is related to other terms having the same meaning, such as the latin "Natura," the Spanish Naturalesa, the English "Nature" and "Nutriment", etc. In a real sense, as we will see, Natur means power manifesting as Neteru and the Neteru are the objects of creation, i.e. "nature."

The Path of Divine Love

Sacred Scriptures of Shetaut Neter

The following scriptures represent the foundational scriptures of Kamitan culture. They may be divided into three categories: Mythic Scriptures, Mystical Philosophy and Ritual Scriptures, and Wisdom Scriptures (Didactic Literature).

MYTHIC SCRIPTURES Literature	**Mystical (Ritual) Philosophy Literature**	**Wisdom Texts Literature**
SHETAUT ASAR-ASET-HERU The Myth of Asar, Aset and Heru (Asarian Resurrection Theology) - Predynastic **SHETAUT ATUM-RA** Anunian Theology Predynastic Shetaut Net/Aset/Hetheru Saitian Theology – Goddess Spirituality Predynastic **SHETAUT PTAH** Memphite Theology Predynastic Shetaut Amun Theban Theology Predynastic	**Coffin Texts** (C. 2040 B.C.E.-1786 B.C.E.) **Papyrus Texts** (C. 1580 B.C.E.- Roman Period)[2] Books of Coming Forth By Day Example of famous papyri: Papyrus of Any Papyrus of Hunefer Papyrus of Kenna Greenfield Papyrus, Etc.	**Wisdom Texts** (C. 3,000 B.C.E. – PTOLEMAIC PERIOD) Precepts of Ptahotep Instructions of Any Instructions of Amenemope Etc. **Maat Declarations** Literature (All Periods) **Blind Harpers Songs**

---
[2] After 1570 B.C.E they would evolve into a more unified text, the Egyptian Book of the Dead.

Neter and the Neteru

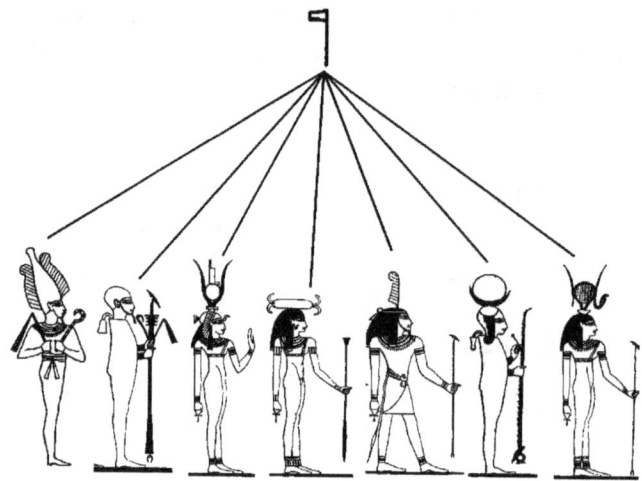

The Neteru (Gods and Goddesses) proceed from the Neter (Supreme Being)

As stated earlier, the concept of Neter and Neteru binds and ties all of the varied forms of Kamitan spirituality into one vision of the gods and goddesses all emerging from the same Supreme Being. Therefore, ultimately, Kamitan spirituality is not polytheistic, nor is it monotheistic, for it holds that the Supreme Being is more than a God or Goddess. The Supreme Being is an all-encompassing Absolute Divinity.

The Neteru

The term "Neteru" means "gods and goddesses." This means that from the ultimate and transcendental Supreme Being, "Neter," come the Neteru. There are countless Neteru. So from the one come the many. These Neteru are cosmic forces that pervade the universe. They are the means by which Neter sustains Creation and manifests through it. So Neterianism is a monotheistic polytheism. The one Supreme Being expresses as many gods and goddesses. At the end of time, after their work of sustaining Creation is finished, these gods and goddesses are again absorbed back into the Supreme Being.

All of the spiritual systems of Ancient Egypt (Kamit) have one essential aspect that is common to all; they all hold that there is a Supreme Being (Neter) who manifests in a multiplicity of ways through nature, the Neteru. Like sunrays, the Neteru emanate from the Divine; they are its manifestations. So by studying the Neteru we learn about and are led to discover their source, the Neter, and with this discovery we are enlightened. The Neteru may be depicted anthropomorphically or zoomorphically in accordance with the teaching about Neter that is being conveyed through them.

The Neteru and Their Temples

Diagram 1: The Ancient Egyptian Temple Network

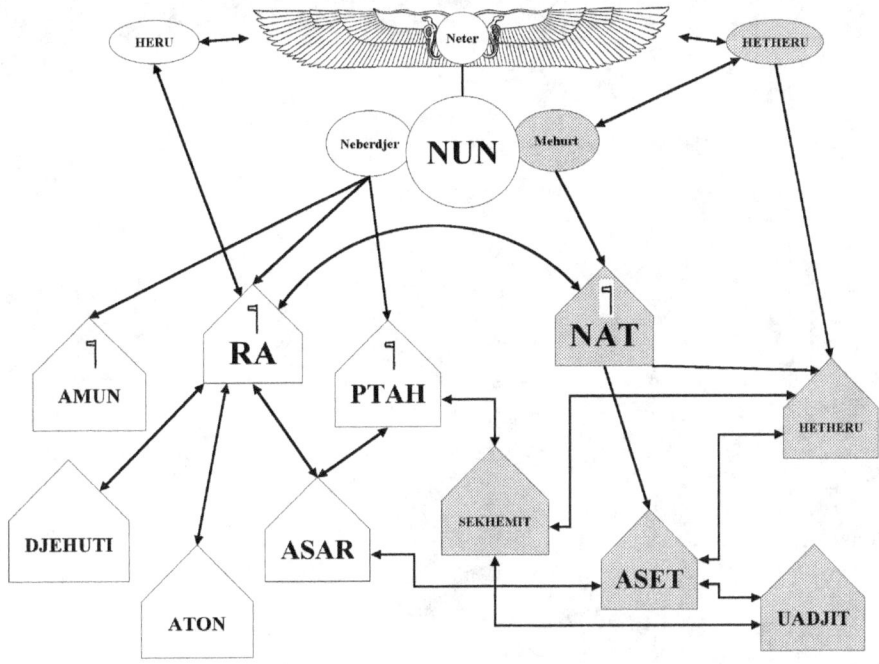

The sages of Kamit instituted a system by which the teachings of spirituality were espoused through a Temple organization. The major divinities were assigned to a particular city. That divinity or group of divinities became the "patron" divinity or divinities of that city. Also, the Priests and Priestesses of that Temple were in charge of seeing to the welfare of the people in that district as well as maintaining the traditions and disciplines of the traditions based on the particular divinity being worshipped. So the original concept of "Neter" became elaborated through the "theologies" of the various traditions. A dynamic expression of the teachings emerged, which though maintaining the integrity of the teachings, expressed nuances of variation in perspective on the teachings to suit the needs of varying kinds of personalities of the people of different locales.

In the diagram above, the primary or main divinities are denoted by the Neter symbol ( ). The house structure represents the Temple for that particular divinity. The interconnections with the other Temples are based on original scriptural statements espoused by the Temples that linked the divinities of their Temple with the other divinities. So this means that the divinities should be viewed not as separate entities operating independently, but rather as family members who are in the same "business" together, i.e. the enlightenment of society, albeit through variations in form of worship, name, form (expression of the Divinity), etc. Ultimately, all the divinities are referred to as Neteru and they are all said to be emanations from the ultimate and Supreme Being. Thus, the teaching from any of the Temples leads to an understanding of the others, and these all lead back to the source, the highest Divinity. Thus, the teaching within any of the Temple systems would lead to the attainment of spiritual enlightenment, the Great Awakening.

The temple is an architectural symbol of devotion to the Divine. Embedded in its very measurements are the symbols and meditative movement that turn the mind of aspirants towards the Divine and thereby awaken the devotional feeling.

Above: The great temple of Amun, Ra and Ptah, commissioned by Per=ahh (pharaoh) Rameses II

The Path of Divine Love

The Neteru and Their Interrelationships

Diagram : The Primary Kamitan Neteru and their Interrelationships

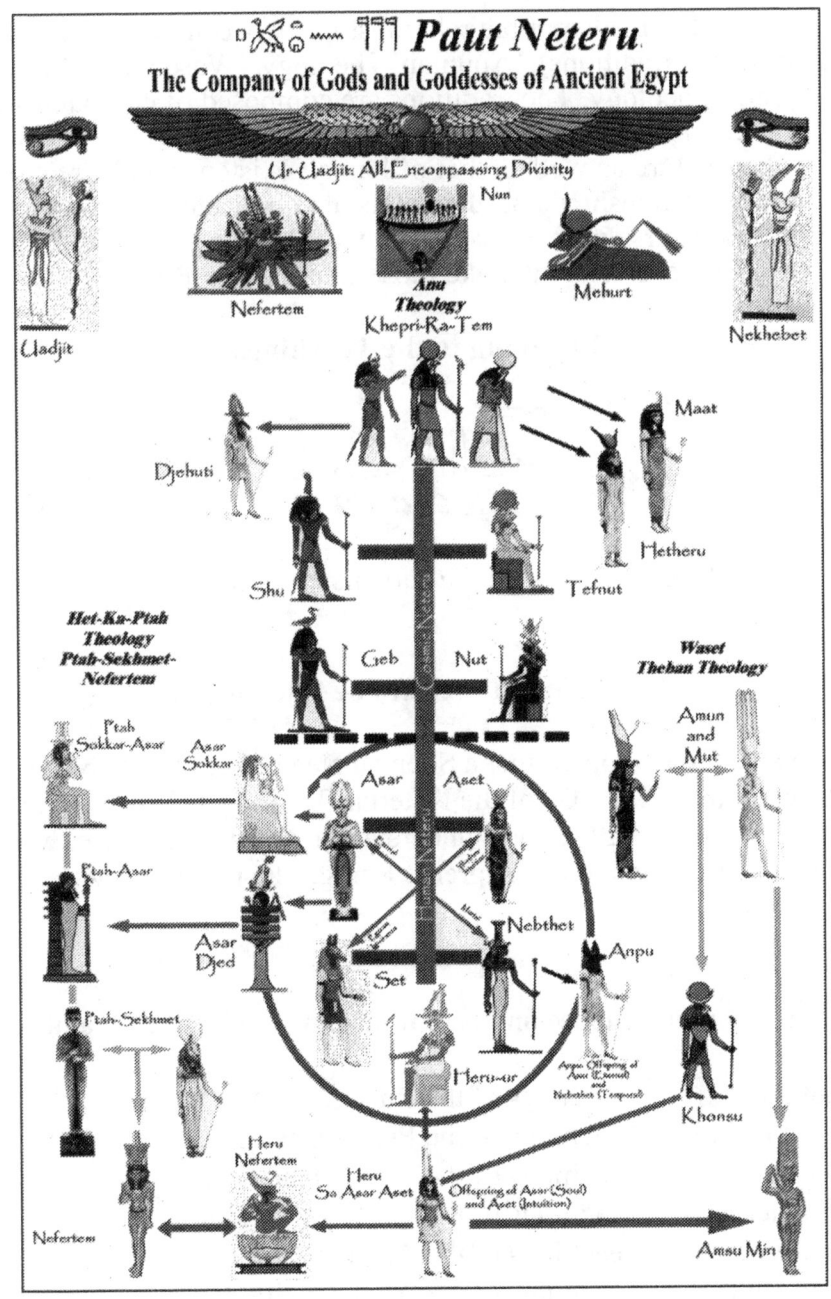

The same Supreme Being, Neter, is the winged all-encompassing transcendental Divinity, the Spirit who, in the early history, is called "Heru." The physical universe in which the Heru lives is called "Hetheru" or the "house of Heru." This divinity (Heru) is also the Nun or primeval substratum from which all matter is composed. The various divinities and the material universe are composed from this primeval substratum. Neter is actually androgynous and Heru, the Spirit, is related as a male aspect of that androgyny. However, Heru in the androgynous aspect, gives rise to the solar principle and this is seen in both the male and female divinities.

The image above provides an idea of the relationships between the divinities of the three main Neterian spiritual systems (traditions): Anunian Theology, Wasetian (Theban) Theology and Het-Ka-Ptah (Memphite) Theology. The traditions are composed of companies or groups of gods and goddesses. Their actions, teachings and interactions with each other and with human beings provide insight into their nature as well as that of human existence and Creation itself. The lines indicate direct scriptural relationships and the labels also indicate that some divinities from one system are the same in others, with only a name change. Again, this is attested to by the scriptures themselves in direct statements, like those found in the Prt m Hru text Chapter 4 (17).[3]

Listening to the Teachings

"*Mestchert*"

"Listening, to fill the ears, listen attentively-"

What should the ears be filled with?

The sages of Shetaut Neter enjoined that a Shemsu Neter (follower of Neter, an initiate or aspirant) should listen to the WISDOM of the Neterian Traditions. These are the myth related to the gods and goddesses containing the basic understanding of who they are, what they represent, how they relate human beings and to the Supreme Being. The myths allow us to be connected to the Divine.

An aspirant may choose any one of the 6 main Neterian Traditions.

- Shetaut Anu – Teachings of the Ra Tradition
- Shetaut Menefer – Teachings of the Ptah Tradition
- Shetaut Waset – Teachings of the Amun Tradition
- Shetaut Netrit – Teachings of the Goddess Tradition
- Shetaut Asar – Teachings of the Asarian Tradition
- Shetaut Aton – Teachings of the Aton Tradition

---

[3] See the book **The Egyptian Book of the Dead** by Muata Ashby

The Path of Divine Love

The Anunian Tradition

 **Shetaut Anu**

The Mystery Teachings of the Anunian Tradition are related to the Divinity Ra and his company of Gods and Goddesses.[4] This Temple and its related Temples espouse the teachings of Creation, human origins and the path to spiritual enlightenment by means of the Supreme Being in the form of the god Ra. It tells of how Ra emerged from a primeval ocean and how human beings were created from his tears. The gods and goddesses, who are his children, go to form the elements of nature and the cosmic forces that maintain nature.

Below: The Heliopolitan Cosmogony.

The city of Anu (Amun-Ra)

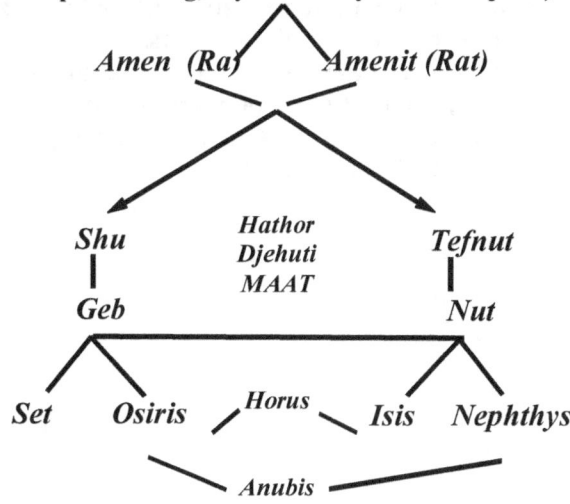

Top: Ra. From left to right, starting at the bottom level- The Gods and Goddesses of Anunian Theology: Shu, Tefnut, Nut, Geb, Aset, Asar, Set, Nebthet and Heru-Ur

---

[4] See the Book Anunian Theology by Muata Ashby

The Memphite Tradition

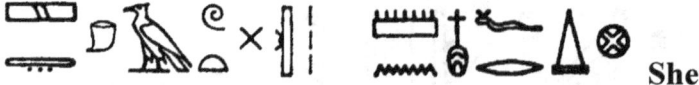 **Shetaut Menefer**

The Mystery Teachings of the Menefer (Memphite) Tradition are related to the Neterus known as Ptah, Sekhmit, Nefertem. The myths and philosophy of these divinities constitutes Memphite Theology.[5] This temple and its related temples espoused the teachings of Creation, human origins and the path to spiritual enlightenment by means of the Supreme Being in the form of the god Ptah and his family, who compose the Memphite Trinity. It tells of how Ptah emerged from a primeval ocean and how he created the universe by his will and the power of thought (mind). The gods and goddesses who are his thoughts, go to form the elements of nature and the cosmic forces that maintain nature. His spouse, Sekhmit has a powerful temple system of her own that is related to the Memphite teaching. The same is true for his son Nefertem.

Below: The Memphite Cosmogony.

The city of Hetkaptah (Ptah)

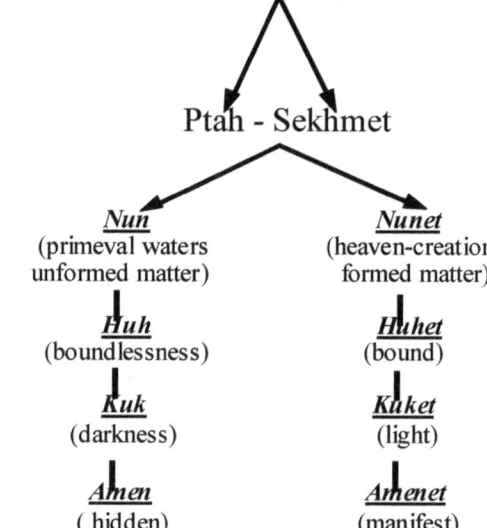

The Neters of Creation -
The Company of the Gods and Goddesses
Neter Neteru
Nebertcher - Amun (unseen, hidden, ever present Supreme Being, beyond duality and description)

Ptah - Sekhmet

Nun (primeval waters unformed matter) — *Nunet* (heaven-creation formed matter)

Huh (boundlessness) — *Huhet* (bound)

Kuk (darkness) — *Kuket* (light)

Amen (hidden) — *Amenet* (manifest)

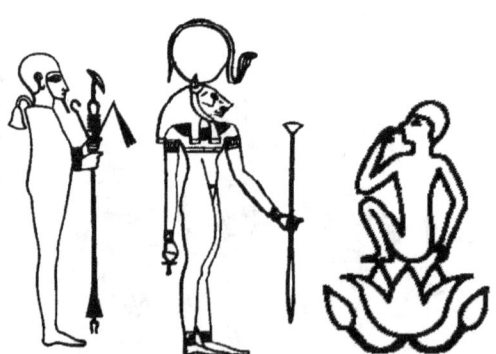

Ptah, Sekhmit and Nefertem

---

[5] See the Book Memphite Theology by Muata Ashby

The Path of Divine Love

The Theban Tradition

Shetaut Amun

The Mystery Teachings of the Wasetian Tradition are related to the Neterus known as Amun, Mut Khonsu. This temple and its related temples espoused the teachings of Creation, human origins and the path to spiritual enlightenment by means of the Supreme Being in the form of the god Amun or Amun-Ra. It tells of how Amun and his family, the Trinity of Amun, Mut and Khonsu, manage the Universe along with his Company of Gods and Goddesses. This Temple became very important in the early part of the New Kingdom Era.

Below: The Trinity of Amun and the Company of Gods and Goddesses of Amun

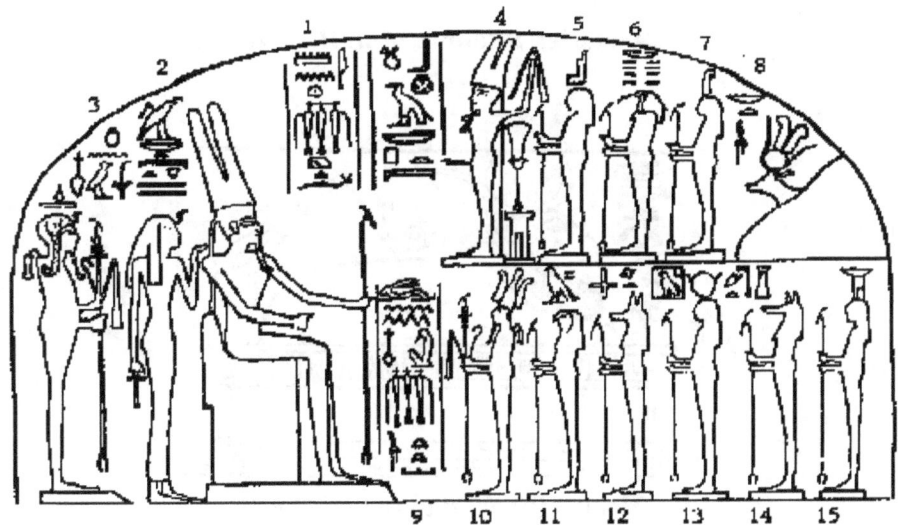

See the Book *Egyptian Yoga Vol. 2* for more on Amun, Mut and Khonsu by Muata Ashby

The Goddess Tradition

Shetaut Netrit

"Arat"

The hieroglyphic sign Arat means "Goddess." General, throughout ancient Kamit, the Mystery Teachings of the Goddess Tradition are related to the Divinity in the form of the Goddess. The Goddess was an integral part of all the Neterian traditions but special temples also developed around the worship of certain particular Goddesses who were also regarded as Supreme Beings in their own right. Thus as in other African religions, the goddess as well as the female gender were respected and elevated as the male divinities. The Goddess was also the author of Creation, giving birth to it as a great Cow. The following are the most important forms of the goddess.[6]

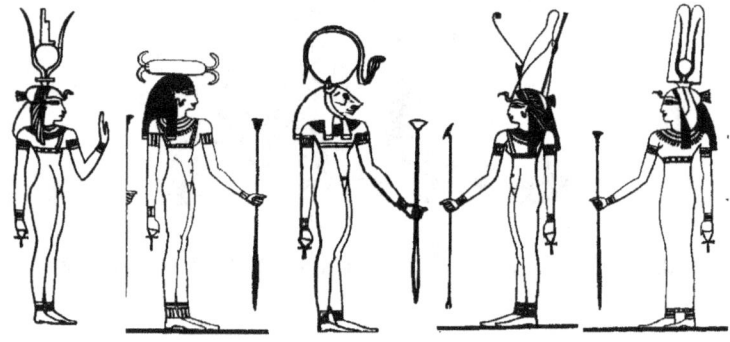

Aset, Net, Sekhmit, Mut, Hetheru

Mehurt ("The Mighty Full One")

---

[6] See the Books, **The Goddess Path, Mysteries of Isis, Glorious Light Meditation, Memphite Theology** and **Resurrecting Osiris** by Muata Ashby

The Path of Divine Love

The Asarian Tradition

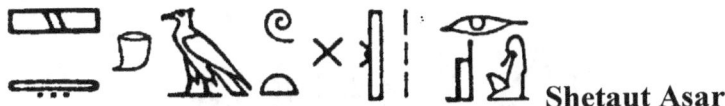 **Shetaut Asar**

    This temple and its related temples espoused the teachings of Creation, human origins and the path to spiritual enlightenment by means of the Supreme Being in the form of the god Asar. It tells of how Asar and his family, the Trinity of Asar, Aset and Heru, manage the Universe and lead human beings to spiritual enlightenment and the resurrection of the soul. This Temple and its teaching were very important from the Pre-Dynastic era down to the Christian period. The Mystery Teachings of the Asarian Tradition are related to the Neterus known as: **Asar, Aset, Heru (Osiris, Isis and Horus)**

The tradition of Asar, Aset and Heru was practiced generally throughout the land of ancient Kamit. The centers of this tradition were the city of Abdu containing the Great Temple of Asar, the city of Pilak containing the Great Temple of Aset[7] and Edfu containing the Ggreat Temple of Heru.

---
[7] See the Book Resurrecting Osiris by Muata Ashby

Neter Merri

The Aton Tradition

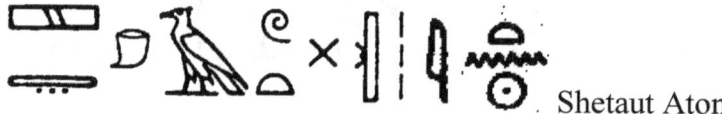 Shetaut Aton

This temple and its related temples espoused the teachings of Creation, human origins and the path to spiritual enlightenment by means of the Supreme Being in the form of the god Aton. It tells of how Aton with its dynamic life force created and sustains Creation. By recognizing Aton as the very substratum of all existence, human beings engage in devotional exercises and rituals and the study of the Hymns containing the wisdom teachings of Aton explaining that Aton manages the Universe and leads human beings to spiritual enlightenment and eternal life for the soul. This Temple and its teaching were very important in the middle New Kingdom Period. The Mystery Teachings of the Aton Tradition are related to the Neter Aton and its main exponent was the Sage King Akhnaton, who is depicted below with his family adoring the sundisk, symbol of the Aton.

Akhnaton, Nefertiti and Daughters

For more on Atonism and the Aton Theology see the Essence of Atonism Lecture Series by Sebai Muata Ashby ©2001

The Path of Divine Love

The General Principles of Shetaut Neter
(Teachings Presented in the Kamitan scriptures)

1. The Purpose of Life is to Attain the Great Awakening-Enlightenment-Know thyself.

2. SHETAUT NETER enjoins the Shedy (spiritual investigation) as the highest endeavor of life.

3. SHETAUT NETER enjoins that it is the responsibility of every human being to promote order and truth.

4. SHETAUT NETER enjoins the performance of Selfless Service to family, community and humanity.

5. SHETAUT NETER enjoins the Protection of nature.

6. SHETAUT NETER enjoins the Protection of the weak and oppressed.

7. SHETAUT NETER enjoins the Caring for hungry.

8. SHETAUT NETER enjoins the Caring for homeless.

9. SHETAUT NETER enjoins the equality for all people.

10. SHETAUT NETER enjoins the equality between men and women.

11. SHETAUT NETER enjoins the justice for all.

12. SHETAUT NETER enjoins the sharing of resources.

13. SHETAUT NETER enjoins the protection and proper raising of children.

14. SHETAUT NETER enjoins the movement towards balance and peace.

The Forces of Entropy

In Neterian religion, there is no concept of "evil" as is conceptualized in Western Culture. Rather, it is understood that the forces of entropy are constantly working in nature to bring that which has been constructed by human hands to their original natural state. The serpent Apep (Apophis), who daily tries to stop Ra's boat of creation, is the symbol of entropy. This concept of entropy has been referred to as "chaos" by Western Egyptologists.

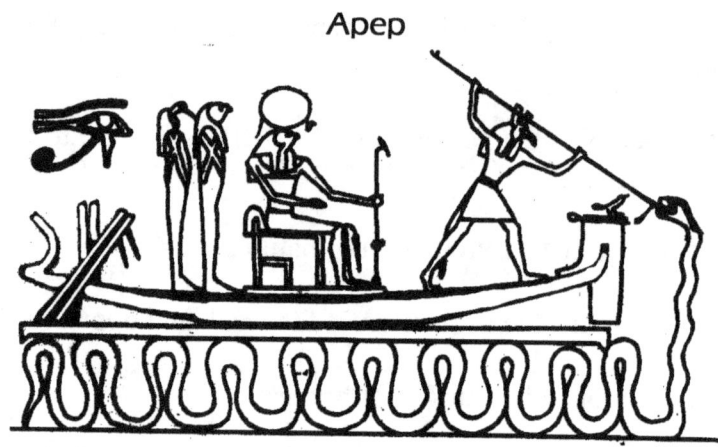

Above: Set protecting the boat of Ra from the forces of entropy (symbolized by the serpent Apep).

As expressed previously, in Neterian religion there is also no concept of a "devil" or "demon" as is conceived in the Judeo-Christian or Islamic traditions. Rather, it is understood that manifestations of detrimental situations and adversities arise as a result of unrighteous actions. These unrighteous actions are due to the "Setian" qualities in a human being. Set is the Neteru of egoism and the negative qualities which arise from egoism. Egoism is the idea of individuality based on identification with the body and mind only as being who one is. One has no deeper awareness of their deeper spiritual essence, and thus no understanding of their connectedness to all other objects (includes persons) in creation and the Divine Self. When the ego is under the control of the higher nature, it fights the forces of entropy (as above). However, when beset with ignorance, it leads to the degraded states of human existence. The vices (egoism, selfishness, extraverted ness, wonton sexuality (lust), jealousy, envy, greed, gluttony) are a result.

Set

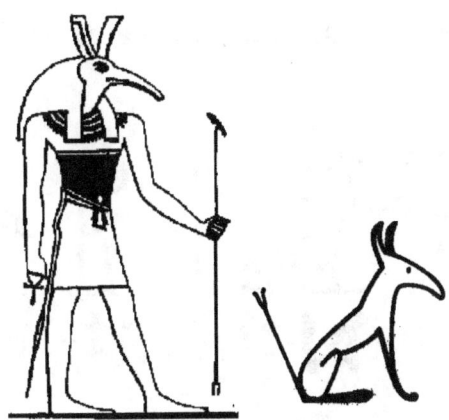
Set and the Set animal

The Great Awakening of Neterian Religion

"Nehast"

Nehast means to "wake up," to Awaken to the higher existence. In the Prt m Hru Text it is said:

Nuk pa Neter aah Neter Ujah asha ren

"I am that same God, the Supreme One, who has myriad of mysterious names."

The goal of all the Neterian disciplines is to discover the meaning of "Who am I?," to unravel the mysteries of life and to fathom the depths of eternity and infinity. This is the task of all human beings and it is to be accomplished in this very lifetime.

This can be done by learning the ways of the Neteru, emulating them and finally becoming like them, Akhus, (enlightened beings), walking the earth as giants and accomplishing great deeds such as the creation of the universe!

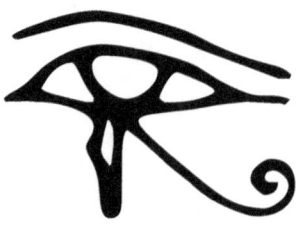

Udjat
The Eye of Heru is a quintessential symbol of awakening to Divine Consciousness, representing the concept of Nehast.

---
[8] (Prt M Hru 9:4)

Who Were the Ancient Egyptians and What is Yoga Philosophy?

The Ancient Egyptian religion (Shetaut Neter), language and symbols provide the first "historical" record of Yoga Philosophy and Religious literature. Egyptian Yoga is what has been commonly referred to by Egyptologists as Egyptian "Religion" or "Mythology", but to think of it as just another set of stories or allegories about a long lost civilization is to completely miss the greatest secret of human existence. Yoga, in all of its forms and disciplines of spiritual development, was practiced in Egypt earlier than anywhere else in history. This unique perspective from the highest philosophical system which developed in Africa over seven thousand years ago provides a new way to look at life, religion, the discipline of psychology and the way to spiritual development leading to spiritual Enlightenment. Egyptian mythology, when understood as a system of Yoga (union of the individual soul with the Universal Soul or Supreme Consciousness), gives every individual insight into their own divine nature and also a deeper insight into all religions and Yoga systems.

Diodorus Siculus (Greek Historian) writes in the time of Augustus (first century B.C.):

"Now the Ethiopians, as historians relate, were the first of all men and the proofs of this statement, they say, are manifest. For that they did not come into their land as immigrants from abroad but were the natives of it and so justly bear the name of autochthones **(sprung from the soil itself)**, is, they maintain, conceded by practically all men..."

"They also say that the Egyptians are colonists sent out by the Ethiopians, Asar having been the leader of the colony. For, speaking generally, what is now Egypt, they maintain, was not land, but sea, when in the beginning the universe was being formed; afterwards, however, as the Nile during the times of its inundation carried down the mud from Ethiopia, land was gradually built up from the deposit...And the larger parts of the customs of the Egyptians are, they hold, Ethiopian, the colonists still preserving their ancient manners. For instance, the belief that their kings are Gods, the very special attention which they pay to their burials, and many other matters of a similar nature, are Ethiopian practices, while the shapes of their statues and the forms of their letters are Ethiopian; for of the two kinds of writing which the Egyptians have, that which is known as popular **(demotic)** is learned by everyone, while that which is called sacred **(hieratic)**, is understood only by the priests of the Egyptians, who learnt it from their Fathers as one of the things which are not divulged, but among the Ethiopians, everyone uses these forms of letters. Furthermore, the orders of the priests, they maintain, have much the same position among both peoples; for all are clean who are engaged in the service of the gods, keeping themselves shaven, like the Ethiopian priests, and having the same dress and form of staff, which is shaped like a plough and is carried by their kings who wear high felt hats which end in a knob in the top and are circled by the serpents which they call asps; and this symbol appears to carry the thought that it will be the lot who shall dare to attack the king to encounter death-carrying stings. Many other things are told by them concerning their own antiquity and the colony which they sent out that became the Egyptians, but about this there is no special need of our writing anything."

The Ancient Egyptian texts state:

> "Our people originated at the base of the mountain of the Moon,
> at the origin of the Nile river."

"KMT"
"Egypt", "Burnt", "Land of Blackness","Land of the Burnt People."

KMT (Ancient Egypt) is situated close to Lake Victoria in present day Africa. This is the same location where the earliest human remains have been found, in the land currently known as Ethiopia-Tanzania. Recent genetic technology as reported in the new encyclopedias and leading news publications has revealed that all peoples of the world originated in Africa and migrated to other parts of the world prior to the last Ice Age 40,000 years ago. Therefore, as of this time, genetic testing has revealed that all humans are alike. The earliest bone fossils which have been found in many parts of the world were those of the African Grimaldi type. During the Ice Age, it was not possible to communicate or to migrate. Those trapped in specific locations were subject to the regional forces of weather and climate. Less warmer climates required less body pigment, thereby producing lighter pigmented people who now differed from their dark-skinned ancestors. After the Ice Age when travel was possible, these light-skinned people who had lived in the northern, colder regions of harsh weather during the Ice Age period moved back to the warmer climates of their ancestors, and mixed with the people there who had remained dark-skinned, thereby producing the Semitic colored people. "Semite" means mixture of skin color shades.

Therefore, there is only one human race who, due to different climactic and regional exposure, changed to a point where there seemed to be different "types" of people. Differences were noted with respect to skin color, hair texture, customs, languages, and with respect to the essential nature (psychological and emotional makeup) due to the experiences each group had to face and overcome in order to survive.

From a philosophical standpoint, the question as to the origin of humanity is redundant when it is understood that <u>ALL</u> come from one origin which some choose to call the "Big Bang" and others "The Supreme Being."

> "Thou makest the color of the skin of one race to be different from that of another, but however many may be the varieties of mankind, it is thou that makes them all to live."
>
> —Ancient Egyptian Proverb from The Hymns of Amun

> "Souls, Heru, son, are of the self-same nature, since they came from the same place where the Creator modeled them; nor male nor female are they. Sex is a thing of bodies not of Souls."
>
> —Ancient Egyptian Proverb from The teachings of Aset to Heru

Historical evidence proves that Ethiopia-Nubia already had Kingdoms at least 300 years before the first Kingdom-Pharaoh of Egypt.

> "Ancient Egypt was a colony of Nubia - Ethiopia. ...Asar having been the leader of the colony..."

> "And upon his return to Greece, they gathered around and asked, "tell us about this great land of the Blacks called Ethiopia." And Herodotus said, "There are two great Ethiopian nations, one in Sind (India) and the other in Egypt."

Recorded by Egyptian high priest Manetho **(300 B.C.)**
also Recorded by Diodorus **(Greek historian 100 B.C.)**

The pyramids themselves however, cannot be dated, but indications are that they existed far back in antiquity. The Pyramid Texts (hieroglyphics inscribed on pyramid walls) and Coffin Texts (hieroglyphics inscribed on coffins) speak authoritatively on the constitution of the human spirit, the vital Life Force along the human spinal cord (known in India as "Kundalini"), the immortality of the soul, reincarnation and the law of Cause and Effect (known in India as the Law of Karma).

What is Yoga Philosophy and Spiritual Practice

Since a complete treatise on the theory and practice of yoga would require several volumes, only a basic outline will be given here.

When we look out upon the world, we are often baffled by the multiplicity which constitutes the human experience. What do we really know about this experience? Many scientific disciplines have developed over the last two hundred years for the purpose of discovering the mysteries of nature, but this search has only engendered new questions about the nature of existence. Yoga is a discipline or way of life designed to promote the physical, mental and spiritual development of the human being. It leads a person to discover the answers to the most important questions of life such as Who am I?, Why am I here? and Where am I going?

The literal meaning of the word YOGA is to "YOKE" or to "LINK" back. The implication is: to link back to the original source, the original essence, that which transcends all mental and intellectual attempts at comprehension, but which is the essential nature of everything in CREATION. While in the strict or dogmatic sense, Yoga philosophy and practice is a separate discipline from religion, yoga and religion have been linked at many points throughout history. In a manner of speaking, Yoga as a discipline may be seen as a non-sectarian transpersonal science or practice to promote spiritual development and harmony of mind and body thorough mental and physical disciplines including meditation, psycho-physical exercises, and performing action with the correct attitude.

The disciplines of Yoga fall under five major categories. These are: Yoga of Wisdom, Yoga of Devotional Love, Yoga of Meditation, Tantric Yoga and Yoga of Selfless Action. Within these categories there are subsidiary forms which are part of the main disciplines. The important point to remember is that all aspects of yoga can and should be used in an integral fashion to effect an efficient and harmonized spiritual movement in the practitioner. Therefore, while there may be an area of special emphasis, other elements are bound to become part of the yoga program as needed. For example, while a yogin may place emphasis on the yoga of wisdom, they may also practice devotional yoga and meditation yoga along with the wisdom studies.

While it is true that yogic practices may be found in religion, strictly speaking, yoga is neither a religion or a philosophy. It should be thought of more as a way of life or discipline for promoting greater fullness and experience of life. Yoga was developed at the dawn of history by those who wanted more out of life. These special men and women wanted to discover the true origins of creation and of themselves. Therefore, they set out to explore the vast reaches of consciousness within themselves. They are sometimes referred to as "Seers", "Sages", etc. Awareness or consciousness can only be increased when the mind is in a state of peace and harmony. Thus, the disciplines of meditation (which are part of Yoga), and wisdom (the philosophical teachings for understanding reality as it is) are the primary means to controlling the mind and allowing the individual to mature psychologically and spiritually.

The teachings which were practiced in the Ancient Egyptian temples were the same ones later intellectually defined into a literary form by the Indian Sages of Vedanta and Yoga. This was discussed in my book Egyptian Yoga: The Philosophy of Enlightenment. The Indian Mysteries of Yoga and Vedanta represent an unfolding and intellectual exposition of the Egyptian Mysteries. Also, the study of Gnostic Christianity or Christianity before Roman Catholicism will be useful to our study since Christianity originated in Ancient Egypt and was also based on the Ancient Egyptian Mysteries. Therefore, the study of the Egyptian Mysteries, early Christianity and Indian Vedanta-Yoga will provide the most comprehensive teaching on how to practice the disciplines of yoga leading to the attainment of Enlightenment.

The question is how to accomplish these seemingly impossible tasks? How to transform yourself and realize the deepest mysteries of existence? How to discover "who am I?" This is the mission of Yoga Philosophy and the purpose of yogic practices. Yoga does not seek to convert or impose religious beliefs on any one. Ancient Egypt was the source of civilization and the source of religion and Yoga. Therefore, all systems of mystical spirituality can coexist harmoniously within these teachings when they are correctly understood.

The goal of yoga is to promote integration of the mind-body-spirit complex in order to produce optimal health of the human being. This is accomplished through mental and physical exercises which promote the free flow of spiritual energy by reducing mental complexes caused by ignorance. There are two roads which human beings can follow, one of wisdom and the other of ignorance. The path of the masses is generally the path of ignorance which leads them into negative situations, thoughts and deeds. These in turn lead to ill health and sorrow in life. The other road is based on wisdom and it leads to health, true happiness and enlightenment.

Our mission is to extol the wisdom of yoga and mystical spirituality from the Ancient Egyptian perspective and to show the practice of the teachings through our books, videos and audio productions. You may find a complete listing of other books by the author in the back of this volume.

How to study the wisdom teachings:

There is a specific technique which is prescribed by the scriptures themselves for studying the teachings, proverbs and aphorisms of mystical wisdom. The method is as follows:

The spiritual aspirant should read the desired text thoroughly, taking note of any particular teachings which resonates with him or her. The aspirant should make a habit of collecting those teachings and reading them over frequently. The scriptures should be read and re-read because the subtle levels of the teachings will be increasingly understood the more the teachings are reviewed. One useful exercise is to choose some of the most special teachings you would like to focus on and place them in large type or as posters in your living areas so as to be visible to remind you of the teaching.

The aspirant should discuss those teachings with others of like mind when possible because this will help to promote greater understanding and act as an active spiritual practice in which the teachings are kept at the forefront of the mind. In this way, the teachings can become an integral part of everyday life and not reserved for a particular time of day or of the week.

The study of the wisdom teachings should be a continuous process in which the teachings become the predominant factor of life rather than the useless and oftentimes negative and illusory thoughts of those who are ignorant of spiritual truths. This spiritual discipline should be observed until Enlightenment is attained.

May you discover supreme peace in this very lifetime!

(HETEP - Supreme Peace)

Introduction to Egyptian Yoga

The Path of Divine Love

What is Yoga?

Most students of yoga are familiar with the yogic traditions of India consider that the Indian texts such as the Bhagavad Gita, Mahabharata, Patanjali Yoga Sutras, etc. are the primary and original source of Yogic philosophy and teaching. However, upon examination, the teachings currently espoused in all of the major forms of Indian Yoga can be found in Ancient Egyptian scriptures, inscribed in papyrus and on temple walls as well as steles, statues, obelisks and other sources.

Yoga is the practice of mental, physical and spiritual disciplines which lead to self-control and self-discovery by purifying the mind, body and spirit, so as to discover the deeper spiritual essence which lies within every human being and object in the universe. In essence, the goal of Yoga practice is to unite or yoke one's individual consciousness with Universal or Cosmic consciousness. Therefore, Ancient Egyptian religious practice, especially in terms of the rituals and other practices of the Ancient Egyptian Temple system known as Shetaut Neter (the way of the hidden Supreme Being), also known in Ancient times as Smai Tawi "Egyptian Yoga," should as well be considered as universal streams of self-knowledge philosophy which influenced and inspired the great religions and philosophers to this day. In this sense, religion, in its purest form, is also a Yoga system, as it seeks to reunite the soul with its true and original source, God. In broad terms, any spiritual movement or discipline that brings one closer to self-knowledge is a "Yogic" movement. The main recognized forms of Yoga disciplines are:

- Yoga of Wisdom,
- Yoga of Devotional Love,
- Yoga of Meditation,
    - Physical Postures Yoga
- Yoga of Selfless Action,
- Tantric Yoga
    - Serpent Power Yoga

The diagram below shows the relationship between the Yoga disciplines and the path of mystical religion (religion practiced in its three complete steps: 1st receiving the myth {knowledge}, 2nd practicing the rituals of the myth {following the teachings of the myth} and 3rd entering into a mystical experience {becoming one with the central figure of the myth}).

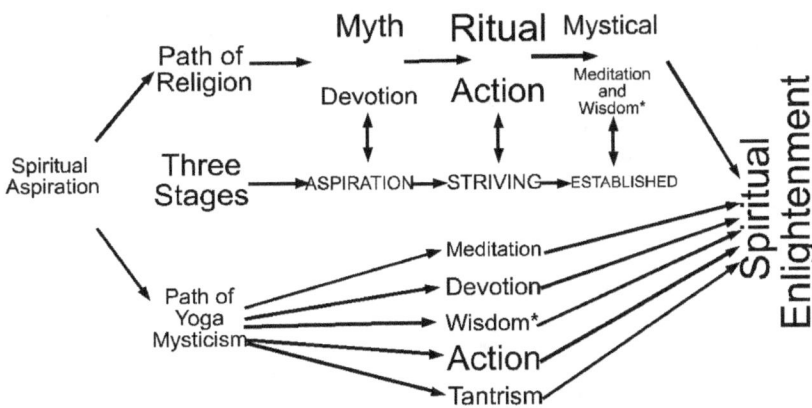

The disciplines of Yoga fall under five major categories. These are: Yoga of Wisdom, Yoga of Devotional Love, Yoga of Meditation, Tantric Yoga and Yoga of Selfless Action. When these disciplines are practiced in a harmonized manner this practice is called "Integral Yoga." Within these categories there are subsidiary forms which are part of the main disciplines. The emphasis in the Kamitan Asarian (Osirian) Myth is on the Yoga of Wisdom, Yoga of Devotional Love and Yoga of Selfless Action. The important point to remember is that all aspects of Yoga can and should be used in an integral fashion to effect an efficient and harmonized spiritual movement in the practitioner. Therefore, while there may be an area of special emphasis, other elements are bound to become part of the Yoga program as needed. For example, while a Yogin (practitioner of Yoga, aspirant, initiate) may place emphasis on the Yoga of Wisdom, they may also practice Devotional Yoga and Meditation Yoga along with the wisdom studies. So the practice of any discipline that leads to oneness with Supreme Consciousness can be called Yoga. If you study, rationalize and reflect upon the teachings, you are practicing Yoga of Wisdom. If you meditate upon the teachings and your Higher Self, you are practicing Yoga of Meditation.

Thus, whether or not you refer to it as such, if you practice rituals which identify you with your spiritual nature, you are practicing Yoga of Ritual Identification (which is part of the Yoga of Wisdom {Kamitan-Rekh, Indian-Jnana} and the Yoga of Devotional Love {Kamitan-Ushet, Indian-Bhakti} of the Divine). If you develop your physical nature and psychic energy centers, you are practicing Serpent Power (Kamitan-Uraeus or Indian-Kundalini) Yoga (which is part of Tantric Yoga). If you practice living according to the teachings of ethical behavior and selflessness, you are practicing Yoga of Action (Kamitan-Maat, Indian-Karma) in daily life. If you practice turning your attention towards the Divine by developing love for the Divine, then it is called Devotional Yoga or Yoga of Divine Love. The practitioner of Yoga is called a Yogin (male practitioner) or Yogini (female practitioner), or the term "Yogi" may be used to refer to either a female or male practitioner in general terms. One who has attained the culmination of Yoga (union with the Divine) is also called a Yogi. In this manner, Yoga has been developed into many disciplines which may be used in an integral fashion to achieve the same goal: Enlightenment. Therefore, the aspirant is to learn about all of the paths of Yoga and choose those elements which best suit {his/her} personality or practice them all in an integral, balanced way.

Enlightenment is the term used to describe the highest level of spiritual awakening. It means attaining such a level of spiritual awareness that one discovers the underlying unity of the entire universe as well as the fact that the source of all creation is the same source from which the innermost Self within every human heart arises.

The Path of Divine Love

What is Egyptian Yoga?

The Term "Egyptian Yoga" and The Philosophy Behind It

As previously discussed, Yoga in all of its forms were practiced in Egypt apparently earlier than anywhere else in our history. This point of view is supported by the fact that there is documented scriptural and iconographical evidence of the disciplines of virtuous living, dietary purification, study of the wisdom teachings and their practice in daily life, psychophysical and psycho-spiritual exercises and meditation being practiced in Ancient Egypt, long before the evidence of its existence is detected in India (including the Indus Valley Civilization) or any other early civilization (Sumer, Greece, China, etc.).

The teachings of Yoga are at the heart of Prt m Hru. As explained earlier, the word "Yoga" is a Sanskrit term meaning to unite the individual with the Cosmic. The term has been used in certain parts of this book for ease of communication since the word "Yoga" has received wide popularity especially in western countries in recent years. The Ancient Egyptian equivalent term to the Sanskrit word yoga is: "Smai." Smai means union, and the following determinative terms give it a spiritual significance, at once equating it with the term "Yoga" as it is used in India. When used in conjunction with the Ancient Egyptian symbol which means land, "Ta," the term "union of the two lands" arises.

In Chapter 4 and Chapter 17 of the Prt m Hru, a term "Smai Tawi" is used. It means "Union of the two lands of Egypt," ergo "Egyptian Yoga." The two lands refer to the two main districts of the country (North and South). In ancient times, Egypt was divided into two sections or land areas. These were known as Lower and Upper Egypt. In Ancient Egyptian mystical philosophy, the land of Upper Egypt relates to the divinity Heru (Heru), who represents the Higher Self, and the land of Lower Egypt relates to Set, the divinity of the lower self. So Smai Taui means "the union of the two lands" or the "Union of the lower self with the Higher Self. The lower self relates to that which is negative and uncontrolled in the human mind including worldliness, egoism, ignorance, etc. (Set), while the Higher Self relates to that which is above temptations and is good in the human heart as well as in touch with transcendental consciousness (Heru). Thus, we also have the Ancient Egyptian term Smai Heru-Set, or the union of Heru and Set. So Smai Taui or Smai Heru-Set are the Ancient Egyptian words which are to be translated as **"Egyptian Yoga."**

Above: the main symbol of Egyptian Yoga: Sma. The Ancient Egyptian language and symbols provide the first "historical" record of Yoga Philosophy and Religious literature. The hieroglyph Sma, ⚊"Sema," represented by the union of two lungs and the trachea, symbolizes that the union of the duality, that is, the Higher Self and lower self, leads to Non-duality, the One, singular consciousness.

The Ancient Egyptians called the disciplines of Yoga in Ancient Egypt by the term "Smai Tawi." So what does Smai Tawi mean?

Neter Merri

Smai Tawi
(From Chapter 4 of the Prt m Hru)

The Ancient Egyptian Symbols of Yoga

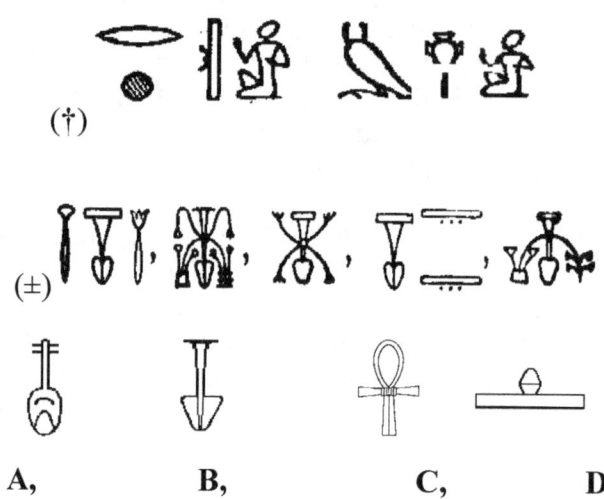

The theme of the arrangement of the symbols above is based on the idea that in mythological and philosophic forms, Egyptian mythology and philosophy merge with world mythology, philosophy and religion. The hieroglyphic symbols at the very top (†) mean: "Know Thyself," "Self knowledge is the basis of all true knowledge" and (±) abbreviated forms of Smai taui, signifies "Egyptian Yoga." The next four below represent the four words in Egyptian Philosophy, which mean "YOGA." They are: (A) "Nefer"(B) "Sema" (C) "Ankh" and (D) "Hetep."

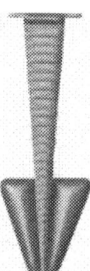

Above: the main symbol of Egyptian Yoga: Sma. The Ancient Egyptian language and symbols provide the first "historical" record of Yoga Philosophy and Religious literature. The hieroglyph Sma, "Sema," represented by the union of two lungs and the trachea, symbolizes that the union of the duality, that is, the Higher Self and lower self, leads to Non-duality, the One, singular consciousness.

58

The Path of Divine Love

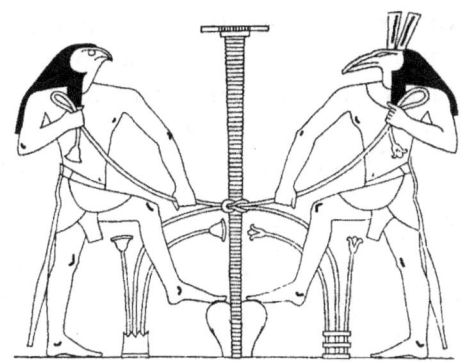

Above left: Smai Heru-Set, Heru and Set join forces to tie up the symbol of Union (Sema –see (B) above). The Sema symbol refers to the Union of Upper Egypt (Lotus) and Lower Egypt (Papyrus) under one ruler, but also at a more subtle level, it refers to the union of one's Higher Self and lower self (Heru and Set), as well as the control of one's breath (Life Force) through the union (control) of the lungs (breathing organs). The character of Heru and Set are an integral part of the Pert Em Heru.

The central and most popular character within Ancient Egyptian Religion of Asar is Heru, who is an incarnation of his father, Asar. Asar is killed by his brother Set who, out of greed and demoniac (Setian) tendency, craved to be the ruler of Egypt. With the help of Djehuti, the God of wisdom, Aset, the great mother and Hetheru, his consort, Heru prevailed in the battle against Set for the rulership of Kemit (Egypt). Heru's struggle symbolizes the struggle of every human being to regain rulership of the Higher Self and to subdue the lower self.

The most ancient writings in our historical period are from the Ancient Egyptians. These writings are referred to as hieroglyphics. The original name given to these writings by the Ancient Egyptians is Metu Neter, meaning "the writing of God" or Neter Metu or "Divine Speech." These writings were inscribed in temples, coffins and papyruses and contained the teachings in reference to the spiritual nature of the human being and the ways to promote spiritual emancipation, awakening or resurrection. The Ancient Egyptian proverbs presented in this text are translations from the original hieroglyphic scriptures. An example of hieroglyphic text was presented above in the form of the text of Smai Taui or "Egyptian Yoga."

Egyptian Philosophy may be summed up in the following proverbs, which clearly state that the soul is heavenly or divine and that the human being must awaken to the true reality, which is the Spirit, Self.

"Self knowledge is the basis of true knowledge."

"Soul to heaven, body to earth."

"Man is to become God-like through a life of virtue and the cultivation of the spirit through scientific knowledge, practice and bodily discipline."

"Salvation is accomplished through the efforts of the individual.
There is no mediator between man and {his/her} salvation."

Neter Merri

"Salvation is the freeing of the soul from its bodily fetters, becoming a God through knowledge and wisdom, controlling the forces of the cosmos instead of being a slave to them, subduing the lower nature and through awakening the Higher Self, ending the cycle of rebirth and dwelling with the Neters who direct and control the Great Plan."

Egyptian Yoga is a revolutionary new way to understand and practice Ancient Egyptian Mysticism, the Ancient Egyptian mystical religion (Shetaut Neter). Egyptian Yoga is what has been commonly referred to by Egyptologists as Egyptian "Religion" or "Mythology," but to think of it as just another set of stories or allegories about a long lost civilization is to completely miss the greatest secret of human existence. What is Yoga? The literal meaning of the word YOGA is to "YOKE" or to "LINK" back. The implication is to link back individual consciousness to its original source, the original essence: Universal Consciousness. In a broad sense Yoga is any process which helps one to achieve liberation or freedom from the bondage to human pain and spiritual ignorance. So whenever you engage in any activity with the goal of promoting the discovery of your true Self, be it studying the wisdom teachings, exercise, fasting, meditation, breath control, rituals, chanting, prayer, etc., you are practicing yoga. If the goal is to help you to discover your essential nature as one with God or the Supreme Being or Consciousness, then it is Yoga. Yoga, in all of its forms as the disciplines of spiritual development, as practiced in Ancient Egypt earlier than anywhere else in history. The ancient scriptures describe how Asar, the first mythical king of Ancient Egypt, traveled throughout Asia and Europe establishing civilization and the practice of religion. This partially explains why the teachings of mystical spirituality known as Yoga and Vedanta in India are so similar to the teachings of Shetaut Neter (Ancient Egyptian religion - Egyptian Yoga. This unique perspective from the highest philosophical system which developed in Africa over seven thousand years ago provides a new way to look at life, religion, psychology and the way to spiritual development leading to spiritual Enlightenment. So Egyptian Yoga is not merely a philosophy but a discipline for promoting spiritual evolution in a human being, allowing him or her to discover the ultimate truth, supreme peace and utmost joy which lies within the human heart. These are the true worthwhile goals of life. Anything else is settling for less. It would be like a personality who owns vast riches thinking that he is poor and homeless. Every human being has the potential to discover the greatest treasure of all existence if they apply themselves to the study and practice of the teachings of Yoga with the proper guidance. Sema (☥) is the Ancient Egyptian word and symbol meaning union or Yoga. This is the vision of Egyptian Yoga.

The Study of Yoga

When we look out upon the world, we are often baffled by the multiplicity, which constitutes the human experience. What do we really know about this experience? Many scientific disciplines have developed over the last two hundred years for the purpose of discovering the mysteries of nature, but this search has only engendered new questions about the nature of existence. Yoga is a discipline or way of life designed to promote the physical, mental and spiritual development of the human being. It leads a person to discover the answers to the most important questions of life such as, Who am I? Why am I here? Where am I going?

As explained earlier, the literal meaning of the word Yoga is to "Yoke" or to "Link" back, the implication being to link the individual consciousness back to the original source, the original essence, that which transcends all mental and intellectual attempts at comprehension, but which is the essential nature of everything in Creation, termed "Universal Consciousness. While in the strict sense, Yoga may be seen as a separate discipline from religion, yoga and religion have been linked at many points throughout history and continue to be linked even today. In a manner of speaking, Yoga as a discipline may be seen as a non-sectarian transpersonal science or practice to promote spiritual development and harmony of mind and body thorough mental and physical disciplines including meditation, psycho-physical exercises, and performing action with the correct attitude.

The teachings which were practiced in the Ancient Egyptian temples were the same ones later intellectually defined into a literary form by the Indian Sages of Vedanta and Yoga. This was discussed in our book Egyptian Yoga: The Philosophy of Enlightenment. The Indian Mysteries of Yoga and Vedanta may therefore be understood as representing an unfolding exposition of the Egyptian Mysteries.

The question is how to accomplish these seemingly impossible tasks? How to transform yourself and realize the deepest mysteries of existence? How to discover "Who am I?" This is the mission of Yoga Philosophy and the purpose of yogic practices. Yoga does not seek to convert or impose religious beliefs on any one. Ancient Egypt was the source of civilization and the source of religion and Yoga. Therefore, all systems of mystical spirituality can coexist harmoniously within these teachings when they are correctly understood.

The goal of yoga is to promote integration of the mind-body-spirit complex in order to produce optimal health of the human being. This is accomplished through mental and physical exercises which promote the free flow of spiritual energy by reducing mental complexes caused by ignorance. There are two roads which human beings can follow, one of wisdom and the other of ignorance. The path of the masses is generally the path of ignorance which leads them into negative situations, thoughts and deeds. These in turn lead to ill health and sorrow in life. The other road is based on wisdom and it leads to health, true happiness and enlightenment.

The central and most popular character within ancient Egyptian Religion of Asar is Heru who is an incarnation of his father, Asar. Asar is killed by his brother Set who, out of greed and demoniac (Setian) tendency, craves to be the ruler of Egypt. With the help of Djehuti, the God of wisdom, Aset, the great mother and Hetheru, his consort, Heru prevails in the battle against Set for the rulership of Egypt. Heru' struggle symbolizes the struggle of every human being to regain rulership of the Higher Self and to subdue the lower self. With this understanding, the land of Egypt is equivalent to the Kingdom/Queendom concept of Christianity.

The most ancient writings in our historical period are from the ancient Egyptians. These writings are referred to as hieroglyphics. Also, the most ancient civilization known was the ancient Egyptian civilization. The proof of this lies in the ancient Sphinx which is over 12,000 years old. The original name given to these writings by the ancient Egyptians is Metu Neter, meaning "the writing of God" or Neter Metu or "Divine Speech." These writings were inscribed in temples, coffins and papyruses and contained the teachings in reference to the spiritual nature of the human being and the ways to promote spiritual emancipation, awakening or resurrection. The Ancient Egyptian Proverbs presented in this text are translations from the original hieroglyphic scriptures. An example of hieroglyphic text is presented on the front cover.

Egyptian Philosophy may be summed up in the following proverbs which clearly state that the soul is heavenly or divine and that the human being must awaken to the true reality which is the spirit Self.

Neter Merri

"Self knowledge is the basis of true knowledge."

"Soul to heaven, body to earth."

"Man is to become God-like through a life of virtue and the cultivation of the spirit through scientific knowledge, practice and bodily discipline."

"Salvation is accomplished through the efforts of the individual. There is no mediator between man and his / her salvation."

"Salvation is the freeing of the soul from its bodily fetters, becoming a God through knowledge and wisdom, controlling the forces of the cosmos instead of being a slave to them, subduing the lower nature and through awakening the Higher Self, ending the cycle of rebirth and dwelling with the Neters who direct and control the Great Plan."

Smai Tawi (From Chapter 4 of the Prt m Hru)

The Sema Tawi of Wisdom

One discipline of Yoga requires special mention here. It is called Wisdom Yoga or the Yoga of Wisdom. In the Temple of Aset (Isis) in Ancient Egypt the Discipline of the Yoga of Wisdom is imparted in three stages:

1-<u>Listening</u> to the wisdom teachings on the nature of reality (creation) and the nature of the Self.
2-<u>Reflecting</u> on those teachings and incorporating them into daily life.
3-<u>Meditating</u> on the meaning of the teachings.

Aset (Isis) was and is recognized as the goddess of wisdom and her temple strongly emphasized and espoused the philosophy of wisdom teaching in order to achieve higher spiritual consciousness. It is important to note here that the teaching which was practiced in the Ancient Egyptian Temple of Aset[9] of **<u>Listening</u>** to, **<u>Reflecting</u>** upon, and **<u>Meditating</u>** upon the teachings is the same process used in Vedanta-Jnana Yoga of India of today. **The Yoga of Wisdom** is a form of Yoga based on insight into the nature of worldly existence and the transcendental Self, thereby transforming one's consciousness through development of the wisdom faculty. Thus, we have here a correlation between Ancient Egypt that matches exactly in its basic factor respects.

THE THREE-FOLD PROCESS OF WISDOM YOGA IN EGYPT:

According to the teachings of the Ancient Temple of Aset the Yoga of Wisdom, entails the process of three steps:

Discipline of Wisdom Yoga in Ancient Egypt
1-<u>Listening</u> to the wisdom teachings on the nature of reality (creation) and the nature of the Self.
2-<u>Reflecting</u> on those teachings and incorporating them into daily life.
3-<u>Meditating</u> on the meaning of the teachings.

---

[9] See the book **The Wisdom of** Aset by Dr. Muata Ashby

Figure 1: The image of goddess Aset (Isis) suckling the young king is the quintecential symbol of initiation in Ancient Egypt.

Temple of Aset
GENERAL DISCIPLINE

Fill the ears, listen attentively- Meh mestchert.

Listening
1- Listening to Wisdom teachings. Having achieved the qualifications of an aspirant, there is a desire to listen to the teachings from a Spiritual Preceptor. There is increasing intellectual understanding of the scriptures and the meaning of truth versus untruth, real versus unreal, temporal versus eternal. The glories of God are expounded and the mystical philosophy behind the myth is given at this stage.

MAUI

"to think, to ponder, to fix attention, concentration"

Reflection
2- Reflection on those teachings that have been listened to and living according to the disciplines enjoined by the teachings is to be practiced until the wisdom teaching is fully understood. Reflection implies discovering, intellectually at first, the oneness behind the multiplicity of the world by engaging in intense inquiry into the nature of one's true Self. Chanting the hekau and divine singing Hesi, are also used here.

"Devote yourself to adore God's name."

—Ancient Egyptian Proverb

 *uaa* "Meditation"

Meditation
3- Meditation in Wisdom Yoga is the process of reflection that leads to a state in which the mind is continuously introspective. It means expansion of consciousness culminating in revelation of and identification with the Absolute Self.

Note: It is important to note here that the same teaching which was practiced in ancient Egypt of **Listening** to, **Reflecting** upon, and **Meditating** upon the teachings is the same process used in Vedanta-Jnana Yoga (from India) of today.

The Path of Divine Love

The Sema Tawi of Right Action

**GENERAL DISCIPLINE
In all Temples especially
The Temple of Heru and Edfu**

Scripture: Prt M Hru and special scriptures including the Berlin Papyrus and other papyri.

1- Learn Ethics and Law of Cause and Effect-Practice right action
(42 Precepts of Maat)
to purify gross impurities of the personality
<u>Control Body, Speech, Thoughts</u>

2- Practice cultivation of the higher virtues
(selfless-service)
to purify mind and intellect from subtle impurities

3- Devotion to the Divine
See maatian actions as offerings to the Divine

4- Meditation
See oneself as one with Maat, i.e. United with the cosmic order which is the Transcendental Supreme Self.

Plate 1: The Offering of Maat-Symbolizing the Ultimate act of Righteousness (Temple of Seti I)

Neter Merri

The Sema Tawi of Divine Love

GENERAL DISCIPLINE
In all Temples

Scripture: Prt M Hru and Temple Inscriptions.

<u>Discipline of Devotion</u>

1– Listening to the myth
    Get to know the Divinity
    Empathize
    Romantisize

2- Ritual about the myth
    Offerings to Divinity – propitiation
    act like divinity
    Chant the name of the Divinity
    Sing praises of the Divinity
    COMMUNE with the Divinity

3– Mysticism
    Melting of the heart
    Dissolve into Divinity

    IDENTIFY-with the Divinity

In the Kamitan teaching of Devotional love:

God is termed Merri, "Beloved One"

Love and Be Loved
"That person is beloved by the Lord." PMH, Ch 4

The Path of Divine Love

Offering Oneself to God-Surrender to God- Become One with God

Figure 2: The Dua Pose- Upraised arms with palms facing out towards the Divine Image

The Sema Tawi of Meditation

Posture-Sitting With Hands on Thighs

It is well known and commonly accepted that meditation has been practiced in India from ancient times. Therefore, there is no need to site specific references to support that contention. Here we will concentrate on the evidence supporting the existence of the philosophy of meditation in Ancient Egypt.

The Paths of Meditation Practiced in Ancient Egypt

System of Meditation: **Glorious Light System**
Location where it was practiced in ancient times: **Temple of Seti I, City of Waset (Thebes)** [10]

System of Meditation: **Wisdom System**
Location where it was practiced in ancient times: **Temple of Aset – Philae Island, Aswan**

System of Meditation: **Serpent Power System**
Location where it was practiced in ancient times: **Temple of Asar- City of Abdu**

System of Meditation: **Devotional Meditation**
Location where it was practiced in ancient times: **IN ALL TEMPLES- GENERAL DISCIPLINE**

Formal meditation in Yoga consists of four basic elements: Posture, Sound (chant-words of power), Visualization, Rhythmic Breathing (calm, steady breath). The instructions, translated from the original hieroglyphic text contain the basic elements for formal meditation.

---

[10] For More details see the book **The Glorious Light Meditation System of Ancient Egypt** by Dr. Muata Ashby.

The Path of Divine Love

(1)-Posture and Focus of Attention

                 iuf iri-f ahau maq b-phr nty hau iu
                body do make stand, within the Sundisk (circle of Ra)

This means that the aspirant should remain established as if in the center of a circle with a dot in the middle.

(2)- Words of power-chant[11]

Nuk Hekau (I am the word* itself)
Nuk Ra Akhu (I am Ra's Glorious Shinning** Spirit)
Nuk Ba Ra (I am the soul of Ra)
Nuk Hekau (I am the God who creates*** through sound)

(3)- Visualization

                Iuf mi Ra heru mestu-f n-shry chet
                "My body is like Ra's on the day of his birth

This teaching is what in Indian Vedanta Philosophy is referred to as Ahamgraha Upashama – or visualizing and meditating upon oneself as being one with God. This teaching is the main focus of the Prt m Hru (Book of Enlightenment) text of Ancient Egypt. It is considered as the highest form of meditation practice amongst Indian mystics.[12]

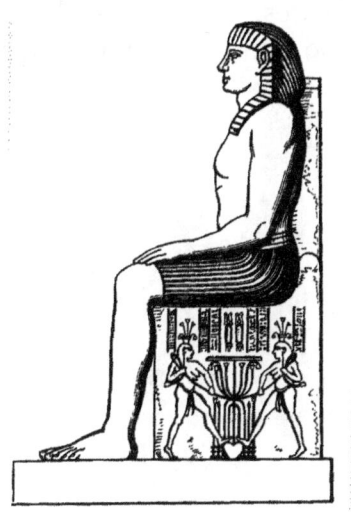

---

[11] The term "Words of Power" relates to chants and or recitations given for meditation practice. They were used in a similar way to the Hindu "Mantras."
[12] Statement made by Swami Jyotirmayananda in class with his disciples.

Plate 2: Basic Instructions for the Glorious Light Meditation System- Given in the Tomb of Seti I. (c. 1350 B.C.E.)

As we have seen, the practice of meditation in Ancient Egypt and its instruction to the masses and not just to the priests and priestesses, can be traced to at least 800 years earlier. If the instructions given by sage Seti I and those given by sage Patanjali are compared, many similarities appear.

The Path of Divine Love

The Yogic Postures in Ancient Egypt

Since their introduction to the West, the exercise system of India known as "Hatha Yoga" has gained much popularity. The disciplines related to the yogic postures and movements were developed in India around the 10th century A.C.E. by a sage named Goraksha.[13] Up to this time, the main practice was simply to adopt the cross-legged meditation posture known as the lotus for the purpose of practicing meditation. The most popular manual on Hatha Yoga is the Hatha Yoga-Pradipika ("Light on the Forceful Yoga). It was authored by Svatmarama Yogin in mid. 14th century A.C.E.[14]

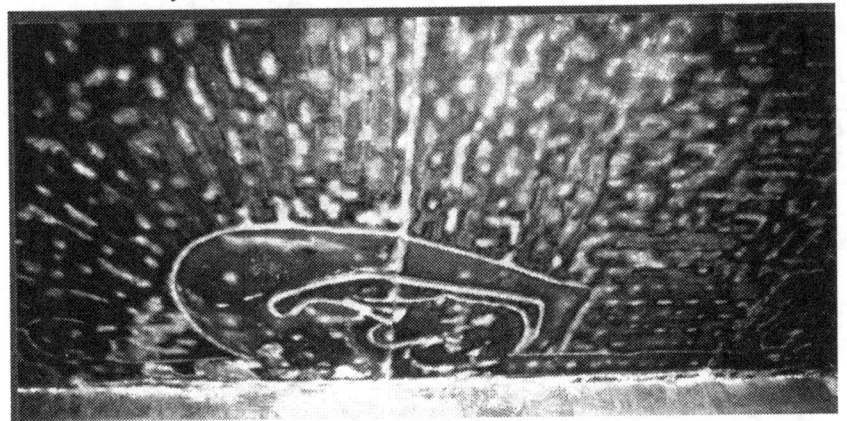

Plate 3: Above- The god Geb in the plough posture engraved on the ceiling of the antechamber to the Asarian Resurrection room of the Temple of Hetheru in Egypt. (photo taken by Ashby). Below: Illustration of the posture engraved on the ceiling.

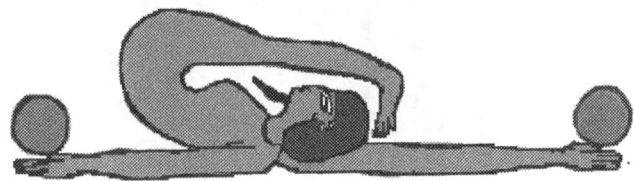

Prior to the emergence of the discipline of the physical movements in India just before 1000 A.C.E.,[15] a series of virtually identical postures to those which were practiced in India can be found in various Ancient Egyptian papyruses and inscribed on the walls and ceilings of the temples. The Ancient Egyptian practice can be dated from 10,000 B.C.E to 300 B.C.E and earlier. Examples: Temple of Hetheru (800-300 B.C.E.), Temple of Heru (800-300 B.C.E.), Tomb of Queen Nefertari (reigned 1,279-1,212 B.C.E.), and various other temples and papyruses from the New Kingdom Era (c. 1,580 B.C.E). In Ancient Egypt the practice of the postures, called Tjef Sema Paut Neteru which means "Movements to promote union with the gods and goddesses" or simply Sema Paut (Union with the gods and goddesses), were part of the ritual

---

[13] Yoga Journal, {The New Yoga} January/February 2000
[14] Hatha-Yoga-Pradipika, <u>The Shambhala Encyclopedia of Yoga</u> by Georg Feuerstein, Ph. D.
[15] <u>The Shambhala Encyclopedia of Yoga</u> by Georg Feuerstein, Ph. D.

aspect of the spiritual myth, which when practiced, served to harmonize the energies and promote the physical health of the body and direct the mind in a meditative capacity to discover and cultivate divine consciousness. These disciplines are part of a larger process called Sema or Smai Tawi (Egyptian Yoga). By acting and moving like the gods and goddesses one can essentially discover their character, energy and divine agency within one's consciousness, and thereby also become one of their retinue, that is, one with the Divine Self. In modern times, most practitioners of Indian Hatha Yoga see it primarily as a means to attain physical health only. However, even the practice in India had an origin in myth and a mythic component which is today largely ignored by modern practitioners.

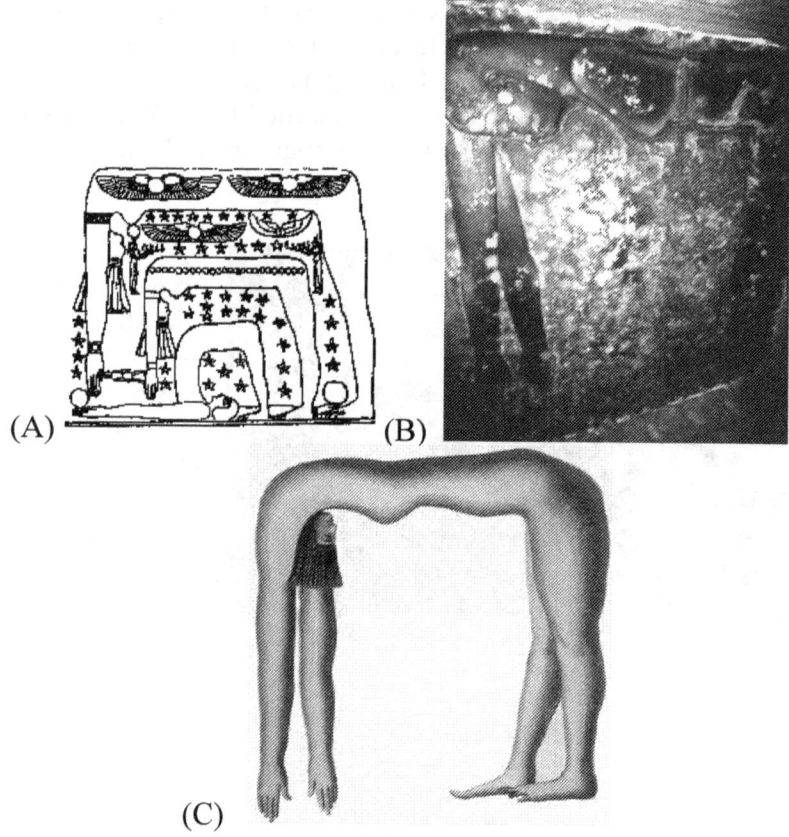

Figure 3: Above left: The Kamitan goddess Nut and god Geb and the higher planes of existence. Above center and right: The goddess Nut performs the forward bend posture.

The figure above (left) depicts another conceptualization of the Netherworld, which is at the same time the body of Nut in a forward bend yoga exercise posture. The innermost goddess symbolizes the lower heaven where the moon traverses, the physical realm. The middle one symbolizes the course of the sun in its Astral journey. This shows a differentiation between the physical heavens and the Astral plane, as well as time and physical space and Astral time and space, i.e., the concept of different dimensions and levels of consciousness. The outermost symbolizes the causal plane.

The Path of Divine Love

Plate 4: Below- The Egyptian Gods and Goddesses act out the Creation through their movements: Forward bend -Nut, Spinal twist -Geb, Journey of Ra – Ra in his boat, and the squatting and standing motions of Nun and Shu.

Figure 4: The varied postures found in the Kamitan papyruses and temple inscriptions.
Figure 5: The practice of the postures is shown in the sequence below.

The Path of Divine Love

The Sema Tawi of Tantrism

> Tantric influence, however, is not limited to India alone, and there is evidence that the precepts of tantrism traveled to various parts of the world, especially Nepal, Tibet, China, Japan and parts of South-East Asia; its influence has also been evident in Mediterranean cultures such as those of Egypt and Crete.[16]
> -Ajit Mookerjee (Indian Scholar-Author –from the book The Tantric Way)

Tantra Yoga is purported to be the oldest system of Yoga. Tantra Yoga is a system of Yoga which seeks to promote the re-union between the individual and the Absolute Reality, through the worship of nature and ultimately the Cosmos as an expression of the Absolute. Since nature is an expression of GOD, it gives clues as to the underlying reality that sustains it and the way to achieve wisdom, i.e. transcendence of it. The most obvious and important teaching that nature holds is the idea that creation is made up of pairs of opposites: Up-down, here-there, you-me, us-them, hot-cold, male-female, Ying-Yang, etc. The interaction, of these two complementary opposites, we call life and movement.

Insight (wisdom) into the true nature of reality gives us a clue as to the way to realize the oneness of creation within ourselves. By re-uniting the male and female principles in our own bodies and minds, we may reach the oneness that underlies our apparent manifestation as a man or woman. Thus, the term Tantra means to create a bridge between the opposites and in so doing the opposites dissolve, leaving unitary and transcendental consciousness. The union of the male and female principles may be effected by two individuals who worship GOD through GOD's manifestation in each other or by an individual who seeks union with GOD through uniting with his or her male or female spiritual partner. All men and women have both female and male principles within themselves.

In the Egyptian philosophical system, all Neteru or God principles emanate from the one GOD. When these principles are created, they are depicted as having a <u>male and female</u> principle. All objects and life forms appear in creation as either male or female, but underlying this apparent duality, there is a unity which is rooted in the pure consciousness of oneness, the consciousness of GOD, which underlies and supports all things. To realize this oneness consciously deep inside is the supreme goal.

In Tantrism, sexual symbolism is used frequently because these are the most powerful images denoting the opposites of Creation and the urge to unify and become whole, for sexuality is the urge for unity and self-discovery albeit limited to physical intercourse by most people. If this

---
[16] <u>The Tantric Way</u> by Ajit Mookerjee and Madhu Khanna

force is understood, harnessed and sublimated it will lead to unity of the highest order that is unity with the Divine Self.

Figure 6: Above- the Kamitan God Geb and the Kamitan Goddess Nut separate after the sexual union that gave birth to the gods and goddesses and Creation. Below: three depictions of the god Asar in tantric union with Aset.

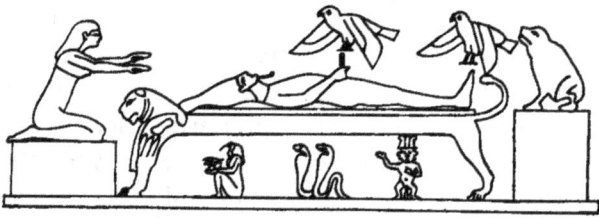

Figure 7: Above-The virgin birth of Heru (The resurrection of Asar - higher, Heru consciousness). Isis in the winged form hovers over the reconstructed penis of dead Asar. Note: Asar uses right hand.

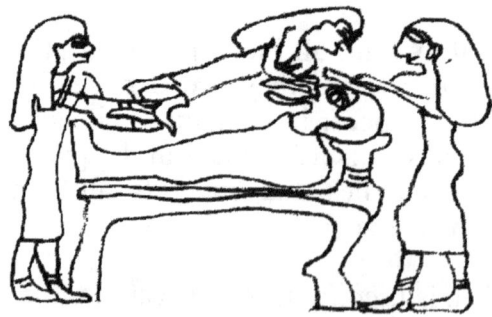

Figure 8: Drawing found in an Ancient Egyptian Building of The Conception of Heru[17]

---

[17] Sexual Life in Ancient Egypt by Lise Manniche

The Path of Divine Love

Isis (representing the physical body-creation) and the dead body of Asar (representing the spirit, that essence which vivifies matter) are shown in symbolic immaculate union (compare to the "Kali Position" on the following page) begetting Heru, symbolizing to the immaculate conception which takes place at the birth of the spiritual life in every human: the birth of the soul (Ba) in a human is the birth of Heru.

-From a Stele at the British Museum 1372. 13th Dyn.

Figure 9: Above- the god Shiva and his consort Shakti

The "Kali position" (above) features **Shiva and Shakti (Kundalini-Prakriti)** in divine union (India). As with Asar and Isis of Egypt, Shiva is the passive, male aspect who "gives" the life essence (spirit) and creative impetus and Shakti is energy, creation, the active aspect of GOD. Thus Creation is akin to the idea of GOD making love with him/herself. Shiva and Shakti are the true essence of the human being, composed of spirit and matter (body). In the active aspect, the female is in the "active" position while the male is in the "passive" position. In Kamitan philosophy, the god Geb is the earth and the goddess Nut is the sky. Just as the earth is sedentary and the sky is dynamic so too are the divinities depicted in this way in Southern (African) and Eastern (India) iconography.

Figure 10: Above- Buddha and his consort.

Above: Tibetan Buddhist representation of The Dharmakaya, the cosmic father-mother. expressing the idea of the Supreme Being as a union of both male and female principals.

Notice that the female divinities are always on the top position. This is classic in Eastern and Kamitan mysticism. It is a recognition that the spirit (male aspect) is sedentary while matter, the female aspect, is in perpetual motion and the two complement and complete each other.

Figure 11: Below left- The Triune ithyphallic form of Asar[18]

Figure 12: Below right- the Trilinga (Triune ithyphallic form) of Shiva.[19]

Figure 13: Below far right- the multi-armed (all-pervasive) dancing Shiva-whose dance sustains the Creation.

Figure 14: Below- left Ashokan[20] pillar with lion capital-Kamitan pillar with lion capitals. Center: Ancient Egyptian pillar with lion capitals. Far right: the Ethiopian divinity Apedemak, displaying the same leonine trinity concept and the multi-armed motif.

---

[18] For more details see the book Egyptian Yoga Volume 1
[19] For more details see the book Egyptian Yoga Volume 1
[20] Constructed in the period of the Indian King Asoka (Ashoka) who adopted Buddhism.

The Path of Divine Love

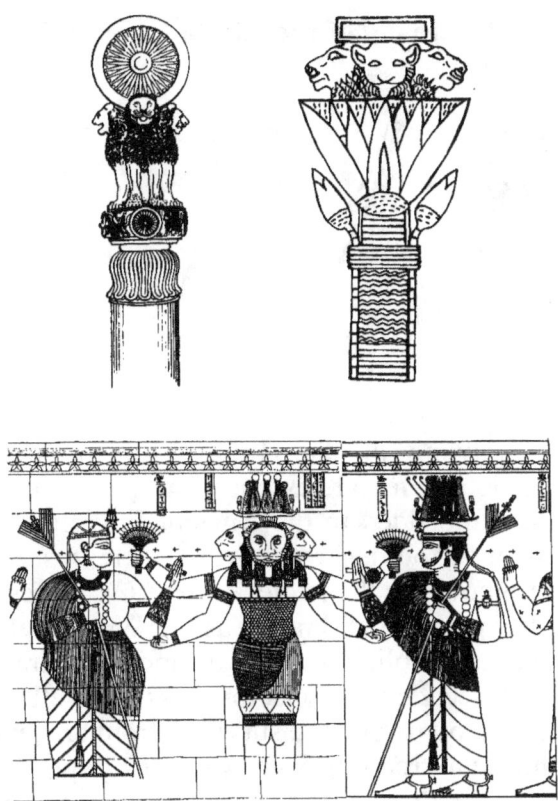

The trinity symbolically relates the nature of the Divine, who is the source and sustenance of the three worlds (physical, astral and causal), the three states of consciousness (conscious, subconscious and unconscious), the three modes of nature (dull, agitated and lucid), the three aspects of human experience (seer, seen and sight), as well as the three stages of initiation (ignorance, aspiration and enlightenment). This triad idea is common to Neterianism, Hinduism and Christianity. The idea of the multi-armed divinity is common in Indian Iconography. However, the depiction above from Ethiopia spiritual iconography shows that it was present in Africa as well.

In the path of Tantra, Divine love is integral to the tantric movement. Through its expression as the sexual union, the emotion of love for the Divine is reveal through sexuality. In this discipline the aspirant abstains from love with other human beings and with worldly objects and reserves this love for the Divine, through the forms of iconographic symbolisms and its expression as Creation itself. Thereby a Divine union is created and upon experiencing that union it is consummated it the enlightenment experience itself, the Nehast or Great Awakening. This is the great "Divine Marriage" of the mystics. It is the mystical teaching behind the procession the Divine Boat, up the center of the temple into the inner shrine, and the Divine embrace in the holy of holies, which remains today as a shadow of its original teaching, in the ritual procession of the Christian Mass sacrament.

Figure 15: Below (A)- Line art drawing of the Hindu Lingam-Yoni (Phallus-Vulva) of India and the Crowns of Ancient Egypt.

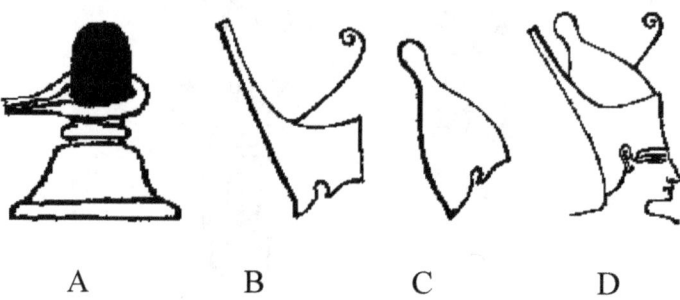

A   B   C   D

Above left, (A)- Line art drawing of the Hindu Lingam-Yoni (Phallus-Vulva) of India symbolizes the unity of the male and female essence into one non-dualistic whole. Figures B-D display the Tantric symbolism embedded in the Ancient Egyptian Pharaonic Crowns. The Red Crown of Lower Egypt, known as the deshret crown (B), represents the female principle. The white Crown of Upper Egypt, known as the hedjet crown (C), represents the male principle. The Crown of Upper and Lower Egypt together, known as the Wereret crown (D), represent the male principle going into the female- symbolizing unity, balance, and transcendence of duality, i.e. it signifies the attainment of transcendental consciousness as well as rulership over the lower nature and the Higher. As, no crowns of have survived from ancient times and no references to it have been discovered in the extant records from Ancient Egypt, Egyptologists have speculated on the nature and symbolism of the Pharaonic crowns from the beginning of modern Egyptology up to the present. The understanding of the crowns in light of tantric symbolism has eluded western Egyptologists partly because of the refusal to admit the possibility that there is tantric, yogic, or mystical symbolism and metaphor in Kamitan culture. Therefore, it should be no surprise that the tantric symbolism of the crowns was first noticed in modern times by the Indian scholar Sudhansu Kumar Ray in 1956.[21]

---

[21] Ray, Kumar Sudhansu, <u>Prehistoric India and Ancient Egypt</u> 1956

PART 1: The Teachings Which Lead To The Unfoldment of Divine Love

"Seekest thou God, thou seekest for the Beautiful...

One is the Path that leadeth unto It - Devotion joined with Wisdom."

INTRODUCTION TO NETER MERRI

Many people shy away from sentimentality saying I am not emotional or sentimental. Yet even intellectuals are sentimental about their particular form of philosophy. So every one is sentimental in one way or another. Furthermore, deep within the heart of every human being there lies an innate desire to love. This desire is often expressed in limited ways, loving individuals, objects, jobs, etc. What is really desired by the soul is to express unlimited love. Therefore, any limitation of love constitutes a falling short of the possibility to achieve emotional fulfillment. Therefore, one should understand that if the emotional aspect of oneself is harnessed and channeled, it can be a formidable force toward self-discovery. The Self is the true objective of all love. When you love a person you are really loving the Soul (God) which is the sustaining reality of that person. When you love an object you are really loving the Soul which is the sustaining reality of that object. This is the basis of the discipline known as Devotional Yoga. It involves developing greater and greater attachment to God first by learning about God through the spiritual scriptures (wisdom teachings) and from here developing faith that there truly is an entity which transcends all. Ordinary love for objects is limited. If you love a car or a house it cannot reciprocate and you could even lose it. Similarly if you love a human being sometimes they cannot reciprocate either due to their own egoism or impairment or death. They may someday even hate you. When you discover love for God who is within you there can be no separation and no reduction in the feeling; it goes on increasing and expanding. This is the glory of true Devotion to God. It is like a perpetual feeling of joy and bliss not unlike the feeling of young lovers or a mother for her child. In both of these cases there is a constant awareness of the loved one no matter what activity one may be engaged in. Love for God is more exalted and more magnanimous because it is infinite and eternal.

As stated earlier, the Yoga of Devotional Love is one of the most powerful forms of spiritual evolution. Throughout this texts we will see how it was the very basis of religion in Ancient Egypt. However, many people sometimes frown upon devotion as a means of spiritual practice. Sometimes it is equated with fanaticism or with that which is opposite to rationality or reason. Indeed, many people have become religious fanatics and many have become insane due to their form of practice. It must be clearly understood that the true practice of Yoga of Devotional Love will lead to increasing clarity, peace and happiness in life through the integration of the whole personality. If there is some other outcome, then it is not Yoga of Devotional Love which is being practiced but something else. The understanding of the correct practice of Yoga of Devotional Love will not lead to any form of insanity, fanaticism or irrationality. Rather, true devotional feeling is a fulfillment of correct reason. This is why the Yoga of Devotional Love is a two-fold movement in spirituality. It is a development of the feeling or emotional capacity in a human being as well as the reasoning capacity. This is because when one allows the devotional feeling to emerge in the heart, there is automatic wisdom which grows in the intellect. Wisdom is defined as knowledge combined with experience. True devotional feeling is not blind love or faith. It is a channeling of the sentimental values and feelings which are directed toward worldly objects and personalities toward the object of supreme love, God. This process leads to a growing awareness of the Divine within one's very heart as the glowing reality. So even if a person were to say "I will practice only the Yoga of Devotional Love and no other form of spirituality", there will be a development in reasoning or the wisdom aspect of the heart. True practice of Devotional Love requires the effacement of the ego-personality. When this occurs, the mind is freed from the egoistic illusions, desires and agitation. The purified mind reveals the transcendental reality which was always there. This is the blooming movement wherein the mind with its knowledge, turn into intuitional realization of the transcendental reality, the Supreme Divinity. In this way, through wisdom and devotion, a human being can discover the underlying essence of the universe and within the heart. This is the true Blossoming of the Lotus of Divine Love. The movement in the Yoga of Devotional Love may be seen in the schematic drawing below.

$$\begin{array}{c} \text{The Self} \\ \Uparrow \\ \text{Wisdom} \; \swarrow \; \nwarrow \; \text{Devotion} \\ \swarrow \quad \nearrow \\ \swarrow \quad \nearrow \\ \Uparrow \\ \text{Human Existence} \end{array}$$

Many people speak ill of devotees or do not want to hear any talk of loving God yet they direct their love toward perishable objects such as cars, houses, countries, their bodies, family, etc. This understanding leads to pain and suffering in life. So why do this? Why devote one's love toward that which is imperfect and fleeting? The answer is that they are ignorant as to the true purpose of life and the ultimate reality which is beyond physical existence. Therefore, we must first understand the practices and way of life which lead to the purification of the intellect and allow the emotional capacity in a human being to develop freely.

Kemetic Hieroglyphs of the Chant and Divine Singing Tradition

Shmait - female mucisian singer

Shmai - male mucisian singer

Hesi - Chant, sing repeatedly praises

Dua - praises, adorations to the divine (standing or sitting)

Dua Neter - title of the priestess of Amun

Dua Neter - title of the priestess of Amun

Smai Tawi - Egyptian Yoga

Uash - praise worship

Uashu - praises, words of worship

S-uash - to praise to worship

The Path of Divine Love

Why are the Gods and Goddesses worshipped?

Neter and the Neteru
**The Neteru (Gods and Goddesses) proceed
from the Neter (Supreme Being)**

As stated earlier, the concept of Neter and Neteru binds and ties all of the varied forms of Kamitan spirituality into one vision of the gods and goddesses all emerging from the same Supreme Being. Therefore, ultimately, Kamitan spirituality is not polytheistic, nor is it monotheistic, for it holds that the Supreme Being is more than a God or Goddess. The Supreme Being is an all-encompassing Absolute Divinity.

Shetaut Neter religion recognizes that there is one supreme and transcendental Divinity- as in all other African religions. However, this divinity cannot be known by the unenlightened mind. For that reason images that the mind can grasp have been created by the sages of ancient times to allow a person to direct their attention and devotion towards an aspect of the Divine. Since all aspects (the gods and goddesses) are regarded as manifestations of the transcendental Divine Self which has no form or name, the worship (directing the heart and mind) of these divinities gradually leads to the discovery of their transcendental essence. In this manner the worship of any of the divinities (neteru) if entered into correctly, will lead to awakening. So the worship of the gods and goddesses is a proper way to lead the mind to discovery of the perspective of higher consciousness. In order to have success it is necessary to worship in two ways, by ritual, chant and offering to the divinity and next by study of the qualities, myth and teaching of the divinity (Devotion and Wisdom). As a divinity is discovered an aspect of the transcendental divine is discovered and if all divinities are known then the transcendental divine is also known.

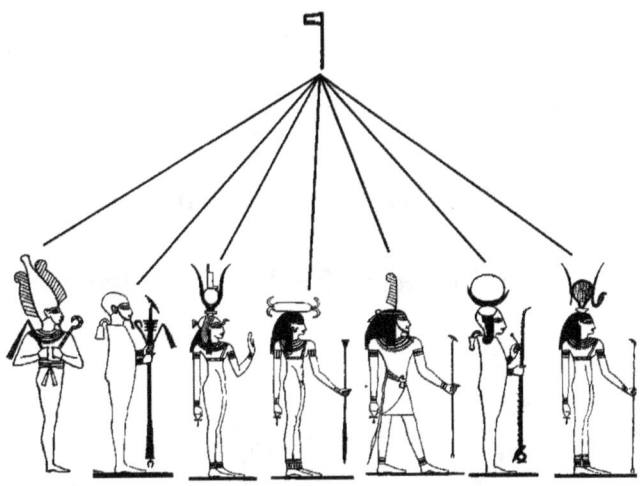

The purpose of Ushet is to engender understanding and closeness with the Divine. So as you study and practice the teachings their deeper subtle and mystical meaning will be revealed to you automatically.

The Main Characters from the Ausarian Resurrection

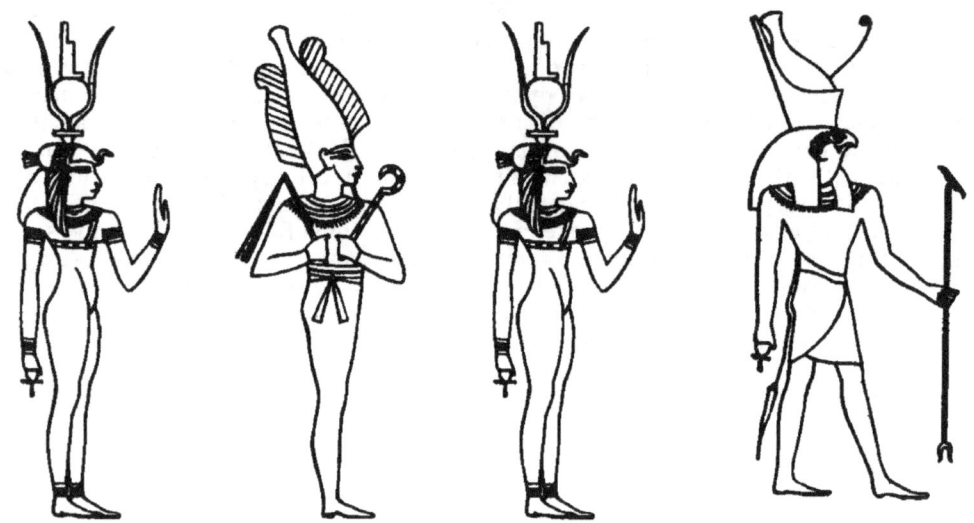

Above from left to right: Aset, Asar, Nebthet, Heru.

Below from left to right: Anpu, Ra, Djehuti, Hetheru.

The Path of Divine Love

The Main Characters from the Ausarian Resurrection

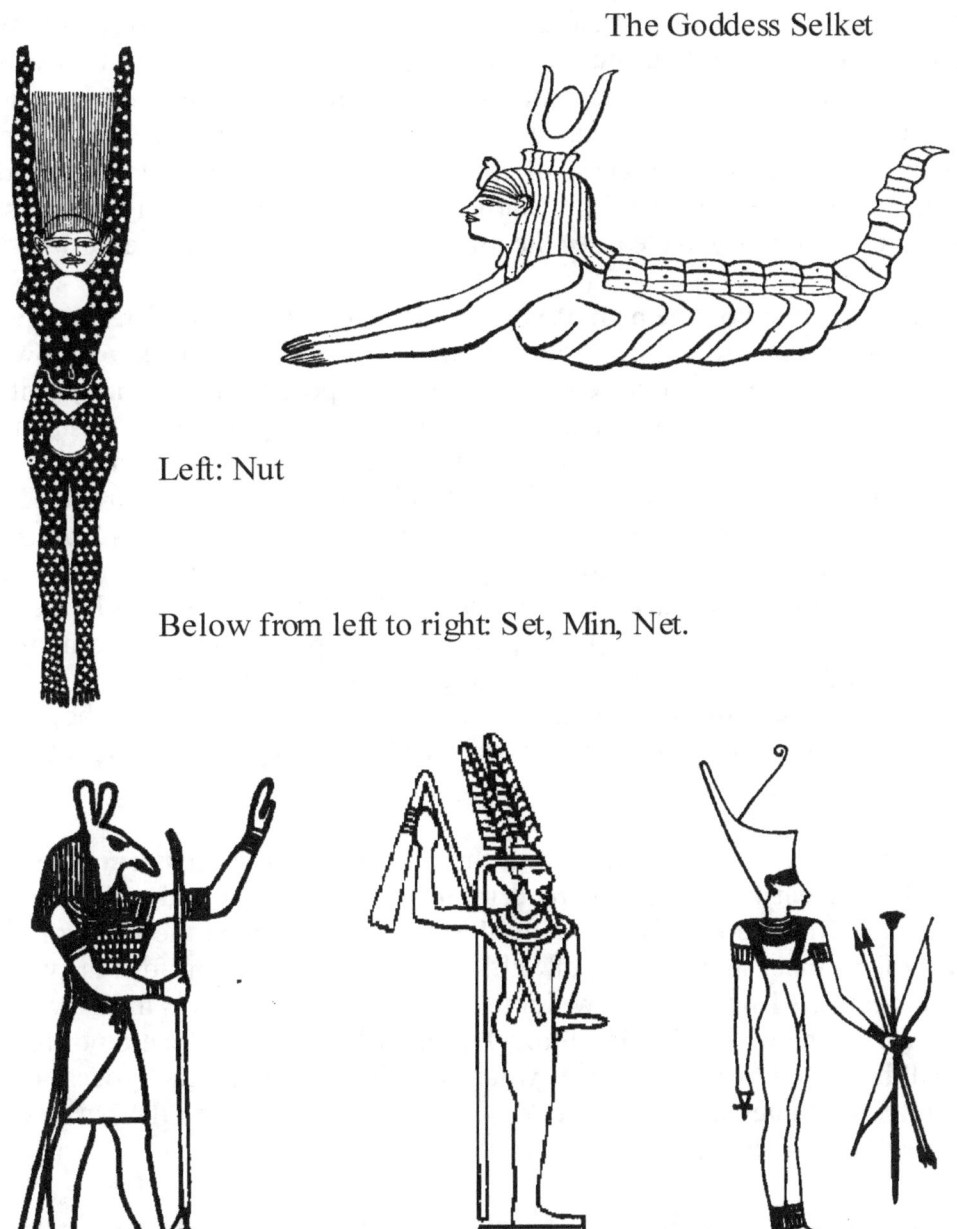

The Goddess Selket

Left: Nut

Below from left to right: Set, Min, Net.

The Practice of The Teachings

The practice of the teachings is the most important part of yoga after the teachings have been received and understood. Many aspirants and lay people believe that the mind may be transformed by simply reading a particular book or some special exercises. This would be like discovering a map for a buried treasure but then not putting in the effort to follow the directions of the map to find the location and not putting in the time and effort necessary to dig for the treasure. While many breakthroughs can occur wherein the subject may experience bursts of enlightening experiences, the process of psycho-spiritual transformation leading to full Enlightenment and transcendence of the karmic process requires many small strides which together amount to a force which cleanses the mind of all illusions and all egoism.

As a developing aspirant on the path of yoga, you must learn how to determine when your are progressing and when you are falling back into the old ways. You will know how to recognize your progress on the path by your level of increasing peace and harmony within yourself. However you should not place overwhelming importance in day to day assessments of yourself since the battle between the higher and lower self often fluctuates from day to day. Some days you may feel harmonious and at peace while on other days you may feel troubled and agitated. You should look at your life in a much more holistic fashion. Ask questions like: Am I slower to anger than I was a month ago? Six months ago? A year ago? These questions will give you a better indication of your current stage of development. Most importantly, be honest with yourself and never be afraid or too full of pride to ask for help and advice from more advanced personalities. When the troubles of life are no longer insurmountable, when you become slow to anger, when you begin to discover a higher vision of yourself which goes beyond any mental conception, that is when you are moving towards self-discovery. This is the art and practice of Yoga in Life.

The process of yoga may be divided into three major sections: **Listening, Reflection and Meditation.** Most of what you have learned up to this point falls under the phase of learning about the teachings. In the book The wisdom of Maati, we presented the value of Maat in action and the basics of the inner implications of Selfless Service and Action for Purity of Heart rather than for exterior gains. Also we saw how finding an occupation which is in line with your karmic personality as the divine will is flowing through you will lead to purification of the heart. In this volume we will begin to practice exercises which will serve to begin the process of reflecting on and practicing the teachings in your day to day life which will lead to the purity of heart which will allow correct reasoning and feeling to develop in your being.

Ritualism Versus True Spiritual Work Which Leads To Real Transformation

> 4f Then said the Majesty of this god, "Your transgressions of violence are placed behind you, for the slaughtering of the enemies is above the slaughter of sacrifice;" thus came into being the slaughter of enemies. And the Majesty of this god said unto Nut, "I have placed my self upon my back in order to stretch myself out."
>
> From the Ancient Egyptian story of
> "The Destruction of Humankind"

Ritualistic acts of worship of God are less important than the actual work towards destroying the enemies of God. Of course, the enemies being referred to here are not some army from another country or alien invaders from space. The enemies of God are anger, hatred, greed, desire for sense enjoyments, unrest, unrighteousness, etc. which lie within the human heart. They distract the mind from awareness of the Divine essence (God). Thus, the "slaughtering" of the enemies" implies any movement against one's conscience and against nature which signifies the removal of hatred, anger, greed, and most importantly ignorance of the Self, from one's psycho-spiritual personality. These enemies must be defeated or slain, as it were, in much the same way as Hetheru slew those who were sinful. Sin here refers to a life based on egoistic values, a life of greed and selfishness, and activities which engender pride, conceit and individuality. They are feelings, thoughts and actions which distract the mind and make you feel you are a separate individual. Sin is that which leads to egoism and egoism is separation from one's own Divine nature.

Images From The Ausarian Resurrection

The birth of Heru

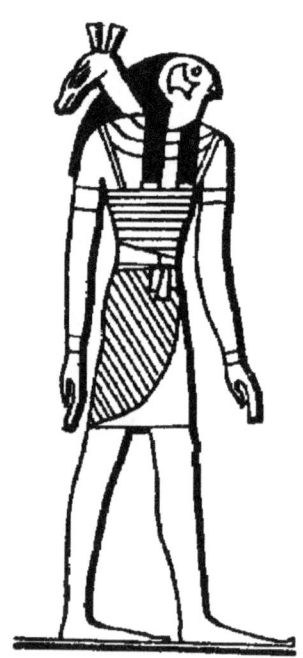

Heru and Set in one personality.

Below: Heru spearing a hippopotamus fiend with the help of Aset

The Path of Divine Love

All things in nature are Divine. They exist and are sustained by God. If you deny someone in need or if you hurt someone or hurt nature, you are in reality committing a sin against God and ultimately against yourself since deep within your heart you are one with God. In this manner, due to ignorance of this knowledge, people hurt one another and create unrest in their own deep unconscious mind which creates indelible impressions that will lead them to experience unrest and suffering while alive on earth, and also in the after-life period.

Therefore, those who only go through the motions of religious rituals and do not seek to understand the deeper implications of spirituality by eradicating their negative qualities will suffer the consequences of their negative karmas (actions). Negative karmas lead to entanglements in the world of time and space. This keeps the soul from discovering its true nature as it incarnates into the world, again and again, using different bodies, in a futile search for human experiences which will provide true fulfillment of its desires. This endless search to fulfill the desires leads to a cycle of birth and death called reincarnation wherein the soul experiences countless embodiments along with the birth, growth, old age and death of each body. This negative karma is known as hell and it is the fate of all who are ignorant about their true spiritual nature.

However, those who seek to change their lives by performing good deeds and who practice yogic techniques for spiritual transformation will experience the fruits of their positive karma. Positive karma implies actions which lead to self-discovery and an end to the cycle of birth and death.

The Ancient Egyptian word for karma is Meskhenet. The more popular word "karma" has been used here for ease of understanding. Karma can be negative or positive and it is up to each individual to watch their thoughts and actions in order to prevent negative karma and to promote positive karma which will lead to spiritual realization.

The destructive power of Hetheru is none other than the destructive force of light when it encounters darkness. Hetheru is the scorching light of her Father, Ra. When you practice gathering will power to control your mind, senses, desires and other negative qualities and concentrate on acquiring spiritual knowledge, a tremendous force builds up within you which can destroy all forms of negativity within and without.

A teaching appears in the Bhagavad Gita which closely resembles the teaching given in hekau 4f (the slaughtering of the enemies is above the slaughter of sacrifice). It states that the sacrifice of the attaining wisdom of the Self (Enlightenment) is better than ritualistic sacrifices because all sacrifices are actions performed in the realm of time and space, and these lead to more actions, desires and thoughts and these lead to more involvement and entanglement into the world of human experience (karma), all of which occurs in the realm of time and space knowledge. When rituals are performed with the higher understanding of the teachings they lead to knowledge that goes beyond the realm of time and space knowledge. They lead to liberation and transcendence of the world (transcendence of karma itself- both positive and negative). This teaching is echoed in the Bhagavad Gita scripture from ancient India.

33. The sacrifice of knowledge, O Scorcher of Foes, is better than the sacrifice of material objects, because all actions, without exception, are terminated when knowledge is attained.

Bhagavad Gita: Chapter 4 Jnan Vibhag Yogah
The Yoga of Wisdom

The knowledge being referred to in the verse from the Gita is intuitive knowledge of the Divine Self, i.e. Enlightenment. Knowledge is of two types, indirect and direct. When you are told about the wisdom teachings of the spirit realm and about your transcendental union with the Divine, you are learning indirect knowledge. When you practice rituals which affirm that reality, you are still in the realm of indirect time and space knowledge, but you are leading yourself toward the transcendental reality by retraining your mind and body. When you actually experience your oneness with the universe (God) then you have gained direct knowledge. This knowledge is what the Gnostics call Gnosis or Knowing. In reality, there is no true knowledge until this experience is achieved. All philosophies and religious theories are transcended (terminated or transcended) in the experience of the truth. Therefore, the spiritual aspirant should never become attached to concepts but should use them in order to gain higher and higher understanding until the ultimate understanding, which transcends the human mind, is finally achieved.

There are many practices which have been devised to effect a change in human consciousness. Collectively they are all called Self Effort:

Study of scriptures, listening to the wisdom teachings, practice of detachment, control of the sexual urge, virtuous action, equanimity of mind, contentment, yogic recreation, discipline, prayer, hekau, good association, receiving instructions from a Spiritual Preceptor, and practicing meditation on the Self - all these are expressions of one's self-effort. Without these, one cannot attain Self-realization (Enlightenment, The Kingdom of Heaven).

The various practices of the personal spiritual discipline may be classified as follows in the process of spiritual development:

<u>Awakening of the spiritual self</u>:

Study of scriptures
Listening to the wisdom teachings (receiving instructions from a Spiritual Preceptor)

The Path of Divine Love

<u>Purgation of the self:</u>

Practice of vigilance
Practice of detachment
Control of the sexual urge
Virtuous action
Equanimity of mind
Contentment
Yogic recreation
Discipline
Prayer
Hekau
Good association
Practicing meditation on the Self

<u>Illumination of the intellect:</u>

All of the various practices listed above are directed to the illumination of your intellect. Therefore you must always keep in mind that the practices themselves are not the object of yoga. You should not develop the idea that you will become a professional meditator, or a dispassionate person just to perfect these practices in themselves. Your goal is to use these practices to lead you to aquire purity of heart which will in turn open the door to the boundless expansion of your true Self.

The next portion of this volume will involve a description of what each element in self-effort means in day to day living along with exercises for your practice.

Purgation of the self:

Practice of Vigilance and Control Over the Mind.

> "To destroy an undesirable rate of mental vibration, concentrate on the opposite vibration to the one to be suppressed."

Whenever an angry thought rises, remember the teachings and remove it with understanding. As soon as you realize that you are becoming aroused with anger, allow reason to flow into your mind. Understand that your ego is angry, then look at it and the motive of its anger from a detached point of view. You are the immutable Soul. You are Absolute Bliss and Peace. Whatever has happened to bring on the anger is only a test of your ability to separate from your hurt ego. Go to a quiet place and recall the teachings. Anger can only be experienced when you associate with the mind and its worries, fears, likes, and dislikes. Disassociate from the mind and you are immediately released from all troubles. Remember who you really are, the supreme abode of peace and bliss, and allow this idea to flow. Take deep breaths so that you can concentrate on the Life Force energy and keep it in the body instead of venting it through negative or evil thoughts, words and deeds. In this manner you can control the body and mind at the same time. When you are in control, then tackle the problem or respond to the situation with reason, in complete control. This practice will become more and more automatic and eventually you will not be affected by situations which in the past would have caused you much anger.

Whenever a greedy thought comes in, remember that your goal is Enlightenment and realize that all objects are God anyway. When you attain God-realization you will become One with all objects in consciousness so there is no need to pursue external objects which in the end are perishable in their transient physical forms.

Whenever a thought of selfishness arises, substitute it with a thought of charity and reinforce it with acts of charity and selfless service with a spirit of honesty and without seeking for rewards or praise in return. The mind entertains greediness and selfishness because it has learned to believe it is an individual among other individuals and that it can be happy by acquiring objects, or through worldly relationships with others. Therefore, any thought of giving up or losing an object of attachment evokes feelings of selfishness. You feel you are giving away your happiness, and indeed you are because you have linked your happiness to the idea of possessing that object.

Images of Ushet from Ancient Egypt

Right: The characteristic Ancient Egyptian posture for prayer and adoration.

Isis addressing the mummy of Osiris as it lay in her boat ready for removal to the tomb.

Uatchit and Saa presenting life and sovereignty to Horus, the son of Isis and Osiris.

Nekhebit and Hu presenting life and sovereignty to the son of Isis.

Practice of Detachment

You should strive to be detached in all of your dealings in life. This does not mean a detachment of physical separation but it implies an inner understanding that you are not the body or the thoughts you experience. These are merely passing pictures which are presented to your consciousness for your witnessing experience. It is foolish to become egotistically attached to objects and people who are perishable and illusory. Rather become attached to the essence of your loved ones, the Divine Self. That eternal essence is the reality which does not fade with time. Always keep an inward understanding that any object you handle, any activity you perform with another, everything you perceive with your mind and senses is in reality the neters, or as modern physics would say, energy. But what is the source of this energy? The Divine Self. Therefore, do not become attached to your relatives in an egoistic way. Do not become attached to your body. Do not become attached to your situation of adversity or prosperity. These are always subject to change. Do not become attached to any possession, do not become attached to your prowess as a yogi(ni). Do not become attached to the pleasures of the mind which you will experience as you advance in meditation. Do not become attached to the energy centers of the body. Lead a detached form of life based on your yogic training and you will never suffer disappointment or sorrow due to any factor outside of yourself.

The practice of detachment does not mean giving up objects. Rather it is an understanding that allows you to deal with objects correctly in such a way that you live in accordance with nature and divine awareness rather than frustration and covetousness. It means giving up the illusion about objects and waking up to the reality about them.

Discipline - Control of the Sexual Urge.

Discipline and Control of the sexual urge are strongly related. Both are necessary for a viable spiritual discipline and both are the foundations of continued success because they allow you to practice for along enough period of time to see some results of your efforts. What good would it do you to set out on a search for a treasure if you cannot discipline yourself to do what is required to perform the search (read the map, follow the instructions, travel to the location and dig until you find what you know is there)? Similarly, what good would you derive from your search if you could not maintain the required amount of concentration because you are continuously distracted by other objects which also appear to be treasures, but which, as soon as you grasp them, fade into thin air in a short time? In this example the treasure is Enlightenment and the objects which appear to be treasures are in reality objects which you sought to acquire because you thought they would bring you happiness, but after a short time, lost your fascination and ceased to elate you. Enlightenment is a treasure of boundless proportions. It does not fade and is ever full of eternal expansion. Which is the real and which is the illusion?

Whenever an uncontrolled feeling of lust arises use the same process to control it. Sexual desire is a normal part of the animal aspect of the body and it is a tremendous source of energy which may be used to accomplish great deeds. However, if these feelings are unrestricted, the sheer force of the energy behind them is irresistible to the mind. The soul that is identified with the mind will not be able to separate from the mind's feelings and desires. One who is dominated by passion and sexual desire cannot aspire to great accomplishments in the relative world or in

The Path of Divine Love

the spiritual. This is why the Sages and Saint of all faiths have enjoined the practice of celibacy in order to control the sexual urge. Even yoga practices which include the cultivation of sexual energy such as the Left Hand Path of Tantrism, also require the practice of celibacy and control of the sex urge. Celibacy must be practiced along with exercises for sexual sublimation, otherwise, the sexual energy will cause tremendous pressure on the mind and body.

As stated earlier, you must strive to control your urges in any form they may arise. If you strive to control the sexual urge, the desire for compulsive shopping may arise. You may develop a desire for parties, or you may indulge in eating. You must strive for balance and moderation in every aspect of life. This is the Maatian practice of Keeping the balance.

The practice of sexual restraint should not be viewed as a pathetic lifestyle or a loss of the pleasure of life. Modern culture has created an illusory mystique surrounding sex, that it is the greatest thin which can ever occur in human life along with material riches, etc. This is a limited view. Physical sex between two people can only be limited because the human body, mind and senses are limited. Once you expand in consciousness you will discover unbounded sources of pleasure which do not require physical contact of any kind. Actually, in many cases physical contact is an obstruction to the discovery of higher pleasure and satisfaction. Thus, when the mind discovers a higher source of pleasure it automatically leaves the lower form behind. This is the experience which Saints and Sages have attained through the ages in all paths of Yoga and Mystical Spirituality. This is the goal of the Yoga of Divine Love which is being espoused in this volume.

Virtuous Living

In all activities of life you must strive to act virtuously. Always strive to uphold the precepts of Maat under all conditions. Actions which are based on Truth, Justice and Order allow you to always remain in a state of peace and harmony. This harmonious state of mind will allow you to perceive the inner depths of the ocean of your consciousness. You will realize that you are much more than a mortal human being. You are an instrument of the Divine, through which the Supreme Being is carrying out the work of creation at all times.

Equanimity of Mind

When you intuitively know that you know that all objects, all people, all thoughts and all feelings are expressions of Divine energy, and that your own deeper self is that Divine Self who emanates the energy of which all things are composed, and that all situations of life are merely the interplay of that energy in the form of two opposite poles which manifest as the various forms of duality in creation, you can relax at all times. Now that you know (at least intellectually) that the changing situations of life are merely waves of energy which are meant for your evolution you can relax in the feeling that they are temporary challenges developed for you as part of the Divine plan for your yogic practice. They are not permanent developments but are transient conditions which you can easily endure. This feeling will lead you in the direction of mental peace no matter how negative or how positive your situations may appear to be. As your practice yoga continues and your intuitional understanding grows, you will experience increasing levels of equanimity, culminating in Enlightenment.

Contentment

Contentment is a profound yogic teaching. Contentment is the understanding that you are provided with all of the necessary tools for your spiritual growth in the form of the necessities of life such as shelter, food as well as your intellectual ability, health, wealth and overall situation in life. Through a combination of your own conscious desires and your soul's unconscious longings you have developed a situation which is your own unique life experience.

You must realize that everything you have at this particular moment is sufficient for your needs. [**Also you need to understand that this feeling does not conflict with your efforts to improve your situation.**] It simply means that you should feel satisfied with what you have at present and that you are supremely fulfilled through your inner realization of the Divine rather than through outer expressions of prosperity. Outer wealth is good when it is used for promoting your own possibilities for spiritual growth. The problem comes when people feel that outer wealth is the measure of success and inward peace. In this miserable condition people strive desperately to accomplish some notion of what they believe will bring them a measure of success in life. When this comes they are still unfulfilled and even more agitated and discontent than before. Their inner peace was based on their outer achievements, and these are always subject to changes and loss. Therefore, inward contentment through spiritual realization is more important than outer forms of success in business or society.

What use would it serve to live in a mansion or palace while your mind is bereft with thoughts and feelings which allow you no rest at any point in your waking state? Why are sleeping pills and other addictive drugs so rampantly abused by people who are wealthy so they can sleep at night? Contentment is a key to spiritual realization which must be developed through constant retraining and re-focusing of the mind from its old habits of coveting what others have or what is advertised as a product which will bring happiness to your life. Contentment also means not engendering egoistic desires within yourself but accepting what providence brings with love and gratitude even while striving for success and peace.

Similarly, what is the use of placing value on physical looks when in the end, all humans, no matter how glamorous or how beautiful, will have a common end wherein the bodies will be ground to dust and fade into the swirling mass of creation from whence it came? Be content in all situations. Accept what the soul has provided for you and strive to come into attunement with your inner music. This attunement will lead you to true prosperity and peace which abides in eternity and reality. Avoid the general feeling of the masses which tends to appreciate outer forms of beauty and wealth as an emblem of success. Many people feel good about themselves because they have nice possessions such as cars, boats, houses, etc. But what would happen if they could not afford the payments on those objects? What would happen to their feeling if they were laid off from their job for even a month? Their lives would be turned upside down due to the inability to hold onto the possessions which they trained themselves to believe would bring them happiness.

Your happiness should not be based on something outside of yourself which you have no control over and which in themselves are illusory and nonexistent anyway. Your happiness should not be based on some activity which you want to do to produce happiness. What would happen if you enjoy playing sports and the weather spoils your week? What would happen if you lose the television and cannot watch the sports channel or the soap opera? You need to develop a philosophical way of life which will lead you to inner fulfillment and spiritual expansion. In

The Path of Divine Love

order for this to occur you must learn to control your mind and direct it towards what is true, righteous and good.

Images of Ushet from Ancient Egypt

Above: The gods and goddesses are worshipping the Supreme Self.

Prayer and Worship of the Divine, Hekau-Ushet

Ushet or Uashu is the Ancient Egyptian word meaning to worship the Divine. Prayer and Hekau should be an integral part of your daily practice of spiritual life. The Ancient Egyptian steles are replete with images of devotional prayer and worship of the Divine. The symbol of adoration to the Divine is the characteristic pose with arms raised, palms facing toward the Divine image, . When you pray with devotion and understanding, your mind turns to the Divine. This turning creates spiritual vibrations which bring solace and peace at all times. Hekau is an intensive way to create spiritual vibrations in the mind which attune it to the Divine vibrations. The recitation of hekau also has the effect of purifying the heart and of bringing you closer to the Divine.

When repeating hekau, bring about a feeling that you are repeating the Divine Name of the Supreme Being, who is Absolute Love, and Absolute Peace and that you are touching that Supreme Being with every utterance. In a short time you will develop a peaceful feeling around your chosen hekau. As soon as you introduce it to your mind you will achieve calm and peacefulness as if by magic.

Hekau has other important benefits. You can begin practicing it at anytime you are not involved in some constructive activity. You will find that when you are not consciously practicing it, it will arise on its own and remind you of the Divine Self. Your mind will automatically be moving toward the Divine at all times, even when you are involved in day to day activities. Chanting (Hekau) can act as a way to release and relieve stress and tension. Instead of going to a drunken party or distracting yourself through various forms entertainment which only drain the mind and take it to a state of dullness, you should practice spiritual chanting.

The recitation of hekau is not in conflict with any other Divine name or prayer. It is a medium which you have chosen to retrain your mind and charge it with spiritual vibrations which will act as an armor against negative feelings of your unconscious or from those outside of yourself (which is still a reflection of your own karma). Hekau is one of the most potent elements in the personal spiritual discipline and it is especially effective when attempting to lead the mind into a meditative state.

The Path of Divine Love

Good Association

One of the most important ways of promoting awareness and constant reflection is keeping the company of wise teachers or Sages. In Ancient Egypt the Temple system served the purpose of instructing aspirants in the wisdom teachings and then allowing them back into the world regularly in order to practice the teachings when confronted with ordinary, worldly minded people. The Temple was a place where the initiate could go on a regular basis to be instructed on the teachings of mystical spirituality and to be reminded of their Divine Nature. They could receive teaching and counseling on the correct application of the teachings in day to day life. The idea is reflected in the Stele of Djehuti-Nefer:

"Consume pure foods and pure thoughts with pure hands, adore celestial beings, become associated with wise ones: sages, saints and prophets; make offerings to GOD..."

The association with Sages (Good Association) is seen as a primary way to accelerate the spiritual development of the aspirant. An important definition of the symbols associated with Sma or Sema is to render clear or visible 𓊃𓌳𓌳𓏏. In Ancient Egypt, the gathering, assembly or reunion was called Smait, 𓊃𓌳𓏏𓏤, and Smai 𓊃𓌳𓇋𓇋 is a name for the Temple, the gathering place. In Ancient Egypt, the priest assumes the role of preceptor, Sbai 𓊹𓇼𓏤𓇋𓇋𓀀𓌳, leading the aspirant to understand the teachings of the hieroglyphs, to purification of the mind and body, and eventually to intuitional realization through the practice of mental exercises and the application of the wisdom teachings. In ancient papyruses this is symbolized by the scenes where deities such as Heru (Horus), Djehuti (Thoth, Hermes), Anpu (Anubis), Hetheru (Hathor), Aset (Isis), etc. lead the initiate to meet Asar (him/her self). In India the process is known as "Satsanga" or "association with truth" where the aspirant receives teaching from the Guru (Spiritual Preceptor) on a continuous basis, until Enlightenment is reached. In Christianity this idea was reflected in the relationship between Jesus and John the Baptist and later with Jesus and his disciples. Keeping the company of wise ones is an important and powerful tool for spiritual development because the nature of the mind allows it to make subtle mistakes which can lead it astray from the correct interpretation of the teachings.

Therefore, the teacher, guru, priest, etc. who is "close" to God (Enlightened) as it were, is seen as greater than God because he or she can lead the aspirant towards God, knowing who and where God is. Otherwise it would be very difficult for the aspirant to realize the truth. It would take millions of incarnations, wherein untold sufferings would occur in the process of gaining experiences which would teach the proper way to discover God.

Finding those around you who are sincerely interested in practicing yoga for spiritual development can be a powerful means for spiritual growth. When people come together their energies are multiplied toward the task which they have chosen to undertake provided that they are being guided by an authentic Spiritual preceptor. This is also true of spiritual practice. Therefore, those who meet and help each other can keep the enthusiasm and level of interest up in positive as well as hard times. Also, in a group setting the subtle vibrations are more strongly attuned to the study process which in turn helps the process of concentration and understanding.

The group learning process is a powerful practice which helps toward the goal of purification of the heart, especially when it is conducted under the guidance of an authentic spiritual preceptor.

PART II Sema (Yoga) of Devotion: Becoming One With The Divine

The Path of Divine Love

INTRODUCTION

Part II of this volume in Egyptian Yoga will focus on two of the most powerful aspects of the spiritual discipline. All of the previous disciplines have been preparing you to understand the inner teachings of the process of union with the Divine through Devotion and Meditation. We have previously discussed the yogic disciplines of Devotion and Meditation in other volumes, however, in this volume we will focus on them exclusively. In this volume, the teachings of Wisdom and Action will come together with Devotion and Meditation to produce a powerful combination toward your spiritual movement. This movement is called Integral Yoga. A human being has four aspects: Emotion, Intellect, Action, and Willing. Through the yoga of Devotion, the emotions of an individual are purified and directed to the Divine Self. Through the yoga of wisdom, the mind and intellect are purified so that they come into harmony with Divine Will. Through the yoga of action, the heart is purified with the practice of selfless service so that it can serve the Divine. Through meditation one's will power is developed so that one is no longer distracted by objects and is able to commune with the Divine always. Thus, the combination of aspects of all of these paths of yoga offers the best method to integrate and spiritualize the human personality.

It is important to understand that devotional yoga involves more than simply mindlessly or fanatically praising God or praying or singing devotional songs with emotional force. An integrated process of Devotional Yoga involves an understanding of the metaphysical teachings of wisdom and a blending of all of the other Yogic systems. This integrated process which involves wisdom or intuitional understanding of the metaphysical realities behind creation serves to close any gaps in the mind of the aspirant as to whether or not there is any doubt of the existence of the divine. Further, an integral movement in yoga is more effective because it employs all aspects of the personality (mind, body, intellect, Sexual Life Force) and all are being led by the power of human emotion toward the Divine. An unbalanced movement will create a dislocated and ineffective discipline, having one part of the aspirant seeking the Divine and the other seeking worldly excitement. In the advanced stages, the meditative movement in Devotional Yoga leads to a merging of the aspirant with the Divine.

WHAT ARE
Uashu and Shedy?

Uashu or Ushet means "to worship the Divine," "to propitiate the Divine." Ushet is of two types, external and internal. When you go to pilgrimage centers, temples, spiritual gatherings, etc., you are practicing external worship or spiritual practice. When you go into your private meditation room on your own and your utter words of power, prayers and meditation you are practicing internal worship or spiritual practice.

Ushet needs to be understood as a process of not only an outer show of spiritual practice, but it is also a process of developing love for the Divine. Therefore, Ushet really signifies a development in Devotion towards the Divine. This practice is also known as sma uash or Yoga of Devotion. Ushet is the process of discovering the Divine and allowing your heart to flow towards the Divine. This program of life allows a spiritual aspirant to develop inner peace, contentment and universal love, and these qualities lead to spiritual enlightenment or union with the Divine. It is recommended that you see the book "The Path of Divine Love" by Dr. Muata Ashby. This volume will give details into this form of Sema or Yoga.

Hekau or "words of power" are utterances which can be used to promote spiritual wisdom, health and well being, mental concentration and the transformation in consciousness. More will be elaborated on hekau in the section on words of power.

Shedy or Sheti: Spiritual discipline or program, to go deeply into the mysteries, to study the mystery teachings and literature profoundly, to penetrate the mysteries. Thus, Sheti signifies "spiritual discipline or program for promoting the understanding of Shetai (Hidden Supreme Being) and growing spiritually in a process leading towards spiritual enlightenment."

"O behold with thine eye God's plans. Devote thyself to adore God's name. It is God who giveth Souls to millions of forms, and God magnifyeth whosoever magnifieth God."

GOD is hidden to Gods and men...GOD's name remains hidden...It is a mystery to his children (men, women, Gods) GOD's names are innumerable, manifold and no one knows their number."

"If you seek GOD, you seek for the Beautiful. One is the Path that leads unto GOD - Devotion joined with Knowledge."

"Seekest thou God, thou seekest for the Beautiful. One is the Path that leadeth unto It - Devotion joined with wisdom."

-Ancient Egyptian-African Proverbs

This teaching means that the path to the Divine is achieved with devotion to the Divine, implying the practice of developing increasing love for the Divine that gradually becomes all-encompassing and enlightening. That devotion is to be expressed in love for all things, primarily, the forms of the Divine that have been handed down by the sages of ancient Kamit. Then to its manifestations in creation. Further, it means the practice of that devotion through disciplines of the devotional path (chant, divine singing, meditation, etc.) including the performance of ritual. Increasing devotion leads to opening of the heart and melting the egoistic aspects of the personality which form the mental obstructions to spiritual realization.

Also the proverb implies that that devotion cannot be based on blind faith and emotionality. Rather, feeling in the practice of religion is to be tempered and augmented with wisdom. Wisdom comes from the study of spiritual texts, reflecting on the exposition of the teaching by qualified sages and then meditating upon that teaching, allowing it and it alone to occupy the mental space so that eventually one becomes one with the knowledge and that knowledge reveals itself as the experience of the innermost Self, the same object of supreme devotion. Then having experienced the knowledge it is realized as wisdom. This is what it means to truly be a shemsu (follower) of the religion.

THE PATH OF DIVINE LOVE

Scriptures: Prt M Hru and Temple Inscriptions.

1– Listening to the myth
    Get to know the Divinity
    Empathize
    Romantisize

2-Ritual about the myth

The Path of Divine Love

    Offerings to Divinity – propitiation
    act like divinity
    Chant the name of the Divinity
    Sing praises of the Divinity (Divine Singing)
    COMMUNE with the Divinity

3– Mysticism
    Melting of the heart
    Dissolve into Divinity
    IDENTIFY-with the Divinity

Uash Neter or The Path of Divine Love is an essential element of Shetaut Neter or Neterianism-Ancient Egyptian (African Religion). The practice of Devotion to the Divine is an integral part of the movement towards spiritual awakening and enlightenment. Devotion to and the repetition of the Divine Name is an integral part of the Path of Divine Love which encompasses the disciplines for promoting spiritual evolution by harnessing the feeling capacity of the human heart. The chanting and praising of the Divine Name is the process of uttering Hekau (Words of Power) containing the name of the chosen divinity being worshipped in a format of recitation and rhythmic, repetition called Hessi. Divine singing makes use of musical forms to intensify the divine feeling experience. Music has a profound effect on the unconscious mind. Have you wondered at the fact that you may forget things and events of the past but if you hear a song from that time, the feelings come back. Feeling has more staying power than thoughts but without thought (wisdom) feelings degrade to the level of sentimental blind faith. So music is used to "feel" the teaching and allow It to have a more profound effect on the personality. The disciplines of the Path of Divine Love are designed to purify the heart, allow a human being to come closer to the Divine and eventually become one with the Divine. There are three important stages in the process of cultivating Neter Merri (Divine Love); Listening to the mythic teaching, practicing the ritual of the myth and entering into the metaphysical (mystical) reality of the myth. The practice of daily devotional chant, divine singing, and divine worship are integral, though not confined to the second stage of the Path of Divine Love.

In the Kamitan teaching of Devotional Love:
God is termed Merri, "Beloved One"
The aspirant is the Beloved

"That person (the aspirant) is beloved by the Lord." PMH, Ch 4

Neter Merri

PURIFICATION OF THE HEART

The Ancient Egyptian "Book of Coming Forth by Day" is one of the oldest philosophical and spiritual texts. It describes the journey of the human soul that is identified with its death and dismemberment of the body. Most people are identified with their bodies as their identity and say, this is me, while pointing to the body. They are ignorant as to the vastness of their true being and therefore, are caught in the problems and needs of the body and are subject to whatever happens to it. The "Book of Coming Forth by Day" also describes the realm of the after life and what each man and woman must do to survive death and "Come Forth" into the light of "Day" (become Enlightened). The book describes how each human being is in reality experiencing the fate of Asar and Heru. Asar is the spirit which has incarnated in human form and has been killed by sin in the form of Set, the ego. Heru is the reincarnation of the soul which comes to vindicate the evil of the ego and to establish Maat (truth). The "Book of Coming Forth by Day" represents a ritualization of the myth of Asar. In it the heart (consciousness, symbolized by the AB) of each human being (Asar) is weighed against TRUTH, symbolized by the feather of MAAT. Here our ability to live virtuously is judged and it is to the extent that we live virtuously that we are able to realize our true spiritual nature. In the Hall of MAAT, the heart and internal organs of the deceased are judged by 42 judges who are each in charge of one regulation. All 42 regulations or virtuous guidelines for living make up the basis for the 42 "negative confessions" or righteous affirmations which the practitioner of Maatian philosophy must uphold in order to purify the heart.

The Egyptian Book of Coming Forth By Day represents the ritualistic exercises of the mystical teachings hidden in the Asarian Myth. Therefore, it represents the second step in the process of religion, ritual. In its complete form, religion is composed of three aspects, mythology, ritual and metaphysical or the mystical experience (mysticism - mystical philosophy). While many religions contain rituals, traditions, metaphors and myths, there are few professionals trained in understanding their deeper aspects and psychological implications (metaphysics and mystical). Thus, there is disappointment, frustration and disillusionment among many followers as well as leaders within many religions, particularly in the Western Hemisphere, because it is difficult to evolve spiritually without the proper spiritual guidance. Through introspection and spiritual research, it is possible to discover mythological vistas within religion which can rekindle the light of spirituality and at the same time increase the possibility of gaining a fuller experience of life. The exoteric (outer, ritualistic) forms of religion with which most people are familiar is only the tip of an iceberg so to speak; it is only a beginning, an invitation or prompting to seek a deeper (esoteric) discovery of the transcendental truths of existence.

The Ancient Egyptian system of education of the Temple of Aset prescribe a three tiered format for transmitting the teachings of mystical spirituality. These were: 1- Listening to the teachings. 2- Constant study and reflection on the teachings. 3- Meditation on the meaning of the teachings. It is important to note here that the same teaching which was practiced in Ancient Egypt of **Listening** to, **Reflecting** upon, and **Meditating** upon the teachings is the same process used in Vedanta-Jnana Yoga of India today. According to the teachings of Jnana Yoga or the Yoga of Wisdom, the process of yoga consists of three steps: 1- Shravana (Listening), 2- Manana (Reflection) and 3- Niddidhyasana (Meditation). Thus, Religion and Yoga are essentially equivalent endeavors with respect to the basic process of their practice as well as the overall theory of their workings.

In the books Egyptian Yoga: The Philosophy of Enlightenment, The Wisdom of Maati and in Egyptian Proverbs the process of virtuous living was outlined as a science of virtue. Virtuous living has the effect of changing the mind (heart) because it has a profound effect on the unconscious mind. The mind is composed of three basic levels. These are the conscious, subconscious and unconscious. The conscious is what we are aware of during the day to day activities and when an idea comes into the conscious it comes from the subconscious level after it has sprung up as a sprout from its seed form in the deep unconscious level.

The unconscious level is where your ideas about who you are, your desires, aspirations, complexes and fears are buried and awaiting the proper moment to come forth. Also, the unconscious is where new desires and complexes which were created in the conscious level go into storage until they sprout into new desires in the present life or in a future lifetime. These unconscious impressions are what sustain the ideas about the self: who am "I". However, you as the aspirant must understand that "you" are not just an individual human being with a finite mortal existence. Since you have lived in ignorance, and don't have a knowledge of your deeper self you have come to believe that the reality of what your senses have perceived and the teachings you have received from your family and from society are true. All of these erroneous teachings have woven an illusion in your mind and this illusion is blocking your perception of the truth. This veil of illusion is known as the Veil of Aset. When this veil is removed one is able to perceive the truth as it is. This is the process of "unveiling" Aset.

When virtuous actions (of course this includes meditation) are performed, the impressions of calmness, peace and goodwill which they leave in the mind counteract the impressions of ignorance, agitation and unrest. As this process advances until the mind is rendered subtle and reality is seen in its true form, no longer blocked by the illusions and misconceptions of ordinary human understanding.

Ordinary human understanding in the waking state is seen as a dream by those who are enlightened to the higher reality, those who have discovered the true essence of the universe by discovering Asar and resurrecting him within themselves. This is why even in the oldest texts of the Asarian religion the initiate is exhorted and admonished repeatedly to awaken and receive the "Eye" which represents intuitional understanding and transcendental awareness of spiritual reality.

Consider your own experience as an example. When you go to sleep and you are in a dream, it feels and looks quite real and compelling. You feel as though you have been there from beginningless time and that you will continue to exist there forever. You have forgotten your life in the waking state altogether and you are committed to this "other reality". Even though you performed various activities, met other personalities and experienced many situations, nothing of this "world" was "real". It all vanishes when you wake up. If in your dream you found a chest full of diamonds, you cannot take even one diamond with you into your waking state.

In the same way that your dream world arose out of the content of your unconscious mind and was sustained by your consciousness, this phenomenal universe arose out of the "mind" of the Nebertcher-Asar (Supreme Being) and is sustained by Nebertcher at every moment.

This universe is an ocean of consciousness in the mind of Nebertcher. Identified with your ego, you are like a wave in the ocean of this consciousness. However, in reality you are the whole ocean of consciousness. Thus, you are capable of producing an entire universe within your mind because you are essentially one with God who sustains all creation. However, in the same way that you can create a universe in your mind and withdraw it, God has created this universe and at the end of time will withdraw it.

Your task as a spiritual aspirant is to discover your deeper essence, the part of your consciousness which is the dream and the part which is sustaining the dream. The part which is sustaining all of your varying states of consciousness it that which is real: God, the Higher Self, Christ, Buddha, The Tao, Allah, etc.

Therefore, the task of becoming enlightened is in reality a process of cleansing your mind and discovering your unity with the Divine which was, is and will always be there. In this manner practicing and living by the precepts of Maat is the most important factor in developing purity of heart. This process includes continuous reflection on the Divine and developing alertness of mind which does not allow you to fall into the illusion of forgetting "who you really are."

This process is similar to the technique called "mindfulness" in Buddhism and "Sakshin Buddhi" in Vedanta Philosophy. It requires alertness, concentration and vigilance over every thought and action you perform so as to always keep the wisdom teachings in mind as well as always acting according to the precepts of Maat. When you become proficient in this practice, the complexes, desires and illusions about the world, people and yourself begin to dwindle and you begin to discover that part of you which is not changeable like the mind and body. You begin to discover the part of you which is not mortal and subject to the events of time and space in the world of physical "reality". You begin to separate yourself from your ego-personality and begin to discover it as a character or dream personality which is involved in the dream which is going on in the mind of God. Ultimately you will discover that the innermost "you" is the one who is sustaining the universe. Then it is no longer a dream to you but a thought. You have unraveled the mystery of creation and have discovered it to be as "real" as a dream in the mind. This is becoming one with Asar, reaching the innermost shrine wherein you as the initiate Asar meet and join with the resurrected ASAR, the source of all.

The Opening of The Way

In Egyptian mythology, the form of spiritual practice which involves constant awareness or vigilance over the mind is presided over by the jackal deity, Apuat (Anpu). This is due to its canine faculty of discriminating friend from foe. In this teaching, the friend is reality and truth of one's innermost essence as the Divine Self (Asar, Heru), and the foe is egoism (Set, Apophis), and the emotions that lead to egoism and feelings of individuality (anger, hatred, fear, lust, etc. - fetters of Set). This is symbolized in the following prayer from the Egyptian Book of Coming Forth By Day:

> O God, grant that the fetters of Set be taken from me so that I may be in your glory...

It is this faculty, discrimination or discernment which when developed, assists the initiate in practicing Yoga at all times, day or night, in waking or in sleep. It is this practice and faculty which opens the way to spiritual revelation and realization.

The jackal deity has two aspects, Anpu is the embalmer, the one who prepares the initiate, the Shti (one who is in his coffin-the body). Up to this point the initiate is considered to be dead, a mummy, since he/she does not have conscious realization of the transcendental reality beyond the ego-personality. At this stage the aspirant must be prepared through virtue and physical purification to receive the teachings because without preparation, the highest teaching would fall on deaf ears. The next aspect is Apuat, The opener of the Ways. In this context Anpu represents vigilance and constant practice of discrimination and watchfulness (mindfulness) over the ego-self. Apuat represents the development of intuitional realization which occurs in degrees. Gradually, the ego-self becomes effaced and reveals the true self as one with the Divine. Then the mysterious hidden essence of all things is realized as one's very self. All of a sudden it is realized that this was always the true Self and that the individual ego personality was a misunderstanding born out of one's ignorance.

It is Anpu who leads King Unas in the Pyramid Texts by constantly urging him to move ahead and not get distracted with the passing fancies of the waking world or the astral plane (Duat-Amenti, Netherworld-unconscious). The following Utterance (#483) from the Pyramid Texts illustrates the role of Anpu as awakener of souls.

> The libation is poured and Apuat (Wepwawet) is on high. Wake up, you sleepers!
> Rouse up, you watchers! Wake up Heru! Raise yourself, Asar the King...

It is Anpu who leads souls to the abode of the Supreme Being in the Book of Coming Forth By Day by constantly urging them to awaken from the dream of the world process and its illusion. The relief of Anpu sitting atop the chest containing the inner-parts of Asar is to be found at the entrance or purification area of the burial chamber of the initiate, . In the Book of Coming Forth By Day, it is stated that it is Anpu who appointed the Seven Spirits, the followers of their lord Sepa, to be protectors of the dead body of Asar. Sepa is the name of the chief of the seven spirits who guarded Asar and seven is the number of spiritual energy centers in the subtle spiritual body (Serpent Power - Kundalini Chakras). Anpu is an aspect of Heru and Heru is the Soul. Therefore, the true enlightener of the self is the Self. In this manner, it is your innermost Self who is enlightening you as well through the desire to practice spiritual discipline.

THE ETERNAL WITNESS

He the One Watcher who neither slumbers nor sleeps.

From the Ancient Egyptian Hymns of Amun

Many thousands of years prior to the development of the Sakshin Buddhi concept in Vedanta philosophy and the Mindfulness concept of Buddhism in India, the concept of the witnessing consciousness was understood in Ancient Egypt. This watcher or witnessing consciousness of utterance 13 is related to three other important utterances (33-35)* which explain the relationship between the witnessing consciousness of the mind, the perceptions through the senses and the physical world. Here we will focus on understanding the watcher or witnessing consciousness which is the innermost essence of the human mind. *(see the books The Mind of Set and God In the Universe, God in the Heart by Dr. Muata Ashby for a complete study of these utterances.

The Self is the eternal witness to all that goes on in the mind of every human being. It is the mind, composed of memories and desires stored in the subconscious and unconscious, which believes itself to be real and independent. But when you begin to ask "who is this that I call me?", you begin to discover that you cannot find any "me". Is "me" the person I was at five years of age? at twenty? or am I the person I see in the mirror today? Am I the person I will be in ten years from now or am I the person I was 500 or 1000 years ago in a different incarnation? Where is "me"? Is "me" the body? Am "I" the legs?, or am "I" the heart? Am "I" the brain? People have lost half their brains and continue to live, not in a vegetable state but as human beings, with consciousness. Since body parts can be lost or transplanted, these cannot be "me". What does this all mean?

As a child you acted a certain way. As an adolescent you acted in another way. As an adult you acted yet another way. All the while, your body is growing, changing, and gradually moving towards death. You have experienced all of these changes and through mental conditioning, you have come to believe that all of these characters are you. Initiatic teaching proves through philosophical argument and through intuitional enlightenment that these are only transitory characters with no real substance. So what is real? Your witnessing Self is real. It was the witnessing consciousness, identified with the ego-self-consciousness, who experienced the pains and pleasures, disappointments and successes. That witnessing consciousness which withdraws at the time of sleep and experiences dreams, that witnessing consciousness that observed all of the changes like a silent onlooker waiting to be noticed, is your innermost Self.

The real "me" is that which causes the existence of the body and uses it to have worldly experiences. The body-mind complex, its problems and concerns, failures and successes, pleasures and pains, life and death, cannot affect the real "me". The project of Yoga is to discover the illusoriness of the ego-personality (mind and body) and to discover the real "me", the Watcher who never slumbers. From the point of view of the ocean, the problems and concerns, failures and successes, pleasures and pains, life and death of the waves is of no concern since none of these occurrences affect its essential nature. The waves do not add or detract from the fullness of the ocean. The ocean encompasses all of the waves. Regardless of whether the waves are rising or falling, the ocean remains full. Likewise, you, the real you, is always embracing the fullness of the Divine Self at every moment. Just as the sun shines and sustains all the activities of the world, the consciousness of God is as a light which shines on all things and allows them to exist. In the same way that you are the sole witness and support of the entire world which arises out of your mind during a dream, the Self is the unaffected witness and support of this entire world process. This silent witnessing is the kind of vision you must engender in your mind as opposed to the one which is constantly agitated and upset by the passing problems of human existence. This is the Divine vision that leads an aspirant to spiritual Enlightenment.

God is always aware of the fact that the entire creation, the universe and all of the various planes of existence within it are nothing more than a thought. Ordinary human beings who have not practiced Yoga or sought to attain spiritual enlightenment are not aware of the fact that this creation is a dream, so they believe it is a reality and become caught in the dream of the world process as it were. They are caught in the desires and illusions of their own as well as the dreams, desires and illusions of others. This leads to a myriad of human complications and entanglements which all lead to disappointment and sorrow in the end. Along with this needless pain and suffering, it is ironic that in the end all human activities, no matter how grand or glorious they may appear to be, are in reality perishable and fleeting much like a dream, albeit a longer lasting dream. Therefore, unenlightened human life is an ignorant state of consciousness in all states (waking, dream, dreamless-deep-sleep).

As stated earlier, ordinary human experience is as a dream. The ignorance which besets the mind causes a kind of ignorant movement from one state of mind to another. The mind moves from waking to the sleep state, from sleep to dream, and from dream once again back to waking. The soul is caught up in the illusory trap of its own ignorance.

The innermost realm of the unconscious is beyond the mind and senses. Therefore, if life is lived in the realm of the mind and senses alone, you are only aware of that which is temporal and unreal. Consider how life would be if you went to sleep and fell into a dream out of which you could not wake up. Having forgotten about the waking state of consciousness, you would be tumbling from one experience to another because you are "ignorant" as to your "true" Self who is sleeping. Your only salvation would be if someone were to come along within your dream and remind you that this dream character is not the real you, and that the real you is comfortably sleeping, and all you need to do to escape the pain and suffering you are experiencing in the dream is to wake up.

Neter Merri

"The wise wake up early to their lasting gain while the fool is hard pressed."

"Salvation is the freeing of the soul from its bodily fetters, becoming a God through knowledge and wisdom; controlling the forces of the cosmos instead of being a slave to them; subduing the lower nature and through awakening the Higher self, ending the cycle of rebirth and dwelling with the neters who direct and control the Great Plan."
                                                                                    -Ancient Egyptian Proverbs

In the same way, the dreams you have when sleeping as well as your experiences in the waking state are all in the realm of the mind and senses, therefore, all of it is illusory, like a dream. Your mortal existence and all of your incarnations throughout time and space are in reality the experience of a dream from the point of view of your innermost Self. While your mind changes, your dreams change, you are born, grow old and die only to be reborn again in a new family, country, etc., these events are all in the realm of time and space. However, when you discover your innermost reality, then you discover that which is timeless, changeless, immortal and eternal. Therefore, you must "drawn close" to the innermost essence within you in order to discover your true identity beyond the mind and senses.

Just as if you were trying to escape a terrible danger in your dream, the best solution would be to wake up, the only way out of the illusion of the world process is to wake up from the triads of Seer-Seen-Sight, the waking-sleep-dream states, entirely. These three states are part of the relative realm of time and space. The task is to transcend them all and to reach attunement with the level of the ever present Watcher, the witness behind all things, the real "me".

The Path of Divine Love

Continuous meditation on the divine: the key to spiritual realization

The importance of maintaining single-minded devotion to the divine is embodied in the statement: "No man can serve two masters: for either he will hate the one, and love the other; or else he will hold to the one, and despise the other" from Matthew 6:24. In the psychological way of reading, the statement clearly refers to a human outlook which is extroverted and externalized rather than introverted and self fulfilled. Single-minded devotion is of paramount importance because the heart (mind) is the key to our perceptions of the world. Whatever the mind holds most dear will be the object of its undivided attention. Therefore, if the mind is externalized with worldly interests it will lack the will to become calm enough to witness the serenity of the consciousness unclouded with thoughts, and this is the prerequisite for achieving attunement with Christ Consciousness.

Gita: Chapter 2 Samkhya Yogah--The Yoga of Knowledge

14. O Son of Kunti, the objects that are perceived by the senses are subject to birth and death. They give rise to pleasure and pain, to heat and cold; they are transient. Therefore, O Bharata, endure them heroically.

15. O best among men, anyone who is balanced in pleasure and pain and who is not agitated by the senses and their contact with objects, only such a hero is fit to attain Liberation.

Gita: Chapter 5 Karma Sanyas Yoga--The Yoga of Renunciation of Action

7. Perfected in Yoga (of action), with a pure heart, having control over the body and mastery over the senses, he beholds the Self in all beings. Such a Sage is untouched by actions, even though he continues performing them.

In the Secret Book of James there is an important statement concerning one-pointedness of mind:

"From now on, while awake or asleep, remember:
    you have seen,
    you have spoken with,
    and you have listened to the Child of
Humanity." (Chap. 2:4)

The idea of maintaining one idea in one's consciousness through the waking state and the sleep state is an important component of the yoga discipline called Vichar or inquiry into "who am I." The aspirant is exhorted to first study the scriptures and then to continuously assert the truth behind the apparent, though illusory reality of the world, namely, that he or she is essentially one with God and that the world is nothing but a projection of God's mind. In Yoga philosophy this technique is also known as Ishvar Chintan and in Buddhist philosophy it is a form of mindfulness.

The technique of continuous devotional meditation on God receives special treatment in Advaita Vedanta philosophy as it is expressed in the Yoga Vasistha. In this text from India, Lord Shiva a divine incarnation of God, explains to Sage Vasistha the doctrine concerning the "highest form of worship". It consists of causing the mind to flow toward the Divine Self through seeing God in all things. When this is achieved, a meditative state of mind called Samadhi (super-consciousness) is achieved even while engaged in worldly activities. Prior to the scientific advances in modern physics in the last century, aspirants where brought to the understanding that the underlying reality behind all objects is one and the same, the Divine Self (God), through the spiritual practices of listening reflecting and meditating on the teachings. In modern physics, just as in the practice of mystical philosophy, wisdom must transcend faith. Even though atoms, particles and electricity have never been seen by human eyes, the properties of both are well understood.

Today it is possible to pick up many books on modern physics which graphically show, through experimental evidence, that the physical world is not real, that all phenomena is in reality energy in various states of vibration. Therefore, it is no longer necessary to make the initial leap of faith of believing that there is an underlying reality to creation beyond the ordinary human senses. From here we may begin our spiritual practice by simply reminding ourselves constantly, that what we are seeing, feeling, hearing, thinking, etc., is in reality the Divine Self. Further, that what is within us which "perceives" is itself the Divine Self as well. Indeed there is nothing that exists which is not the Divine Self. This is "the Kingdom of God which is spread upon the earth" which Jesus says that "Men do not see".

Though sounding simple, this technique is one of the hardest forms of yogic practice since it requires constant control of the mind by applying it on the continuous realization of the wisdom at an intellectual level until it is realized intuitionally. That is, until it becomes self evident. The idea of one-pointed devotion as a way to realize oneness with God occurs in (a)-Egyptian Mythology (5,000-100 BCE), (b)-Indian Upanishads (900 BCE) and is most explicitly explained in the (c)-Yoga Vasistha (700 ACE) and (d) the Bhagavad Gita:

(a)- Hermetic Philosophy:

"When an idea exclusively occupies the mind, it is transformed into an actual physical state."

"Reason of Divinity may not be known except by a concentration of the senses like onto it."

(b)-Kaivalya Upanishad:

Seek to know Brahman (God-Kingdom of Heaven) by acquiring faith in the word of the scriptures and in your Guru. Be devoted to Brahman. Meditate on him unceasingly. Not by work nor by progeny, nor by wealth, but by devotion to him and by indifference to the world, does a man achieve immortality.

The Path of Divine Love

Svetasvatara Upanishad:

Follow only in the footsteps of the illumined ones, and by continuous meditation merge both mind and intellect in the eternal Brahman. The glorious Lord will be revealed to you.

(c)- Yoga Vasistha:

While talking, opening and closing the eyes, accepting and rejecting objects, and all such activities, at all times be devoted to the Self* by keeping yourself detached from the operations of the mind. Do not forget the Self whether in life or in death, whether in pleasure or in pain...

Be devoted to the Self whether your body is young or old, whether you have prosperity or adversity, whether you are in dream or sleep.

*(underlying reality behind all phenomena -internal and external - God -Kingdom of Heaven)

(d) Gita: Chapter 10 Vibhuti Yogah--The Yoga of Divine Glories

10. To them whose minds rest in the Divine Self, who worship Me ceaselessly with devotion, I give the Yoga of Wisdom by which they attain Me.

The idea behind the technique, described above, is that the mind does not behold transcendental levels of existence, (The Kingdom of Heaven, The Tuat, Nirvana, heaven, etc.) because the mind is variously agitated by worldly thoughts, that reinforce the apparent reality of the world and no other realities. By keeping one idea in the mind constantly, the effect of concentrating the mind is achieved. Therefore, the concentrated mind, thus being focused, is able to behold the reality which it seeks. In this respect many exercises are given in Gnostic Christianity as well as other religious systems to bring about a condition in which the mind is brought to a state wherein it is devoid of agitation. Hence the Christian teachings admonishing one to love one's enemy, having no worry as the lilies of the field, and to treat others as one would like to be treated, etc. If these principles were to be practiced there would develop a condition of mind characterized by indifference or equal vision, accepting pleasure or sorrow equally and seeking nothing from the world while being fulfilled by the peace of mind and contentment which ensues from this way of life.

Luke 6
27. But I say to you who hear, love your enemies, do good to them who hate you,
28 Bless them that curse you, and pray for them who despitefully use you.
29. And to him that smites thee on the [one] cheek offer also the other; and him that taketh away thy cloak forbid not [to take thy] coat also.
30 Give to every man that asks of thee; and of him that taketh away thy goods ask [them] not again.
31 And as ye would that men should do to you, do ye also to them likewise.

This process of maintaining continuous awareness or vigilance of the mind constitutes a form of continuous meditation on the Divine which leads to a condition of absolute transcendence of the phenomenal world of time and space experience. This process is described indirectly or implicitly implied in Christian texts from the Bible and the Koran and more explicitly in Gnostic Christian texts as well as in Egyptian and Eastern spiritual scriptures. This teaching is perhaps the most important element of the spiritual discipline as it is directly related to the transformation of the human heart. It must be clearly understood that this practice of continuous awareness of the teachings cannot be performed halfheartedly or whenever it is found to be convenient. It must be practiced every day, hour and minute of your waking time to the best of your ability, and as we will see, also while asleep. It is essential that all thoughts within the mind are vigilantly watched over so as not to allow egoistic thoughts to enter and take hold of the mind. In this way the egoistic impressions of the past wane while there are less new ones being created. Through this practice, the sense of body consciousness and identification with the mind gradually decrease until they finally disappear. Study the following teachings carefully and reflect on their meaning whenever possible.

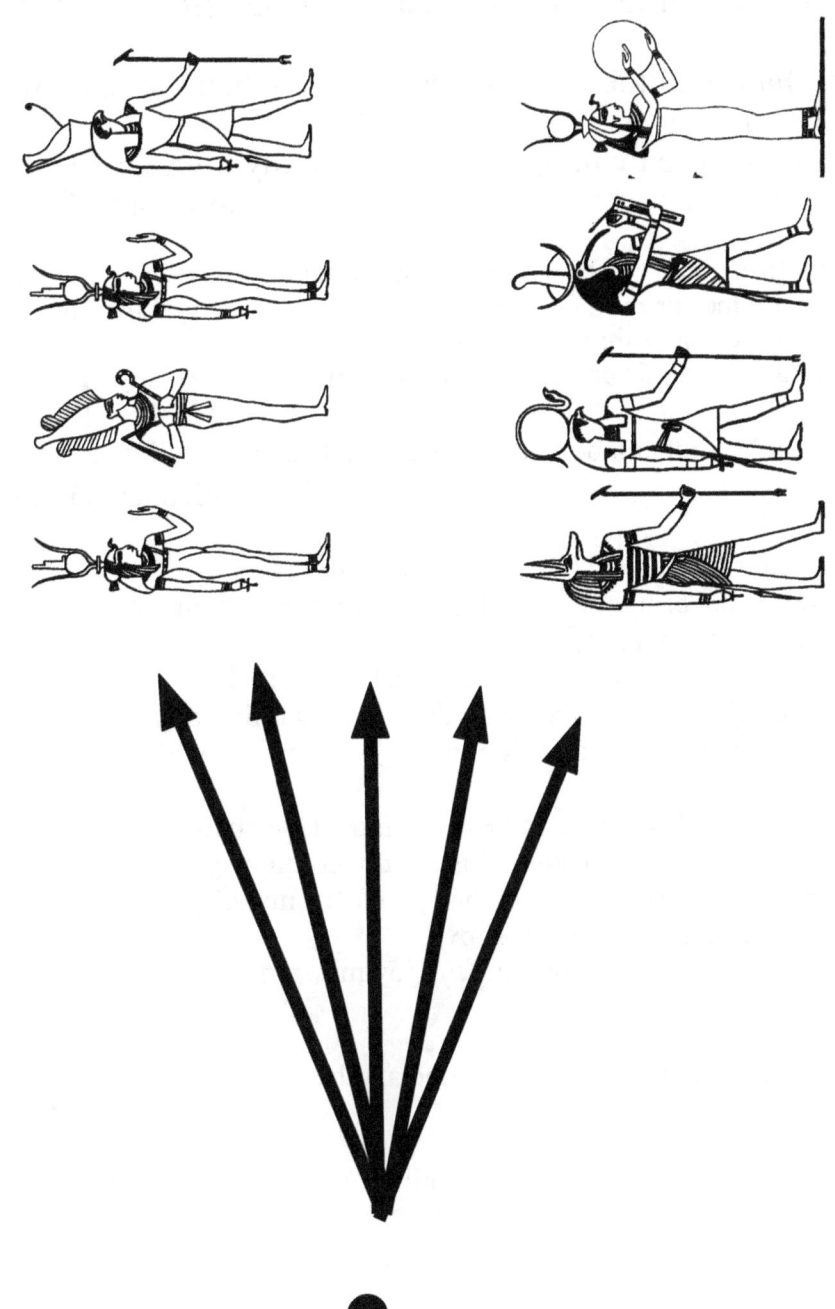

Left: The Supreme Being, Nebertcher, manifests as the various gods and goddesses as well as human beings, nature and the elements. Thus, from the one arise many, however, all objects are in reality a reflection of the one. Since a reflection is not real, only the one is real. So even though there appears to be multiplicity and duality it is only an illusion based on human ignorance. All is one and the one is God

4. Hear, O Israel: The LORD our God [is] one LORD:

5 And thou shalt love the LORD thy God with all thy heart, and with all thy soul, and with all thy might.

6 And these words, which I command thee this day, shall be in thy heart:

7 And thou shalt teach them diligently to thy children, and shalt talk of them when thou sit in thy house, and when thou walk by the way, and when thou liest down, and when thou risest up. {teach: HEB. whet, or, sharpen}

8 And thou shalt bind them for a sign upon thy hand, and they shall be as frontlets between thy eyes.

9 And thou shalt write them upon the posts of thy house, and on thy gates.

-Deuteronomy 6, The Bible

36 And a man's foes [shall be] they of his own household.

37 He that loveth father or mother more than me is not worthy of me: and he that loveth son or daughter more than me is not worthy of me.

38 And he that taketh not his cross, and followeth me, is not worthy of me.

-Matthew 10, The Bible

28 Come to me, all [ye] that labor and are heavy laden, and I will give you rest.

-Matthew 11, The Bible

5 I am the vine, ye [are] the branches: He that abideth in me,
and I in him, the same bringeth forth much fruit: for without me ye can do nothing. {without me: or, severed from me}

6 If a man abideth not in me, he is cast forth as a branch, and
is withered; and men gather them, and cast [them] into the fire, and they are burned.

7 If ye abide in me, and my words abide in you, ye may ask what ye will, and it shall be done to you.

8 In this is my Father glorified, that ye bear much fruit; so shall ye be my disciples.

9. As the Father hath loved me, so have I loved you: continue ye in my love.

10 If ye keep my commandments, ye shall abide in my love; even as I have kept my Father's commandments, and abide in his love.

11 These things have I spoken to you, that my joy may remain in you, and [that] your joy may be full.

12 This is my commandment, That ye love one another, as I have loved you.

-John 15, The Bible

"From now on, while awake or asleep, remember: you have seen, you have spoken with, and you have listened to the Child of Humanity."

-The Secret Book of James Chap. 2:4

2:45 Nay, seek (Allah's) help with patient perseverance and prayer: It is indeed hard, except to those who bring a lowly spirit, --
2:46 Who bear in mind the certainty that they are to meet their Lord, and that they are to return to Him.

35:3 O men! Call to mind the grace of Allah unto you! Is there a Creator, other than Allah, to give you sustenance from heaven or earth? There is no Allah but He: How then are ye deluded away from the Truth?
-The Koran

Give thyself to the GOD, guard thou thyself well for the God daily, and let tomorrow be as today.

The house of God, an abomination to it is much speaking. Pray thou with a loving heart, all its words being hidden. He will do thy business. He will hear what thou sayest and will receive thy offerings.
-Maxims of Ani (Ancient Egypt)

The end and aim of all these toils and labors (spiritual disciplines) is the attainment of the knowledge of the First and Chief Being, who alone is the object of the understanding of the mind; and this knowledge the goddess invites us to seek after, as being near and dwelling continually with her. A Devotee of ISIS is: One who ponders over sacred matters and seeks therein for hidden truth.
-Temple of Aset (Ancient Egypt)

Seek to know Brahman by acquiring faith in the word of the scriptures and in your Guru. Be devoted to Brahman. Meditate on him unceasingly. Not by work nor by progeny, nor by wealth but by devotion to him and by indifference to the world, does a man achieve immortality.
-Kaivalya Upanishad

Follow only in the footsteps of the illumined ones, and by continuous meditation merge both mind and intellect in the eternal Brahman. The glorious Lord will be revealed to you.
-Svetasvatara Upanishad

While talking, opening and closing the eyes, accepting and rejecting objects, breathing in and out, walking, sitting, at play, at work, and all such activities, at all times be devoted to the Self by keeping yourself detached from the operations of the mind. Do not forget the Self whether in life or in death, whether in pleasure or in pain...

The thoughts of near and far depend upon the illusion, "I am the body." Having renounced such thoughts, be devoted to the Self that is eternal and immutable.

Be devoted to the Self whether your body is young or old, whether you have prosperity or adversity, whether you are in dream or deep sleep.

> Though awake, discover the sleepless sleep of the Self. Enjoy the sleep-like tranquillity by meditating upon the truth: "I am not this body. I am the Self that has manifested in all this. I am indeed all this."
>
> -Yoga Vasistha
> Upashama Parkarana 50:12-16

> 8. O Partha! taking recourse to the Yoga of Abhyasa (repeated practice of meditation), possessing a mind that does not go elsewhere, and constantly dwelling upon Me, one goes to the Effulgent Self--the Supreme Purusha.
>
> -Bhagavad Gita: Chapter 8
> Akshara Brahma Yogah--
> The Yoga of Imperishable Brahman

> 10. To them whose minds rest in the Divine Self, who worship Me ceaselessly with devotion, I give the Yoga of Wisdom by which they attain Me.
>
> -Bhagavad Gita: Chapter 10
> Vibhuti Yogah--The Yoga of Divine Glories

> 2. The Blessed Lord said: Those who having immersed their mind in Me endowed with faith, worship Me with ceaseless devotion, they are in my opinion the best skilled in Yoga.
>
> 6. But those who having offered all actions to Me, devoted to Me, meditate upon Me with one-pointed Yoga.
>
> Bhagavad Gita: Chapter 12
> Bhakti Yogah--The Yoga of Devotion

Special attention is drawn here to John 15 and to the Bhagavad Gita Chapter 8:8 where Jesus admonishes his followers to abide in him and Krishna asks his disciple Arjuna, to constantly dwell upon him, and also to Matthew 11:28 and to the Gita: Chapter 10:10 wherein Jesus exhorts his followers to draw themselves to him with one-pointed interest just as Krishna asked Arjuna to worship him with ceaseless devotion. Clearly, the same sentiment and instruction is being given here, using almost the same exact wording. The important idea behind the monastic order and discipleship is the turning away from the phenomenal world and turning attention toward the divine essence behind it with unbroken concentration, allowing the flow of thought (wisdom) and feeling to be continuously directed toward the divine.

The mystical teachings presented in the Asarian mysteries are also found in the Hindu scriptures related to God in the form of a deity, Lord Krishna. In Shetaut Neter (Ancient Egyptian religion) the worship of the Divine with name and form is represented by the name and form of Asar. The Divine Self can be worshipped by using either a concrete name and form or by adoption an abstract ideal. For most people, the name and form provides something for the mind to lean on. This is especially true in the beginning stages of spiritual practice. However, as spiritual sensitivity grows, the name and form are to be transcended. in this manner, the name and form are to be understood as symbols of the Divine or as sign posts to direct the mind towards positive spiritual feelings and not as absolute realities.

The Path of Divine Love

The following passages from the Christian and Hindu Bibles reflect the teaching of single-minded devotion to God. Thus, Shetaut Neter (Ancient Egyptian religion), Christianity and Hinduism, share a common legacy.

Deuteronomy 11:13
    13 And it shall come to pass, if ye shall hearken diligently to my commandments which I command you this day, to love the LORD your God, and to serve him with all your heart and with all your soul,

Deuteronomy 13:3
    3 Thou shalt not hearken to the words of that prophet, or that dreamer of dreams: for the LORD your God tempt you, to know whether ye love the LORD your God with all your heart and with all your soul.

Joshua 22:5
    5 But take diligent heed to perform the commandment and the law, which Moses the servant of the LORD charged you, to love the LORD your God, and to walk in all his ways, and to keep his commandments, and to hold fast to him, and to serve him with all your heart and with all your soul.

1 Samuel 12:20
    20 And Samuel said to the people, Fear not: ye have done all this wickedness: yet turn not aside from following the LORD, but serve the LORD with all your heart;

1 Samuel 12:24
    24 Only fear the LORD, and serve him in truth with all your heart: for consider what great [things] he hath done for you.

Jeremiah 29:13
    13 And ye shall seek me, and find [me], when ye shall search for me with all your heart.

Joel 2:12
    12. Therefore also now, saith the LORD, turn ye [even] to me with all your heart, and with fasting, and with weeping, and with mourning.

Mark 12
    29 And Jesus answered him, The first of all the commandments [is], Hear, O Israel; The Lord our God is one Lord:
    30 And thou shalt love the Lord thy God with all thy heart, and with all thy soul, and with all thy mind, and with all thy strength: this [is] the first commandment.
    31 And the second [is] like, [namely] this, Thou shalt love thy neighbor as thyself. There is no other commandment greater than these.

Gita: Chapter 8 Akshara Brahma Yogah--The Yoga of Imperishable Brahman

8. O Partha! taking recourse to the Yoga of Abhyasa (repeated practice of meditation), possessing a mind that does not go elsewhere, and constantly dwelling upon Me, one goes to the Effulgent Self--the Supreme Purusha.

Gita: Chapter 9 Raja Vidya Raja Guhya Yogah--The Yoga of Royal Knowledge and Royal Secret

22. But those who worship Me by meditating upon Me with a vision of non-separateness, and who are ceaselessly devoted to Me, I look after their Yoga (spirituality) and Kshema (material needs).

As the Gnostic, Egyptian and other texts above explain, this form of religious discipline is essential to the development of higher spiritual consciousness and progress on the path of spirituality cannot occur without whole hearted attention toward the divine. This is because the mind holds the key to bondage and liberation of the soul and if the mind is in the state of bondage (ignorance) it is because it is constantly being bombarded with mental impressions which intensify the erroneous information about the world. The way to counteract this negative process is to reverse the flow of mentation from error or ignorance and distraction to the light of wisdom. The most popular forms of mental distraction in modern times are the pursuit of fulfillment of the sense pleasures and modern entertainments such as the television and other media.

Another important idea given here is that it is not exclusively necessary to remove oneself from society and to seclude oneself from the world in the privacy of the temple walls in order to practice this form of intense spiritual discipline. Unless one is very highly advanced, secluding oneself will actually result in an increase of the illusoriness and egoism within the mind. You may discover peace and you may feel that you have attained enlightenment but once you come out of seclusion and interact with the world of human society you will encounter anxieties, anger, etc. You led yourself into a false sense of attainment and you failed the test which was placed before you by the world. So the best plan for most people is to study the teachings in the temple (may be your own home or with a spiritual preceptor) and then to have interaction with the world on a regular basis in a balanced manner.

Since our state of consciousness is created by our experiences, perceptions, learned behaviors and reasoning, it is possible to relearn new forms of reasoning through the study of wisdom teachings and through practicing them in daily life. These new forms of reasoning can show you how to deal with life situations in the light of spiritual values and in doing this, the flood of ignorance is reversed even while you remain in the world carrying out your day to day duties. For this reason the Ancient Egyptian temple system allowed aspirants to have interaction with the outside world on a regular basis in order to get opportunities to practice the teachings when confronted with worldly minded people, while incorporating periods of intense meditation and withdrawal in a balanced program of spiritual practice. This understanding is the same in Hindu Ashrams and Buddhist Wats.

The Path of Divine Love

The world can be a temple of intensive yogic discipline when the aspirant is equipped with the teachings of wisdom and is backed by competent spiritual guidance. It would be easy to control thoughts and feelings of the flesh (anger, hate, greed, lust, etc.) when in a spiritual environment of peace and harmony. However, a discipline which incorporates constant, intensive provocation as well as regular opportunities for reflection and meditation is preferable in most cases over a temple environment exclusive of outside stimulus. The sages realized that in many instances the mind of the aspirant fools itself into believing it is progressing spiritually and even develops elaborate illusions about what Enlightenment is. In order to avoid this problem, the constant practice of reflection blended with contact with the world and contact with enlightened personalities (Sages, Saints, etc.) is the most desirable method of spiritual discipline because it constantly challenges the aspirant to put the ego down whenever it arises. This is one of the meanings of Matthew 16:24 Then said Jesus to his disciples, If any [man] will come after me, let him deny himself, and take up his cross, and follow me. Jesus is challenging his disciple to follow the path of the Christian teachings, which lead to self-denial (ego-effacement). Christianity must then be understood as a discipline of transpersonal movement in consciousness akin to the Asarian Mystery, Buddhism, Sufism, and other mystery cults which promote the dissolution of the personal ego and the emergence of the transcendental, transpersonal consciousness.

Your life has been designed by the Divine Self to lead you to Enlightenment. The Self has carefully orchestrated all of the situation and events you will need to deal with. As you deal with life in accordance with the teachings you allow a process of transformation to occur wherein you grow in wisdom and self-awareness.

Several of the passages just presented talk about maintaining the teachings in the mind not only in the waking but also in the sleep state of consciousness, but how can this be possible? Have you ever had a dream during the night while asleep about something you have been pondering over intensely while you were awake, something you wanted intensely, a person you fell in love with and could not take your mind off, an experience or an object you wanted to acquire? The conscious desires of the waking state enter the subconscious and unconscious levels of the mind and there lodge as impressions of latent desire. If these impressions are strong enough they surface continually, causing the waking state to experience them as thoughts of the present. The same thing occurs in the dream state. When you intensify your waking efforts toward spirituality they will continue to work in the mind even during the sleep state, and in this manner the sleep state becomes a continuous worship of the Divine teachings of wisdom. This occurs due to the force of habit created through the practice while in the waking state. So just as you practice detachment from the people and objects in the waking state, the mind learns to practice this discipline automatically in the unconscious. Therefore, for a devoted aspirant the sleep state of consciousness is never wasted. In order to be successful, spiritual practice needs to be continuous. This point is explained in the following verse from the Yoga Vasistha IV 43:2-3

> Just as water sustains liquidity, wind is characterized by movement, and the sky is inseparable from spaciousness, in the same way, Atman or the Self is inseparable from His creation of divine beings.

> I perform this Divine worship at all times. During the waking state, I offer Him the flowers of all day-to-day activities; during sleep, I worship the Self by the vritti*-function

of the unconscious mind. (*thought process).

The most important quality to develop is the meditative mind. This is not only to be thought of as the mind of a person that sits in a state of deep catatonic meditation, but a person who, while he or she is involved in the affairs of the world, all the time KNOWS his or her true identity. This is the mind that interacts with every moment of existence unlike the previously discussed automatic mind. This quality represents the vision of Heru which is the vision to be regained. In a sense, people living in the ancient societies such as that of Egypt and India would not have needed to practice formalized forms of meditation as much as today. This is because then, knowledge of the existence of GOD and the Gods was not an object of speculation but it was inherent in the very fabric of the culture. Spirituality was an inseparable part of their practical life. Therefore, their minds would be constantly thinking about and accommodating divinity, regardless of their activities. This attitude in itself constitutes a meditative state of mind. A similar technique of spiritual discipline enjoined by modern day spiritual preceptors is called "mindfulness", wherein one maintains a sense of one's divine essence at every moment while performing one's daily tasks (breathing, walking, resting, or even while answering nature's call). Also known as the "development of the witness", this technique aids the spiritual aspirant in developing an expanded awareness aside from the common waking consciousness. Through this practice, the soul separates itself from the ego-personality and obtains knowledge of itself through identification with itself instead of with the body, mind and sense perceptions.

The Path of Divine Love

The Movement Toward Divine Love

"Seekest thou God, thou seekest for the Beautiful. One is the Path that leadeth unto It - Devotion joined with Wisdom."

—Ancient Egyptian Proverb

All of the previous practices (listening, reflection and meditation on the teachings) have been preparing you to understand the inner teachings of the process of union with the Divine through Intuitional Understanding of the truth and Devotional Meditation on the Divine. We have previously discussed (in Egyptian Yoga: The Philosophy of Enlightenment) the yogic disciplines of Devotion and Meditation, however, in this section we will focus on them exclusively. In this section, the teachings of Wisdom and Action will come together with Devotion and Meditation to produce a powerful combination toward your spiritual movement. When your intellectual attainment (wisdom) is united with your feeling or emotional aspect, these form a formidable force for moving the mind toward the Divine. This is the power of true devotional feeling. It gives wings to the intellect and allows it to fly beyond reason to discover the absolute transcendental existence.

The myth of Asar, Aset and Heru is ritualized in the Books of Coming Forth By Day. These texts are like manuals for initiates who want to follow the path of spiritual enlightenment by practicing the teachings of Maat and identifying with Asar, Aset and Heru, culminating in a spiritual resurrection. As such, the Book of Coming Forth by Day and the rituals surrounding it which were used in the temples of Asar and Aset represent the ritualization of the mythology itself which helps to attune the practitioner to the deeper mysteries of the myth as they apply to him/herself. The religion of Asar, Aset and Heru is essentially a mixture of two forms of yogic practice. These are the Yoga of Wisdom and the Yoga of Devotion to the Higher Self in the form of Asar, Aset and Heru. The devotion and love expressed toward the Asarian Trinity was of immense proportions. While there were several favorite gods and goddesses of many localities, the Asarian Trinity was revered throughout the land of Ancient Egypt as well as in the Near Eastern countries which came into contact with Ancient Egypt. This prodigious quality is what spurred the development of the Christian Trinity and had a profound effect on the Trinity of India.

Indian devotional yoga has attained a high degree of development. It has mainly been popularized as a method of worship for the masses who find it easier to meditate on the divine in the form of a human personality. In other words, devotional meditation is primarily supported by a figure or symbol of the Divine with a name and form rather than an abstract form of meditation which requires no name or form. The following is a brief description of the Devotional Yoga System. Devotional Yoga has developed into a program which involves nine integrated aspects or practices whose purpose is to lead the aspirant to develop a mental process which is one-pointedly directing all thoughts and emotions toward the Divine. These practices are:

Listening to the Teachings

This implies the development of a calm mind which is intent upon understanding the teachings about God. It also implies that the listener must have an open mind and not be arrogant, prideful or prejudiced toward the teachings or the Spiritual Preceptor. The listener should be open to understanding the hidden wisdom which underlies the teachings and should not hold onto erroneous preconceived notions about spirituality. If there is a closed mind, no teaching will be effective. Thus, the spiritual aspirant must approach the teacher with an attitude of humility and reverence in order to properly receive the teachings of mystical spirituality.

Further, this level of practice requires that the aspirant listen to the myths extolling the glory of the Divine and allow him or herself to let the imagination fly freely into the questions like "Who is this Divine Self?", "What are these magnificent deeds being performed for the benefit of humanity?", "What is the message from the Divine Being conveyed through this story?", "How am I related to this Divinity?". As these questions gradually find their answer through the expert instruction by the Spiritual Preceptor, the aspirant should allow the feelings of love for the Divine to develop. The following is a compendium of the Ausarian Resurrection Myth which should be listened to and studied often for developing devotion toward the Divine.

The Path of Divine Love

A COMPENDIUM OF THE AUSARIAN RESURRECTION MYTH

THE CREATION

The process of creation is explained in the form of a cosmological system for better understanding. Cosmology is a branch of philosophy dealing with the origin, processes, and structure of the universe. Cosmogony is the astrophysical study of the creation and evolution of the universe. Both of these disciplines are inherent facets of Ancient Egyptian philosophy through the main religious systems or Companies of the gods and goddesses. A Company of gods and goddesses is a group of deities which symbolize a particular cosmic force or principle which emanates from the all-encompassing Supreme Being, from which they have emerged. The Self or Supreme Being manifests creation through the properties and principles represented by the Pautti Company of gods and goddesses - cosmic laws of nature. The system or Company of gods and goddesses of Anu is regarded as the oldest, and forms the basis of the Asarian Trinity. It is expressed in the diagram below.

Above: The Ancient Egyptian god Ra, traversing throughout creation in his Boat.

Neter Merri

Shetai - Neter Neteru - Nebertcher
(unseen, hidden, omnipresent, Supreme Being, beyond duality and description)

```
                    Ra-Tem      ⇨ ⇨ ⇘
                       ⇩           Hathor
                       ⇩           Djehuti
                       ⇩           Maat
                  Shu ⇔ Tefnut
                       ⇩
                   Geb ⇔ Nut
                    ⇙  ⇩  ⇘
        Set    Asar ⇔ Aset      Asar ⇔ Nebthet
                       ⇩                 ⇩
                     Heru                Anpu
```

The diagram above shows that the Psedjet (Ennead), or the creative principles which are embodied in the primordial gods and goddesses of creation, emanated from the Supreme Being. Ra or Ra-Tem arose out of the "Nu", the Primeval waters, the hidden essence, and began sailing the "Boat of Millions of Years" which included the Company of gods and goddesses. On his boat emerged the "neters" or cosmic principles of creation. The neters of the Ennead are Ra-Atum, Shu, Tefnut, Geb, Nut, Asar, Aset, Set, and Nebthet. Hetheru, Djehuti and Maat represent attributes of the Supreme Being as the very stuff or substratum which makes up creation. Shu, Tefnut, Geb, Nut, Asar, Aset, Set, and Nebthet represent the principles upon which creation manifests. Anpu is not part of the Ennead. He represents the feature of intellectual discrimination in the Asarian myth. "Sailing" signifies the beginning of motion in creation. Motion implies that events occur in the realm of time and space, thus, the phenomenal universe comes into existence as a mass of moving essence we call the elements. Prior to this motion, there was the primeval state of being without any form and without existence in time or space.

Asar, Aset and Heru[22]

Asar and Aset dedicated themselves to the welfare of humanity and sought to spread civilization throughout the earth, even as far as India and China.

During the absence of Asar from his kingdom, his brother Set had no opportunity to make innovations in the state, because Aset was extremely vigilant in governing the country, and always upon her guard and watchful for any irregularity or unrighteousness.

Upon Asar' return from touring the world and carrying the teachings of wisdom abroad there was merriment and rejoicing throughout the land. However, one day after Asar' return, through he became intoxicated with happiness and slept with Set's wife, Nebthet. Nebthet, as a result of the union with Asar, begot Anpu.

Set, who represents the personification of evil forces, plotted in jealousy and anger (the blinding passion that prevents forgiveness) to usurp the throne and conspired to kill Asar. Set secretly got the measurements of Asar and constructed a coffin. Through trickery Set was able to get Asar to "try on" the coffin for size. While Asar was resting in the coffin, Set and his assistants locked it and then dumped it into the Nile river.

The coffin made its way to the coast of Syria where it became embedded in the earth and from it grew a tree with the most pleasant aroma. The tree was cut into the form of a DJED pillar. The Djed is the symbol of Asar' BACK. It has four horizontal lines in relation to a firmly established, straight column. The DJED column is symbolic of the upper energy centers (chakras) that relate to the levels of consciousness of the spirit within an individual human being.

The King of Syria was out walking and as he passed by the tree, he immediately fell in love with the pleasant aroma, so he had the tree cut down and brought to his palace. Aset (Auset, Ast), Asar' wife, the personification of the life giving, mother force in creation and in all humans, went to Syria in search of Asar. Her search led her to the palace of the Syrian King where she took a job as the nurse of the King's son. Every evening Aset would put the boy into the "fire" to consume his mortal parts, thereby transforming him to immortality. Fire is symbolic of both physical and mental purification. Most importantly, fire implies wisdom, the light of truth, illumination and energy. Aset, by virtue of her qualities, has the power to bestow immortality through the transformative power of her symbolic essence. Aset then told the king that Asar, her husband, is inside the pillar he made from the tree. He graciously gave her the pillar (DJED) and she returned with it to Kamit (Kmt, Egypt).

Upon her return to Kmt Aset went to the papyrus swamps where she lay over Asar' dead body and fanned him with her wings, infusing him with new life. In this manner Aset revived Asar through her power of love and wisdom, and then they united once more. From their union was conceived a son, Heru (Heru), with the assistance of the gods Thoth (Djehuti) and Amon.

---

[22] The entire scripture from the text of the Ancient Egyptian Ausarian Myth is presented in the book **The Resurrecting Osiris** by Dr. Muata Ashby.

The Path of Divine Love

On Previous page: The Sacred Triad: Asar, Aset and Heru (1450 B.C.E. Louvre Museum)

One evening, as Set was hunting in the papyrus swamps, he came upon Aset and Asar. In a rage of passion, he dismembered the body of Asar into several pieces and scattered them throughout the land. In this way it is Set, the brute force of our bodily impulses and desires, that "dismembers" our higher intellect. Instead of oneness and unity, we see multiplicity and separateness which give rise to egoistic (selfish) and violent behavior. The Great Mother, Aset, once again sets out to search, now for the pieces of Asar, with the help of Anpu and Nebthet.

After searching all over the world they found all the pieces of Asar' body, except for his phallus which was eaten by a fish. In Eastern Hindu-Tantra mythology, the God Shiva, who is the equivalent of Asar, also lost his phallus in one story. In Ancient Egyptian and Hindu-Tantra mythology, this loss represents seminal retention in order to channel the sexual energy to the higher spiritual centers, thereby transforming it into spiritual energy. Aset, Anpu and Nebthet remembered the pieces, all except the phallus which was eaten by the fish. Asar thus regained life in the realm of the dead, the duat.

Heru, therefore, was born from the union of the spirit of Asar and the life giving power of Aset (Creation). Thus, Heru represents the union of spirit and matter and the renewed life of Asar, his rebirth. When Heru became a young man, Asar returned from the realm of the dead and encouraged him to take up arms (vitality, wisdom, courage, strength of will) and establish truth, justice and righteousness in the world by challenging Set, its current ruler.

The Battle of Heru (Heru) and Set

The battle between Heru and Set took many twists, sometimes one seeming to get the upper hand and sometimes the other, yet neither one gaining a clear advantage in order to decisively win. At one point Aset tried to help Heru by catching Set, but due to the pity and compassion she felt towards him she set him free. In a passionate rage Heru cut off her head and went off by himself in a frustrated state. Even Heru is susceptible to passion which leads to performing deeds that one later regrets. Set found Heru and gouged out Heru' eyes. During this time Heru was overpowered by the evil of Set. He became blinded to truth (as signified by the loss of his eyes) and thus, was unable to do battle (act with MAAT) with Set. His power of sight was later restored by Hetheru (goddess of passionate love, desire and fierce power), who also represents the left Eye of Ra. She is the fire spitting, destructive power of light which dispels the darkness (blindness) of ignorance.

When the conflict resumed, the two contendants went before the court of the Ennead gods (Company of the nine gods who ruled over creation, headed by Ra). Set, promising to end the fight and restore Heru to the throne, invited Heru to spend the night at his house, but Heru soon found out that Set had evil intentions when he tried to have intercourse with him. The uncontrolled Set also symbolizes unrestricted sexual activity. Juxtaposed against this aspect of Set (uncontrolled sexual potency and desire) is Heru in the form of ithyphallic (erect phallus) MIN, who represents not only the control of sexual desire, but its sublimation as well. Min symbolizes the power which comes from the sublimation of the sexual energy.

Through more treachery and deceit Set attempted to destroy Heru with the help of the Ennead, by tricking them into believing that Heru was not worthy of the throne. Asar sent a letter pleading with the Ennead to do what was correct. Heru, as the son of Asar, should be the rightful heir to the throne. All but two of them (the Ennead) agreed because Heru, they said, was too young to rule. Asar then sent them a second letter (scroll of papyrus with a message) reminding them that even they cannot escape judgment for their deeds; they too will be judged in the end when they have to finally go to the West (abode of the dead).

This signifies that even the gods cannot escape judgment for their deeds. Since all that exists is only a manifestation of the absolute reality which goes beyond time and space, that which is in the realm of time and space (humans, spirits, gods, angels, neters) are all bound by its laws. Following the receipt of Asar' scroll (letter), Heru was crowned King of Egypt. Set accepted the decision and made peace with Heru. All the gods rejoiced. Thus ends the legend of Asar, Aset, and Heru.

The Resurrection of Asar and his reincarnation in the form of Heru is a symbol for the spiritual resurrection which must occur in the life of every human being. In this manner, the story of the Asarian Trinity of Asar-Aset-Heru and the Egyptian Ennead holds hidden teachings, which when understood and properly practiced, will lead to spiritual enlightenment.

Horus spearing Apap (Apôphis)

The Path of Divine Love

The Mystical Implications of the Ausarian Resurrection Myth and the Path of Devotion Toward the Divine

The myth of Asar, Aset and Heru holds great mystical implications for every spiritual aspirant. It shows how devotion, in the form of the actions by Aset and Nebthet, was able to bring Asar back from death to life again. In the same manner, the practice of the Yoga of Devotional Love can lead any human being to engender a rebirth of the spirit, a resurrection from the degradation, dismemberment and suffering which is being imposed on it by the ego (Set) and its negative qualities. The intense practice of the Yoga of Devotional Love has been outlined below.

Singing, Chanting and Divine Music

Singing songs and praises to God both in the form of a male deity or as a female deity. If you review utterance #12 (see below) in the Asarian Drama, music is spoken of as one of the means by which Asar taught the teachings as he traveled the earth. Music is an extremely potent force for spiritual development because it tends to carry the mind to a higher, trance like level of experience. Also, if the mind is correctly attuned the "music of the spheres", the name of God can be heard. In this way, specially designed Words of Power are used in repeated recitation and in songs to draw the mind closer to the Divine.

> 12   Asar, having become king of Egypt, applied himself to civilizing his countrymen by turning them from their former indigent and barbarous course of life. Aset discovered the use of barley and wheat and Asar developed the cultivation process for these and established the custom of offering the first fruits to the neters. He taught them how to cultivate and improve the fruits of the earth, and he gave them a body of laws whereby to regulate their conduct, and instructed them in the reverence and worship which they were to pay to the gods. With the same good disposition he afterwards traveled over the rest of the world, inducing the people everywhere to submit to his discipline, not indeed compelling them by force of arms, but persuading them to yield to the strength of his reasons, which were conveyed to them in the most agreeable manner, in ***hymns and songs***,[23] accompanied with instruments of music.

Another perspective of singing in mystical spirituality implies that you must allow your divine essence to be the driving force in your life. This means that everything you do should be an expression of Divine harmony. You should praise the Divine at all times and acknowledge the Divine presence everywhere and in all things. When prosperity is at hand there should be praises. When there is adversity then too there should be praises.

---

[23] See the Egyptian Yoga Chant and Songbook for more information.

The Names of God (Asar, Aset Amun, Jesus, Buddha, Krishna, Rama, etc.) can be sung in the form of chants, hekau or mantras. This practice was well developed in Ancient Egypt and was used extensively in the Temple proceedings. It is a well developed practice called Kirtana in the Hindu system of religion as well as the Vedanta-Yoga system of India. The vocalization of hekau or mantras draws the mind toward the Divine especially when the meaning of the words is well understood. These words of power have the effect of cleansing the unconscious mind and thus engender a profound transformation leading the human being to Divine awareness. This form of devotional religious practice is the central form of yoga practiced by the followers of Krishna popularly known as the "Hare Krishnas."

This singing need not be an external exercise. It is more important that you internally remain aware and thoughtful of the Divine and remind others of their Divine basis, especially when they are "miraculously" delivered from some problem or adversity of life. By acknowledging that there is a Divine Hand directing your path at all times you are putting down your ego and its illusions and desires which prevent Divine awareness and realization. The most important musical instruments in the practice of devotion to the Divine in Ancient Egyptian mysticism were the voice, sistrum, harp and hand drum. In ancient times music was given high value in the practice of devotion because through music the mind and emotions can be affected and turned towards the Divine more easily. Therefore, music was strictly controlled by the priests and priestesses. Unlike modern society, music for personal pleasure or entertainment was not allowed because in this capacity it can turn the mind more intensely towards worldliness. See the Egyptian Yoga Chant and Songbook for more on Ancient Egyptian Music.

In a broad perspective, one's entire life should be a devotional hymn to the Divine. In this manner, one should strive to promote harmony, peace, selflessness and cheerfulness in life as well as sacrifice, forbearance and forgiveness. These are the most spiritual melodies that can be sung, essentially using one's entire personality as a musical instrument, allowing the Divine to play it.

NOTE In the year 1999 Dr. Muata Ashby composed several chanting and music compositions based on the ancient Egyptian hieroglyphic texts of devotion to the Divine.
The Music of Ancient Egypt collection is an exploration of ancient Egyptian musical forms and concepts using ancient Egyptian musical instrument reproductions to discover the mysteries of Kemetic (Kamitan – ancient Egyptian) devotional musical feeling. The fruit of years of research have given fruit to a unique sound and musical conception which at times sounds ancient and at other times fuses Ancient Egyptian feeling with modern writhyms of the world including West African, Middle Eastern, Soul, Jazz, and East Indian styles. Using authentic the Ancient Egyptian words derived from inscriptions, hymns and papyri such as the Ancient Egyptian Book of the Dead, a wonderful and special musical vision has emerged. A must for lovers of Ancient Egyptian culture and mysticism and alternative music. For more on the music and chants of Ancient Egypt see the Egyptian Yoga Chant and Devotional Songbook by Muata Ashby.

©1999 **Muata Ashby**

Above: The Temple of Aset (Isis) where the myth of Asar was reenacted and the divine worship program was carried out.

Above: Temple of Aset Peristyle Hall

Neter Merri

Service to the Divine

Service here refers to service at the feet of the Lord. This implies developing a spirit of selfless service towards the entire world which is in essence. Everything is an emanation and expression of God, therefore all is to be served as God. This point is directly referred to in the Egyptian Book of Coming Forth By Day in Chapter 125, 8-12 which reads as follows:

"I have not borne false witness; 8. therefore let nothing; [evil] be done to me. I have lived upon truth (Maat), I have fed upon truth, I have performed the ordinances of men, and the things which gratify the gods. 9. I have propitiated The God (Asar, Nebertcher, Neter) by doing God's will, I have given bread to the hungry man, and water to him that was athirst, and clothes to the naked man, 10. and a ferry-boat to him that had no boat. I have made propitiatory offerings and given cakes to the gods, and the " things which appear at the word " to the Spirits. Deliver then ye me 11, protect then ye me and make ye no report against me in the presence of The God [Great God]. I am pure in respect of my mouth, and I am clean in respect of my hands, therefore let it be said unto me by those who shall behold me: "Come in peace, 12. Come in peace...."

The passage above is from the section where the initiate declares that he or she has served humanity and God and that this service has purified their heart and therefore, they are worthy of entering into the deepest mysteries of the soul. Providing selfless service to humanity, especially when it is understood that one is actually serving God, has a profoundly purifying effect on the conscious and unconscious levels of the mind (the heart). You do not need any external reward for performing this service because you are gaining purity of heart and inner peace from the doing itself. Thus, you must strive to see the entire world as an expression of the Divine and also you must strive to see all human beings as expressions of the Divine.

With this understanding you should give thanks when someone approaches you in need since they are indeed a channel through which God is expressing in order to give you an opportunity to practice humility and selfless service. Indeed it is God who expresses as the sick, the downtrodden, the child in need of love or discipline, the elderly person in need of assistance, the person in need of guidance and so on. When you perform a good deed it has a positive effect on your mind and it will lead you to experience heavenly conditions while you live on earth as well as when you leave the body. However, when you practice performing good deeds with the understanding provided by mystical philosophy, your good deeds will lead you on a journey wherein you will transcend heavenly pleasures as you discover and abide in Pa Neter, "The God," directly and eternally.

"Consume pure foods and pure thoughts with pure hands, adore celestial beings, become associated with wise ones: sages, saints and prophets; make offerings to GOD."

-Ancient Egyptian Proverb from
The Stele of Djehuti Nefer

Also, service implies service to the spiritual preceptor by helping to disseminate the teachings of yoga. The main goal of the Spiritual Preceptor is to promote peace and harmony in the world and to disseminate the teachings of mystical philosophy while making every effort to present them in such a way that they are correctly understood. As you assist your spiritual preceptor to disseminate the teachings, you are actually purifying yourself because in order to teach you must learn and in learning there is knowledge, and as knowledge and practice progress they turn into experience. When knowledge and experience come together, wisdom is born, and wisdom eventually blossoms into spiritual realization or enlightenment.

Ritual Worship

This implies ritual worship of the Divine. The thought of worship usually draws ideas of bringing flowers, incense and other offerings to the altar created for a particular deity or representation of the Divine. This is the ritualistic level of worship. In succeeding levels of devotional practice, this ritualism will turn into true and ardent worship of the Divine which is actually practiced in India of today exactly as it was practiced in the Temples of Aset and Asar, Heru and Hetheru over 2,000 years ago. It implies a gradually increasing devotion toward the Divine which is transformed into an assimilation into the Divine. Succeeding stages of devotional worship involve prostration before the image of God and a "slavish" devotion to God. This movement culminates in a "self offering," an absolute surrendering of the individual will through which the worshiper gives up his/her ego to and enters into the immortal body of God. This is the stage wherein the Ancient Egyptian initiate in the ritual procession into the holy of holies is renamed and given the name of Asar. Then the initiate is led to actually meet Asar, his/her Higher Self, and thereby become absorbed or one in consciousness with the Supreme Being.

It is important to understand that devotional yoga involves more than simply mindlessly or fanatically praising God, praying or singing devotional songs with emotional force. An integrated process of Devotional Yoga involves an understanding of the metaphysical teachings of wisdom and a blending of all of the other Yogic systems. This integrated process which involves wisdom or intuitional understanding of the metaphysical realities behind creation serves to close any gaps in the mind of the aspirant as to whether or not there is any doubt of the existence of the divine.

It must be clearly understood that true worship of God means becoming one with God. This can only occur if the individual ego is left behind and the worshiper discovers his/her oneness with the Divine. It is necessary to give one's heart, soul and personality to the Divine as an offering of humility as well as reason. In reality the personality in you is an illusion anyway. It is like a cloud preventing you from seeing the sun. Therefore it must be understood and effaced. When this effacement occurs it is like the clouds dispersing and allowing the light of the sun to shine forth in an unobstructed manner, revealing the absolute reality of the transcendental Self and the illusoriness of the ego and human existence. Any other form of worship with any other idea besides this is only occurring at the level of the ego, and this implies a surface experience and not the real experience of the Divine. Divine love is a universal love which transcends all barriers of egoism. Egoistic love is love with attachments, infatuations and expectations. You love someone up to the point of when they do something you don't like, and then you don't love them as before. If a person does not act in a way which you expect them to, your feelings wane. This is not true love. True love means giving oneself completely and utterly to the object of one's love. However, this giving is not a blind offering of one's being to any object of love. Supreme Love should be reserved for that which is real and abiding. Objects in the world and human personalities are neither real nor abiding, therefore, they are not deserving of your supreme love, except as emanations of the Supreme Self. Their spirit is real and abiding. It survives after death and is indeed immutable, all good and peaceful. This is the spiritual essence in every human personality and in every physical object. This is to be revered as the Supreme Self incarnate in every corner of the universe. So the Supreme Self alone is worthy of Supreme Love, thus one should dedicate one's life to developing increasing unconditional love for the Divine Self throughout one's life.

If the worship remains at the level of the ego and intellect, that is, if you pray "to" a divinity who is separate from yourself, the pains and sorrows of the world will continue to be experienced and there will be no liberation from the cycles of birth and death. You will remain in a state of ignorance of your true Self and will be susceptible to the karmic destiny which is based on the egoistic notions, illusions and desires of your unconscious mind. If you realize your Divine nature, all of the accumulated ignorance of the unconscious mind is eradicated as the light of wisdom enters your mind, just as the sun rises over the horizon at dawn and dispels the darkness. This is the state of spiritual Enlightenment and it signifies an end to the cycles of birth and death as well as an end to human suffering, disillusionment and frustration. It implies a constant awareness of the Divine and Supreme Peace which transcends all human situations, be they positive or negative.

From this perspective it must be clearly understood that becoming one with God (Asar) represents actual "Resurrection". In the advanced stages, the meditative movement in Devotional Yoga leads to a merging of the aspirant with the Divine. This is the re-birth from mortal consciousness to cosmic consciousness, immortality, supreme peace and ultimate bliss.

"placing the face to the ground"

Prostration is a sign of humility and reverence accorded to the Divine and exalted personalities. It is the act of reverencing the Divine image and what it represents. This allows the ego to be sublimated and the flow of divine grace showers over the aspirant, leading him/her to spiritual enlightenment.

The Christian Eucharist and the Asarian Mystery

The Eucharist ritual is one of the most powerful devotional practices when completely understood. It originated in the Asarian Mysteries recorded in the Ancient Egyptian Pyramid Texts (forerunner of the Ancient Egyptian Book of Coming Forth By Day) and is used in modern times in the Christian Mass ceremony as well as the Satsanga (good association) meetings between Gurus and spiritual aspirants (Yoga Initiates). We will begin here with a quotation from the Christian Bible.

Matthew 26:
26. And as they were eating, Jesus took bread, and blessed [it], and broke [it], and gave [it] to the disciples, and said, Take, eat; this is my body. {blessed it: many Greek copies have gave thanks}
27. And he took the cup, and gave thanks, and gave [it] to them, saying, Drink ye all of it;
28. For this is my blood of the new testament, which is shed for many for the remission of sin.

The Eucharist (Christian sacrament) originated with the Asarian mystery of Egypt and can be found as early as the Ancient Egyptian Pyramid Texts (5,500 B.C.E.). It became popular in many other cults and mystery traditions prior to its practice in the Christian mystery. According to Hippolitus, a writer on the Naasenes, who was one of the Christian heresies, he states that "the ineffable mystery of the Samothracians, which is allowable" only for "the initiated to know" was exactly the same proclaimed by Jesus Christ in the Eucharist ritual where he states: "If ye do not drink my blood, and eat my flesh, ye will not enter the Kingdom of Heaven". Hippolitus states that according to the Naasenes, this ritual of flesh and blood is called Corybas by the Phrygians as well as the "Thracians who dwell around Haemus."

The Eucharist is the central rite of the Catholic mass or church service. It reenacts the Last Supper when Christ gave his disciples bread, saying, "This is my body," and wine, saying, "This is my blood." This sacrament is also known as the Holy Communion. However, there has been a controversy over what the communion is supposed to be since the rise in prominence of the Orthodox Roman Catholic Church.

At the Lateran Council in 1215, a doctrine called Transubstantiation, was defined. It stated that there is a change in substance of the Eucharistic elements after the consecration. The substance of bread and wine changes to Christ's actual body and blood. The doctrine is opposed by that of Consubstantiation which holds that after the words of consecration in Communion, the substances of bread and wine remain along with the body and blood of Christ.

Over 5,500 before the Christian era the Egyptian Mystery Religion of Asar incorporated an elaborate system of mental, physical and spiritual transformation through the use of ritual worship of the divine. The process is well described in the Ancient Egyptian Pyramid Texts and the Egyptian Books of Coming Forth By Day. This ritual worship centered around the figure of Asar, who represents the all-encompassing Divine Self. Through continued ritual offerings to Asar and the identification of the initiate with Asar as the true recipient of the offerings the

The Path of Divine Love

initiate is gradually united with Asar. Thus, a system of Ritual Identification is established. There are hundreds of instances of offerings in the Ancient Egyptian Pyramid Texts and Books of Coming Forth By Day. The following Utterances highlight the offering process and the ritual identification of the initiate with Asar and with the other Gods and Goddesses. These lines taken from various segments throughout the Pyramid Texts and the Book of Coming Forth By Day are only a partial sampling. They show the gradual realization of the initiate that the Gods are in reality aspects of him / herself.

"I am Asar...I am The Great God, the self-created one, Nun...I am Ra...I am Geb...I am Atum...I am Asar...I am Min...I am Shu...I am Anpu...I am Aset...I am Hetheru...I am Sekhmet...I am Orion...I am Saa...I am the Lion... I am the young Bull...I am Hapi who comes forth as the river Nile..."

Below: The ancient Egyptian Eucharist using bread, wine and incense.

The Sem Priest Offering bread.

"This is the Flesh itself of Asar"

From the *Egyptian Book of Coming Forth By Day* (Book of The Dead)

The Sem priest presenting a white vessel of wine.

The Sem priest presenting a ball of incense.

The Lord's Supper

Bread and wine are the main symbols of the Christian Eucharist

The Path of Divine Love

In much the same way as the Christian follower is exhorted to accept the bread and wine as the body and blood of Christ, the initiate is continuously told to accept offerings in the form of bread, fruit, wine, beer, vegetables, etc., which represent Asar. Perhaps the most important offering is the Eye of Heru, which represents the power of intuitional vision, the memory of the true Self which is one with the Divine. The Eye is the most powerful weapon the initiate has against the forces of evil (ignorance about the true Self) because it represents knowledge of the true Self or enlightenment which occurs when the Serpent Power or Kundalini energy-consciousness reaches the sixth energy center in the forehead, also known as the Third Eye. In this sense, the Eye of Heru is the highest offering given to the initiate who is exhorted to accept the Eye which was stolen by Set (egoistic identification with the ego-self or the Tree of Knowledge of Good and Evil which takes the soul away from God). The following selections from the Egyptian Pyramid Texts illustrate the significance of the Eye and its identification with the offering of wine and bread.

Utterance 28
O Asar Unas, Heru has given you his Eye; provide your face with it.

O Asar Unas, take the Eye of Heru which was wrested from Set and which you shall take to your mouth, with which you shall split open your mouth— WINE.

Utterance 51
O Unas, take the Eye of Heru which you shall taste— CAKE.

Utterance 89
O Asar Unas, take the Eye of Heru which Set has pulled out—A LOAF.

Utterance 93
O King, take this bread of yours which is the Eye of Heru.

Through the practice of ritual identification with the Divine the aspirant engenders a state of consciousness which develops into mystical union with the Divine. The Christian Eucharist clearly symbolizes the ritual identification of the Christian practitioner with the Christ. However, the mystical experience necessitates the dissolution of the ego. This is the time when the Christian follower dissolves, in consciousness, into the Christhood state of mind or consciousness. The ritual identification of the aspirant is also important because this very idea is at the heart of the myth which is being played out in the ritual. With this understanding, the true name of the follower of Christianity is Christ, the true name of the follower of Vaishnavism is Vishnu, the true name of the follower Vedanta Philosophy is Brahman, the true name of the follower of Buddhism is Buddha, and the true name of the follower of the Asarian Mysteries is Asar. The same process is applied to the worship of female deities (Aset, Kali, etc.), and this practice is extensively taught and practiced by those who follow Vedanta Philosophy and the Bhagavad Gita. The practice is called Ahamgraha Upashama which means that the worshiper meditates and affirms that he or she is the Divinity and not the individual ego. Hence the Upanishadic texts prescribe the mantra Aham Brahma Asmi "I am the Absolute Supreme Being," or the devotee may use one of the other names of God such as Krishna, Rama in the male (father) aspect or Kali, Saraswati or Durga in the female (mother) aspect.

The Pyramid Texts create a striking image of the initiate as the slayer and eater of gods and they also associate the initiate with Heru who in the process of battling the forces of evil, defeats and drinks the blood of the foes. In the Pyramid Texts of Unas, Asar Unas is said to have cooked and eaten the gods and goddesses and absorbed their essence. These references to consuming the demoniac forces as well as the cosmic forces (neters) is a metaphor of a mystical movement wherein the urges and impulses as well as the positive spiritual energies of the universe are discovered and assimilated into one's consciousness instead of being controlled and by them and being at their mercy. Spiritual practice confers on the practitioner the ability to control anger, hatred, greed, fear and other demoniac forces. Also the consumption symbolizes the assimilation of one's own forces which had gone astray into the realm of ignorance. This is the true meaning of the metaphor of assimilation and it is the basis of the Asarian and Christian ritual of the Eucharist. While here is no evidence that cannibalistic rituals were carried out with live subjects in Egypt, there is some evidence to show that when this ritual was adopted by the Greeks and Asians in the Near East, there were actual mutilations, dismemberments and blood sacrifices. Plutarch, Greek author (c. 46-120 AD), wrote on the mysteries: "the mysteries in which the eating of raw flesh, and the tearing in pieces of victims are in use and the human sacrifices offered of old." Clement of Alexandria reports that "the Bacchanals hold their orgies in honor of the frenzied Dionysus... by the eating of raw flesh."

The important idea here is that identification goes beyond rituals, prayers, austerities, penances or keeping company with the Divine. Identification implies a complete absorption into the Divine which completely excludes the ego self. Some mystery cults such as that of Asar and Attis went further in increasing the identification of the initiate with the death, dismemberment and resurrection of the of the deity by having the initiate lay in a coffin for a period of time and rise up in triumph over death. The Attis cult sometimes went to extremes by having the initiate castrated as the dead deity or slashed themselves with swords or knives. The practices just describes are of course evidence of the degradation to which people fell due to ignorance of the true meaning of the Eucharist ritual. It is ignorance and ignorance alone which allows people to believe in superficial rituals and it also allows people to feel (anger, hatred, etc.) negativity to the point of hurting others or themselves.

The stigmata is another effect of strong psychic identification with the passion of Jesus, however, if the identification with the passion of the deity is not transcended, the experience remains at the level of the senses, mind and intellect. These fall under the heading of egoism. What is required is that these be transcended and for the initiate to enter into an expanded consciousness as a result of the experience in the ritual. Thus, the Eucharist ritual was a long standing ceremony which Christianity adopted from Egyptian religion and other cults which were in existence throughout North Africa, the Near East, Greece and Rome which was practiced in the mysteries of Asar, Pythagoreans, Dionysus, Essenes, Mithras, and Attis.

The ritual of eating the body and blood of the dismembered, reconstituted and resurrected deity needs to be understood for its profound symbolic meaning. Whether or not actual bread, raw meat or some other symbol is used is less important than the understanding of the underlying significance of the wisdom behind it. When the world is understood as being composed of differently arranged atoms which are themselves composed of energy as modern physics has proven, the idea of consuming any kind of substance assumes a strong spiritual import. In this sense, keeping the metaphysical understanding in mind, every time food is consumed is a Eucharistic ritual because all substances are composed of the same underlying essence. This essence may be called Christ, Brahman, Amen, or energy. Therefore, every meal that is consumed is a communion with the Divine. Every breath that is taken is a communion as well because the body is consuming the necessary nutrients of life and in turn, transferring its own essence into the environment. It is easy to understand that the body is constantly in communion with the ocean of energy for its survival. When there is conscious communion with that ocean as being one with it, then there is communion of the highest degree. At this time all who achieve this state of consciousness can partake in the full experience of Christhood expressed by Jesus in the statement: I and the Father are one and The Kingdom of the Father is spread upon the earth and men do not see it.

When an Ancient Egyptian lay person died, the priest would go to his home and together with the deceased person's family, act out the mystery of Asar' death and resurrection in order to assist the deceased's efforts to traverse the Netherworld and to discover the abode of Asar, an attainment which signifies achieving self-knowledge, resurrection, and is identical with the Kingdom of Heaven of Christianity and the Liberation of Buddhism. A similar practice is still performed in Tibetan Buddhism where the priest and the deceased loved ones perform the ritual of reading the text known as The Tibetan Book of The Dead, The Great Liberation through Hearing in the Bardo. It serves the purpose of assisting the newly deceased to find his/her way in the Netherworld in order to reach liberation. Also, it serves the purpose of educating the family members as to the fate after death.

However, the task of the aspirant is to reach a state of purification wherein Asar is met even while still alive and through intense communion with the Divine (Asar), to merge with the Divine (Asar). This process is achieved through devotional practices outlined in this volume.

The Egyptian Book of Coming Forth By Day is a text of wisdom about the true nature of reality and also of "Spells" to assist the initiate in making that reality evident. The affirmations presented in this text are excellent tools to develop a devotional feeling towards the Divine. These special affirmations are only a portion of those found in the Egyptian Book of Coming Forth By Day. They are a special form of affirmation which involves the I am formula of speech.

These spells are in reality Hekau or words of power which the initiate recites in order to assist him or her in changing the consciousness level of the mind. The hekau themselves may have no special power except in their assistance to the mind to change its perception through repetition with understanding and feeling. They assist the mind in becoming still and centered on the deeper reality of the subconscious mind.* Through these affirmations the initiate is able to change the consciousness from body consciousness ("I am a body") to cosmic consciousness ("I am GOD"). This form of "affirmatory" (using affirmation in the first person) spiritual discipline is recognized by Indian Gurus as the most intense form of spiritual discipline. This great formula of devotional meditation is also to be found in the Bible and in the Gnostic Christian Gospels with even more emphasis. The following are examples from the Christian Bible and from the Hindu Bible. The deity Heru, of Egypt, is the prototype for the Gnostic savior Jesus, as well as Krishna and Buddha of India. In reality, Heru is none other than the innermost heroic character which lies deep within the heart of everyone. *(see Meditation, The Ancient Egyptian path to Enlightenment by Dr. Muata Ashby)

John 15

    5 I am the vine, ye [are] the branches: He that abideth in me, and I in him, the same bringeth forth much fruit: for without me ye can do nothing without me.

The following statement by an Egyptian initiate affirms his identity with Heru:

"My heart (mind-memory) is with me and it shall not be taken away, for... I live by truth, in which I exist; I am Heru who is in the heart, that which is in the middle of the body. I live by saying what is in my heart...I have committed no sin against the gods."

The following statements are encountered throughout Egyptian mythology in reference to the symbolism of Heru. These statements are also encountered in Christian mythology.

"The resurrection and the life", "The anointed one", "The WORD made flesh", "The KRST"†, "The WORD made TRUTH", "The one who comes to fulfill the LAW", "The destroyer of the enemies of his father", "The one who walks upon the water of his Father"

The following statements from the Bhagavad Gita impart the same wisdom in reference to the presence of the "Savior" in the form of Krishna being within oneself.

Gita: Chapter 7 Jnana Vijnana Yogah--. The Yoga of Wisdom and Realization

    9. I am the pure fragrance in earth, I am the effulgence in fire,
    I am the life in all living beings, I am the austerity in the ascetics.

The Path of Divine Love

The Supreme Offering

"Suten   Hetep   ta"

The Path of Devotion is symbolized by the offering. Making offerings to the Divine is a symbolic way of giving of oneself to the Divine with the ultimate goal of directing all of ones attention and being towards the Divine and eventually merging with the Divine. In the Temples of Ancient Egypt even today one can visit and see the scenes of offerings, constant offerings. The most important offerings are the offerings of the Food, Libations, the Lotus, offering Maat, symbolized by a small statue of the goddess, sitting in a basket. Another important offering is the Eye of Heru. Another important offering is the supreme peace offering: Hetep. It is this great process that unites and binds Kemetic Philosophy and Mythology as well as the Temple System. No two temples are exactly alike, nor are they dedicated to the same gods or goddesses in the same way or using the same architecture. However, the principle of Devotion is equally manifested in all of them. In fact, the temple itself is an offering to the Divine and it was built to last forever, unlike other buildings. Considering that Ancient Egyptian society was the most powerful culture in ancient times, is it not remarkable that the wealth and intellectual attention was given to the matters of spirituality as opposed to the pursuit of pleasure? In modern times the most energy is placed on pleasure seeking and personal happiness through relationships, money, fame, etc. The movement towards the pursuit of satisfying worldly desires constitutes the degradation of modern culture. Conversely, the pursuit of spiritual awakening constitutes the factor which made Ancient Egypt supreme among all other ancient cultures and what they achieved in ancient times still surpasses modern culture, since modern culture has only progressed in technological areas and not in spiritual enlightenment or in matters of wisdom about life.

The Ancient Egyptian words "Suten Hetep ta" come from the ceremonies of offerings in the liturgy of the Ancient Egyptian pyramid texts of Unas. Suten means the "king" or "initiate". Hetep, as you should know by now, means peace but not peace in the ordinary sense of the word as it is used in modern day society or as literal translations of the word by Egyptologists would suggest. Hetep in this context means the peace which comes when there is extinction of desire. It represents a state of mind wherein there is complete giving of oneself to the Divine. The next word, "ta", means offering. Thus as the priests give offerings to the initiate which symbolize the "Eye of Heru" which the initiate must accept and thereby realize oneness with Asar, the initiate must give the offering of egoism to the Divine. Having given this offering, the initiate is now able to realize the fruits of Supreme Peace. In connection with this ceremony the hekau "Suten Hetep ta" is to be repeated four times in order to propitiate the gods of the four quarter of creation which will enable the initiate to move freely in all realms of existence.

The offering of the Maat

The King offering the Eye

The Path of Divine Love

The Practice of Devotional Meditation

What is Meditation?

Meditation may be thought of or defined as the practice of mental exercises and disciplines to enable the meditator to achieve control over the mind, specifically, to stop the vibrations of the mind due to unwanted thoughts, imaginations, etc.

Consciousness refers to the awareness of being alive and of having an identity. It is this characteristic which separates humans from the animal kingdom. Animals cannot become aware of their own existence and ponder the questions such as: Who am I?, Where am I going in life?, Where do I come from? etc. They cannot write books on history and create elaborate systems of social history based on ancestry, etc. Consciousness expresses itself in three modes. These are: Waking, Dream-Sleep and Dreamless-Sleep.

However, ordinary human life is only partially conscious. When you are driving or walking you sometimes lose track of the present moment. All of a sudden you arrive at your destination without having conscious awareness of the road which you have just traveled. Your mind went into an "automatic" mode of consciousness. This automatic mode of consciousness represents a temporary withdrawal away from the waking world. This state is similar to a day dream (a dreamlike musing or fantasy). This form of existence is what most people consider as "normal" everyday waking consciousness. It is what people consider to be the extent of the human capacity to experience or be conscious.

The "normal" state of human consciousness cannot be considered as "whole" or complete because if it was there would be no experience of lapses or gaps in consciousness. In other words, consciousness would be accounted for in every instant. There would be no trance like-states wherein one loses track of time or awareness of one's own activities, even as they are being performed. In the times of trance or lapse, full awareness or consciousness is not present, otherwise it would be impossible to not be aware of the passage of time while engaged in various activities. Trance here should be differentiated from the religious or mystical form of trance-like state induced through meditation. As used above, it refers to the condition of being so lost in solitary thought as to be unaware of one's surroundings. It may further be characterized as a stunned or bewildered condition, a fog, stupor, befuddlement, daze or a muddled state of mind. Most everyone has experienced this condition at some point or another. What most people consider to be the "awake" state of mind in which life is lived is in reality only a fraction of the total potential consciousness which a human being can experience.

The state of automatic consciousness is characterized by mental distraction, restlessness and extroversion. The automatic state of mind exists due to emotions such as anger and hatred, which engender desires in the mind which in turn cause more movement, distractions, delusions, fanatics and lapses or "gaps" in human consciousness. In this condition it does not matter how many desires are fulfilled. The mind will always be distracted and agitated and will never discover peace and contentment. If the mind were under control, meaning, if you were to remain fully aware and conscious of every feeling, thought and emotion in your mind at any given time, it would be impossible for you to be swayed or deluded by your thoughts into a state of relative unconsciousness or un-awareness. Therefore, it is said that those who do not have their minds under control are not fully awake and conscious human beings.

Meditation and Yoga Philosophy are disciplines which are directed toward increasing awareness. Awareness or consciousness can only be increased when the mind is in a state of peace and harmony. Thus, the discipline of Meditation is the primary means to controlling the mind and allowing the individual to mature psychologically and spiritually by integrating all aspects of the mind.

Psychological growth is promoted because when the mind is brought under control, the intellect becomes clear and psychological complexes such as anxiety and other delusions which have an effect even in ordinary people, can be cleared up. Control of the mind and the promotion of internal harmony allows the meditator to integrate their personality and to resolve the hidden issues of the present, of childhood and of past lives.

When the mind has been brought under control, the expansion in consciousness leads to the discovery that one's own individual consciousness is not the total experience of consciousness. Through the correct practice of meditation, the individual's consciousness-awareness expands to the point wherein there is a discovery that one is more than just an individual. The state of "automatic consciousness" becomes reduced in favor of the experiences of increasing levels of continuous awareness. In other words, there is a decrease in daydreaming as well as the episodes of carrying out activities and forgetting oneself in them until they are finished (driving for example). Also, there is a reduced level of loss of awareness of self during the dreaming-sleep and dreamless-sleep states. Normally, most people at a lower level of consciousness-awareness become caught in a swoon or feinting effect which occurs at the time when one "falls" asleep or when there is no awareness of dreams while in the dreamless-sleep state. In the dream state this swooning effect causes an ordinary person to lose consciousness of their own "waking state" identity and to assume the identity of their "dream subject" and thus, to feel that the dream subject as well as the dream world are realities in themselves.

This shift in identification from the waking personality to the dream personality to the absence of either personality in the dreamless-sleep state led ancient philosophers to discover that these states are not absolute realities. Philosophically, anything that is not continuous and abiding cannot be considered as real. Only what exists and does not change in all periods of time can be considered as "real". Nothing in the world of human experience qualifies as real according to this test. Nature, the human body, everything has a beginning and an end. Therefore, they are not absolutely real. They appear to be real because of the limited mind and senses along with the belief in the mind that they are real. In other words, people believe that matter and physical objects are real even though modern physics has proven that all matter is not "physical" or "stable". It changes constantly and its constituent parts are in reality composed of "empty spaces". Think about it. When you fall asleep, you "believe" that the dream world is "real" but upon waking up you believe it was not real. At the same time, when you fall asleep, you forget the waking world, your relatives and life history, and assume an entirely new history, relatives, situations and world systems. Therefore, philosophically, the ordinary states of consciousness which a human being experiences are limited and illusory. The waking, dream and dreamless-sleep (deep sleep) states are only transient expressions of the deeper underlying consciousness. This underlying consciousness which witnesses the other three states is what Carl Jung referred to as the "Collective Unconscious". In Indian Philosophy this "fourth" state of consciousness-awareness is known as Turia. It is also referred to as "God Consciousness" or "Cosmic Consciousness."

The theory of meditation is that when the mind and senses are controlled and transcended, the awareness of the transcendental state of consciousness (superconsciousness) becomes evident. From here, consciousness-awareness expands, allowing the meditator to discover the latent abilities of the unconscious mind. When this occurs, an immense feeling of joy emerges from within and the desire for happiness and fulfillment through external objects and situations dwindles, and a peaceful, transcendental state of mind develops. Also, the inner resources are discovered which will allow the practitioner to meet the challenges of life (disappointments, disease, death, etc.) while maintaining a poised state of mind.

When the heights of meditative experience are reached, there is a more continuous form of awareness which develops. It is not lost at the time of falling asleep. At this stage there is a discovery that just as the dream state is discovered to be "unreal" upon "waking up" in the morning, the waking state is also discovered to be a kind of dream which is transcended at the time of "falling asleep." There is a form of "continuous awareness" which develops in the mind which spans all three states of consciousness and becomes a "witness" to them instead of a subject bound by them.

Further, there is a discovery that there is a boundless source from which one has originated and to which one is inexorably linked. This discovery brings immense peace and joy wherein the worldly desires vanish in the mind and there is absolute contentment in the heart. This level of experience is what the Buddhists call Mindfulness. However, the history of mindfulness meditation goes back to the time of Ancient Egypt and was called Amun. In India, the higher level of consciousness wherein automatic consciousness is eradicated and there is continuous awareness is called Sakshin Buddhi. From Vedanta and Yoga Philosophy, the teaching of the "witnessing consciousness" found even greater expression and practice in Buddhist philosophy and Buddhist meditation. Buddhi or higher intellect, is the source of the word Buddha, meaning one who has attained wakefulness at the level of their higher intellect.

When devotional love develops in the heart, the process of meditation becomes easy, because it is easy to focus the mind on what is well known and cared for, the object of love. Normally, people's love expresses in the form of attachment to objects, people or places that they somehow have come to know as desirable or which they believe will bring them happiness. This idea is based on ignorance because once an object of desire is acquired, the luster and excitement wanes. Therefore, objects, personalities, etc. will not lead to the true satisfaction of love in a human being. When you are firmly established in this idea of detachment from the world you will be ready to start attaching yourself to the Divine. God is limitless and therefore, your potential love relationship with God is limitless and this eternity and infinity is what the soul of every human being really craves for deep down. It is this deep seeded need which has erroneously taken the form of attachment for worldly objects, personalities, earthly existence, etc. So Divine Love means decreasing attachment to the world and increasing attachment to God. Since God is the underlying reality behind all objects, people and other life forms in the universe, then it follows that your love should not be limited to certain members of your family, social group, country or even the world. You must allow a magnanimous love to grow within your heart which will eventually encompass all that exists, in other words, the entire universe. As you develop deeper devotional feelings you will discover God everywhere and in everything. This is the basis for universal love which Sages and Saints have expressed from time immemorial. When you practice formal meditation you will be able to also experience God in an intensive way. Thus you will have an inner and outer experience of expansion and transcendence.

The practice of chanting the Divine Name should be approached with the same principle of divine attachment. You should allow yourself to develop a gradually more intense feeling that you are one with that Divine Being as you consciously utter hymns and Identification Affirmations (affirmations in which you identify yourself with the Divine). Practice uttering them along with your daily spiritual disciplines but don't just utter them as words you are reading which have no life. Let the affirmation reach the depth of your heart and you will find that your faith will turn into experience of the Divine. You will experience the truth of those affirmations and you will be changed for all eternity.

Continue with your affirmatory practice until you reach a point where your mind is no longer straying from divine awareness. At this point your mental affirmation will drop off and you will abide in the pure awareness of the Self. Continue in this practice daily until your divine awareness is continuous, regardless of your day to day activities.

The following are more affirmation formulas from the Egyptian Book of Coming Forth By Day. When you see (Name) substitute your own name here.

I, Asar (Name) have arrived at the abode of Asar, being glorious (Enlightened)...
I am Tmu in rising up. I am the only One. I came into existence in Nu (the primeval waters).
(17:4-5)

I am the Supreme Being great who came into existence by myself. (17:9)

I am yesterday, I (Name) am tomorrow...(17:14)

I am Bennu, that which is in Anu. I am the keeper of the book of that which is, and of that which shall be. (17:26)

I came into existence from unformed matter, I created myself in the image of the God Khepera, and I grew in the form of plants. I am hidden in the likeness of the Tortoise. I am the essence of every god and goddess, I am the origin of the four quarters of the world, I am the seventh of those seven urei who came into existence in the East, I am the mighty one Heru who illumines the world with his person, I am god in the likeness of Set, and Djehuti who dwelleth among us in the Judgment of Him who dwelleth in Sekhem and of the spirits of Anu. I sail among them , and I come; I am crowned, I am become a shining one-glorious, I am mighty, I am become holy among the gods and goddesses...(Ch. 83)

The Path of Divine Love

When reading the devotional texts strive to develop a feeling of surrender to the Divine Self within you. Allow your feeling to rise as you read the texts in such a way that you become more and more exalted and more and more in tune with your inner feeling.

As you study the spiritual texts on your own you may discover many utterances which resonate with your mind. Concentrate on these and use them in your daily practice. Never forget that the utterances are speaking about you, and not about some far off god who lives millions of miles away. God is within you, therefore, the teachings are speaking about and for you.

Above: Heru, the Sun-child, sitting upon the world lotus (creation) which rises out of the primeval ocean. The image is used as an objective for focusing the devotional feeling and for teaching about the Divinity.

Neter Merri

Waking up from the Dream of Ignorance and Awakening to the Wisdom of the Self.

Throughout this work we have explored the ideas of ignorance and illusion in which the human mind is caught. However, one important analogy has been made by the ancient scriptures in reference to the process which must occur in the mind of every human being. In verse #53 of the Asarian Drama as well as many instances in the Pyramid Texts, the oldest scriptures on earth, the teaching is given that we must "Wake Up" from our present state of consciousness, otherwise we are as if "dead," because we have no knowledge of our true being, and thus live in the state of ignorance and human suffering.

Now we may look at the most ancient texts in the world which give the teaching of waking up. These come from the Ancient Egyptian Pyramid Texts and primarily from the pyramid of King Unas. They are excepts from the teachings given to Unas by his spiritual preceptor. You may use them in your own practice of reflection by reading and re-reading them in order to understand their deeper essence, and to lead your mind towards the innermost reality which is discovered when you wake up from all of the ordinary states of consciousness. In the ancient process of the pyramid text ritual, the initiate is identified with Asar and is encouraged to wake up to her/his true essence (Asar - possessor of the intuitional Eye of Heru). There are dozens of Utterances or Hekau (Words of Power) which provide the detailed teaching of the sleep existence and the need to wake up from the dream. The following Utterances are provided to give you a deeper insight into the teaching. Now that you are familiar with the philosophy and with the meaning behind the Neter symbols, you are ready to begin looking at the ancient texts themselves and to discover the subtle teachings within them. When their meaning is known, not just intellectually, but deep within the heart, a mystical transformation occurs. These hekau are the magical words which you can use to transform yourself into a divine being.

The Utterances:

While the teacher (preceptor) has woken up to this deeper reality of existence, the aspirant is caught in the world of time and space and is only aware of the mind and body he or she has always known, and a world full of multitudinous objects with almost infinite variety. However, the Sage with cosmic vision sees the phenomenal world of the ordinary human being as well as the deeper threads that bring all matter into one unified whole of existence. Therefore, the Sage is secure in proclaiming that the world as it appears to the ordinary human is an illusion. This is the inner meaning of the following passages from the Ancient Egyptian Pyramid Texts which urge the initiate (King) to Wake up!

> To the King:
> May you awake in peace!
> May you awake in peace!
> May Taitet awake in peace!
> {May} the Eye of Heru which is in Dep {awake} in peace!
> May the Eye of Heru which is in the Mansions of the

Nt-crown awake in peace! (Utterance 81)
Awake! Turn yourself about! So shout I.
O king...(Utterance 223)
Rouse yourself, O king! Turn yourself about, O king! Go, that you may govern the mounds of Heru, that you may govern the mounds of Set and address the mounds of Asar. (Utterance 225)

It is Anpu who leads King Unas in the Pyramid Texts, by constantly urging him to move ahead and not to get distracted with the passing fancies of the waking world or the astral plane (Duat-Amenti, Netherworld-unconscious). The following Utterance (#483) from the Pyramid Texts illustrates the role of Anpu as awakener of souls.

> The libation is poured and Apuat (Wepwawet) is on high. Wake up, you sleepers! Rouse up, you watchers! Wake up Heru! Raise yourself, Asar the King...

The Supreme Abode: The Goal of All Spiritual Efforts

Earlier, in previous disciplines, we discussed the ideas of the Earth, the Duat and Heaven, as well as the transcendental realm which lies beyond. Now we will define the Supreme Abode, the target towards which all spiritual efforts are to be directed, the supreme good and ultimate purpose of human existence.

According to the mystical teachings the righteous have the choice of two heavens in which to live. One is the Sekhtet-Aaru, or the Abode of Asar which is a section of the Sekhtet-Hetep or realm of peace (Astral world) from which all life emanates and the Barque of Ra or the Abode of Ra, the light of consciousness which illumines the astral world (the Self which illumines the mind and senses). The followers of Asar, preferred the Sekhtet-Aaru, where they could unite with Asar. Those who chose the Barque of Ra sailed with him over the skies. They fed upon light of the Self (Ra), and were arrayed in light (of the Self), and were finally became one with Ra (the Self). Otherwise, the soul would remain in the astral plane, Sekhtet-Hetep, where they could enjoy spiritualized pleasures and an existence which resembled their life upon earth (physical plane). The Sekhtet-Hetep is the realm where astral experiences take place and the Sekhtet-Aaru is a transcendental realm where there are no relative experiences. Here, there is only absolute consciousness beyond the mind and senses. Asar is pure consciousness beyond time and space.

Those who were in the company of Asar assisted him in cultivating the plant of Truth, Maat, which was of the substance of Asar himself, and as they lived upon Maat (God) they finally became absorbed into Asar and lived by and in him for ever.

Thus, as explained in previous disciplines, one of the possibilities upon death is that of going into the Duat and experiencing various situations according to the ideas in the mind at the time of death. This works like a dream world in which the soul continues tumbling from one world system to another in an endless way due to the karmic pressure of desires which impel the soul onward until once again there will be reincarnation on earth.

For those who are truly devoted to the Divine, they will follow a path which will allow them to be in the presence of the Divine rather than to be tumbling from one situation to another in the

Duat or in the physical world. Rather than being in the realms of ignorance (Astral plane or Duat and the physical plane) they will draw ever closer to the Divine until they will merge with the Divine as a wave merges in the ocean, or a river merges with the ocean; never to be born again or to suffer the sorrows of individuality, duality and ignorance. This is the Supreme Abode which is the goal of all spiritual efforts and the supreme good.

Thus in reality there is only one heaven; whether it be called the heaven of Ra, Asar, the Kingdom of Heaven, etc., does not matter. The important point is in the understanding of the meaning of the teaching and its correct practice because only the correct practice and understanding will lead to success. Further, this heaven is transcendental and absolute. It is beyond all relativity and all ignorance. This is why it involves "merging" with the Divine, for only when there is oneness with the Divine can there be true knowledge. All other realms are relative worlds like a dream existence, limited, fleeting and devoid of peace.

Incorporating the Rituals and Mystical Teachings Into Your Life.

If you have practiced Christianity you will have noticed many similarities to the Asarian ritual of the Eucharist. However, you must understand that spirituality need not be reserved for a particular time on a particular day, in a particular place or location. With this understanding it should be easy for you to understand now that every time you eat anything you are consuming matter whose essence is God. Every time you breath you are communing with the universe. Every time you interact with the objects of other living beings you are in holy communion with God who is in reality your very Self.

With this understanding you can spiritualize your life through the knowledge that God is everywhere; the universe is a majestic Temple and every movement and sound is a holy affirmation of the Divine. Wherever you go, whatever you do, whatever thoughts appear in your mind, whatever occurs in the world of time and space, you should realize these as passing, transient and illusory waves in the ocean of primordial consciousness which you are. As waves rise and subside, so too all of the various thoughts and objects in the world are merely waves of energy in different configuration which are being born, grow and will someday die, only to once again become a part of the primordial pool of matter from whence they came. All the while you must be the observer, the detached watcher who is awakening from the long dream of time and space. This is your dream. You are essentially God and therefore, you are the immortal essence of this ocean of consciousness.

As you incorporate this understanding into your consciousness, your spiritual practice will intensify. You will be able to increase your presence of mind many fold because every object in creation will remind you of the Divine. Your wisdom studies, introspection, and meditation will bring you awareness of the Divine within yourself. Wherever you go and whatever you do will be illumined by the Divine presence and by Divine inspiration. In this manner you will remember and reunite the Higher Self and lower self within you and reach the summits of spiritual evolution.

The Path of Divine Love

Consider the path of the masses of ignorant human beings. People love all kinds of things for all kinds of reasons. There is love between parent and child, husband and wife, between friends etc. Also there is love for objects and possessions, power, sensual pleasures, etc. All of the previously mentioned forms of love must be understood as being limited and perishable as well as the source of pain and sorrow in life. Also, they are susceptible to emotions and circumstances. Many times a person will become upset if they do not receive outer forms of affection (hugs, kisses, sex, passion, etc.) because they have learned to associate these acts with love. This form of love is immature and ignorant. A car is desired for its flashiness and when it is acquired, the feeling becomes ordinary and boredom sets in. This is true for possessions in general. people are loved because they make a person feel good. However, when the person does something which is not appreciated, anger and hatred arise. Is this true love? Shouldn't something true be always true? In other words, how can something be true part of the time and not true at other times? The answer is that if it is not true always, in the beginning, middle and end, then it is not really true, even while it appears to be. They are in fact, expressions of a human being's desire to experience true love. The love which is infinite and abiding, not limited by time or emotions.

PROGRESS ON THE PATH

The important factor to remember in developing a spiritual discipline is that it should build gradually to an intensive process, being careful not to go to extremes or to expect much in a short time. The focus should be on developing the will to sustain continued and regular effort even when there does not appear to be any progress and even if the effort seems small (Ex. even if you practice meditation for only five minutes a day). By gradually blending a little worship, a little meditation, awareness practice, etc. each day, progress is sure to follow.

As spiritual practice progresses, psychic experiences will occur. These are encouragements for you to let you know that there is more to existence than the body and the world of time and space but they are not to be held unto. Through the practice of the disciplines of Yoga, glimpses of the divine emerge. These mystical experiences allow you to glimpse into the divine reality which you are. The glimpses will give you inspiration, showing you the way to your essential nature as the Self. As you meet life, having assimilated the wisdom teachings, your problems, mental complexes and faults begin to dwindle in much the same way as you erase an erroneous idea when you learn the correct information. They seem to vanish into nothingness.

When the troubles of life are no longer insurmountable, when you become slow to anger, when you become more content and serene, when you begin to discover a higher vision of yourself which goes beyond any mental conception, that is when you are moving toward self-discovery. Ordinary situations in life are seen in a new light. Every situation is seen as an opportunity to practice sublimation of the ego and you begin to discover the divine intent behind all situations you face through life. In the advanced stages, the flow of thoughts automatically moves toward the divine essence of your self and of creation without effort.

Though, noticing the activities of inimical personalities, you can now understand them and develop compassion toward them. Your past practices of seeking fulfillment in the world begin to lessen because you are discovering it within yourself as an indescribable feeling of peace and contentment which you can share with others without asking for anything in return. You begin to discover that many activities of ordinary human existence are indirect methods which are in reality seeking the same goal of spiritual freedom, though in an ignorant and twisted manner. For example, the myriads of love songs and stories in society, seem to be directed from one individual toward another but in reality they are reflecting a yearning for absolute fulfillment which is the essence of the other individual. However, this ideal is rarely understood an even less acknowledged. Most forms of romance are in reality egoistic love based on externalities such as sexual attraction or a desire to find happiness by entering into a relationship with someone who can make them happy. In reality no one can make another person happy since happiness comes from within, from the Self. If a love song in popular culture is speaking about a "Sweet Love", what sweeter love can there be than the love for the author of creation who is the innermost reality of every human being, every dust particle and every atom of the universe? The creator who caused and sustains the people and objects who are loved so much. These manifestations in song, in lore or as physical acts of love are in reality a reflection of the souls search for the Divine Self. Therefore, the true essence being sought after in marriage is the cosmic marriage of the soul with the Divine. So marital love should not be directed toward the spouses personality, since this is flawed and perishable. This form of love leads to disappointment, anguish and infidelity. It should be directed toward the essence of a human being, to that which is eternal, infinite and perfect. For more on Universal love and Sex Sublimation see the book Egyptian Tantra Yoga by Dr. Muata Ashby.

"Searching for one's self in the world is the pursuit of an illusion."
                                                            Ancient Egyptian Proverb

The universe is like the human mind in a dream. All of the creations of a dream are effective only when the dreamer is dreaming and not when he or she wakes up. There can be no absolute fulfillment in the realm of time and space because everything that is manifest is transitory and illusory. This is the illusion of the masses. The universe is a realm of experience for the soul, providing opportunities for self-discovery. Most people are like miners searching for gold in a coal mine or a thirsty person in a desert looking for water in a dry well. You, as a spiritual aspirant, must turn toward what is real, forever abiding and eternal, the hidden, unmanifest essence. Only this essence can quench the thirst of the soul and when it is quenched it reaches the state of Supreme Peace or Hetep. So as you apply the teachings you begin to see through the egoistic sentimentality and folly of your own mind and the futility of ordinary human life. With this understanding you are now are able to direct your thoughts relentlessly toward the Divine and thereby become more effective and vibrant in your worldly activities (work, recreation, relationships, etc.). These in turn will not lead to painful disappointments but they will help you to reach your sublime goals. No matter where you turn there is the Divine, be it in objects, songs, your work, companions, family, the tree, the air, the sky, the ocean, the stars, etc. These are all names for the same thing: The Self. This is the art and practice of advanced intensive Integral Yoga, which blends the disciplines of yoga in day to day life.

Neter Merri

The Power of Divine Love

What is the power of Divine Love? If God is all-powerful, all-pervasive, and all-knowing what does he/she need with love from a mere mortal human being?

Love is the very essence of the Divine. Therefore, there is no question of the Supreme Being's interest in the devotional feeling of a human being. The feeling of unrestricted love allows the Supreme Being to manifest in a human being. Thus, the devotional feeling is a sure way to attract divine grace.

In the Ausarian Resurrection the goddess Nebthet, who represents mortality and human nature, was able to attract the Supreme Being (Asar) to her. In a manner of speaking, the Supreme Being, God, cannot resist the devotional feeling and the most intense form of devotional feeling is when there is complete and absolute giving of oneself to the object being loved. This implies giving without reservations or expectations, just offering pure love.

Nebthet is the sister of Asar and Aset. She represents the gross aspect of nature and the natural phase of life called death. Nature is what the Spirit impregnates with its life giving essence. Therefore, nature (Nebthet) is the recipient of Asar' seed (spirit). According to natural law, anything that is born must be subject to the laws of nature and ultimately die. In his original form, detached from nature, Asar was timeless, immortal, and untouched by the passions and frailties of human nature. As an incarnation of the Divine, Asar becomes intoxicated with nature, his own Creation, and becomes associated with it through intercourse with Nebthet. Asar, as a symbol of the human soul, is a stark example of the fate of human existence. His situation embodies the predicament of every individual human being. This is why the Ancient Egyptian Pharaohs and all initiates into the mystery of Asar are referred to as Asar and Heru, and are considered to be the daughter or son of Aset. Just as Asar became intoxicated with His own Creation, so too the human soul becomes involved with nature and thereby produces an astral body composed of subtle elements, and a physical body composed of an aggregate of gross physical elements (water, earth, fire, air) which exist within Shu (ether-space).

There is deep mystical symbolism in the images and teachings surrounding the Triad or Asar, Aset and Nebthet. In the temples of Denderah, Edfu and Philae, there are sculptured representations of the Mysteries of Asar. These show The Asar (initiate) lying on a bier (ritual bed), and Aset and Nebthet, who stand nearby, being referred to as the "two widows" of the dead Asar. Aset and Nebthet are depicted as looking exactly alike, the only difference being in their head dresses: Aset ⌒, Nebthet ⌒ or ⌒. However, the symbols of these goddesses are in reality just inverted images of each other. The symbol of Nebthet is the symbol of Aset when inverted ⌒➔⌒. Therefore, each is a reflection of the other. Thus, it can be said that both life and death are aspects of the same principle.

The bodies and facial features of Aset and Nebthet are exactly alike. This likeness which Aset and Nebthet share is important when they are related to Asar. As Asar sits on the throne (see cover), he is supported by the two goddesses, Aset and Nebthet. Symbolically, Asar represents the Supreme Soul, the all-encompassing Divinity which transcends time and space. Aset represents wisdom and enlightened consciousness. She is the knower of all words of power and has the power to resurrect Asar and Heru. Nebthet represents temporal consciousness or awareness of time and space. She is related to mortal life and mortal death. This symbolism is evident in the sistrums which bear the likeness of Aset on one side and of Nebthet on the other, and the writings of Plutarch where he says that Aset represents "generation" while Nebthet represents "chaos and dissolution". Also, in the hieroglyphic texts, Aset is referred to as the "day" and Nebthet as the "night". Aset is the things that "are" and Nebthet represents the things which will "come into being and then die". Thus, the state of spiritual Enlightenment is being referred to here as Aset, and it is this enlightened state of mind which the initiate in the Asarian Mysteries (Asar Shetaiu) has as the goal. The Enlightenment of Asar is the state of consciousness in which one is aware of the transient aspects of Creation (Nebthet) as well as the transcendental (Aset). Aset represents the transcendental aspect of matter, that is, matter when seen through the eyes of wisdom rather than through the illusions produced by the ego. So, an enlightened personality is endowed with dual consciousness. To become one with Asar means to attain the consciousness of Asar, to become aware of the transcendental, infinite and immortal nature (Aset) while also being aware of the temporal and fleeting human nature (Nebthet).

The relationship between Nebthet and Asar gives deep insight into the innermost desires of the human heart. Nebthet is the very embodiment of nature. As such, she is devoted to Asar, because Asar (Supreme Being, the Spirit) is the source and cause of all phenomenal existence (nature). Thus the desire of Nebthet to unite with Asar in reality represents the innermost desire of the soul in every human being to unite with God. Asar is the embodiment of the Self (the Spirit), and it is the innate nature of the Spirit to unite with Nature. Thus nature and the Spirit are in love with each other, and nowhere is this better expressed in Ancient Egyptian iconography than in the images of Geb and Nut, through the mythology surrounding their union and separation. This relationship between Nature and the Spirit is also paramount in the Tantric symbolism of Hindu mythology in the form of Shiva (God, the Spirit) and Shakti (Nature). This is the cause of the proliferation of the myriad forms of life on earth and throughout the universe. Nature is the form or outer expression and the Life Force within nature is an expression of the Divine Spirit.

Thus in the relationship of Asar and Nebthet there are two important teachings. It shows how nature, what is mortal and transient (human existence) attracts the spirit (God, the human soul). Secondly, it shows how the spirit of every human being, which is already essentially one with the Divine, falls into the illusoriness of physical embodiment (human life). In this respect, the union between Asar and Nebthet cannot be seen as an illicit or adulterous relationship. It is to be understood as the fate of the Soul (Asar) in every human being which has become intoxicated, as it were, by the promise of human experience. However, it also shows the means to liberation from human existence and the pain of life through devotion and surrender to the Divine Self.

Neter Merri

The Lotus in Kemetic (Ancient Egyptian Mystical Philosophy

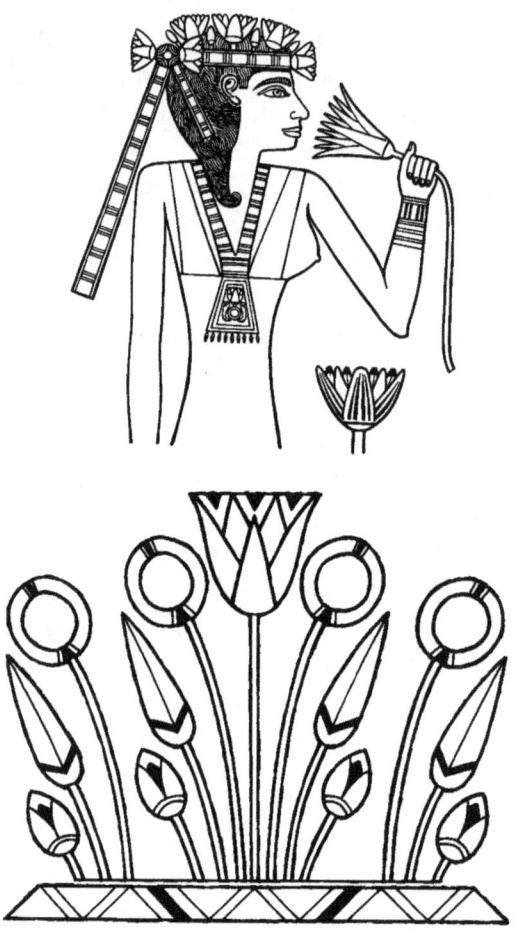

Nefertem and the Mysticism of the Memphite Trinity

The word Nefertem means "beautiful completion." In the Ancient Egyptian Book of Coming Forth By Day it is said that when an initiate attains resurrection, i.e. Spiritual enlightenment, they are actually becoming Nefertem. In the Creation Myth of the city of Anu (Anunian Theology) Tem is the divine aspect of the spirit as the first individuated entity to emerge from the primeval ocean. Tem is the male aspect of the fullness of the ocean. Also, in a separate but related teaching, from the myth of Ra and Aset, Tem is referred to as the third aspects of Ra as follows:

In the myth of Ra and Aset, Ra says: "I am Kheperi in the morning, and Ra at noonday, and Temu in the evening." Thus we have Kheper-Ra-Tem, ☉ ⌒ ⊨ 옷 ⌐, as the Anunian Triad and hekau. In Chapter 4 of the Prt m Hru, the initiate identifies him/herself with Tem, symbolizing that [his/her] life as a human being with human consciousness is coming to an end. Instead of an awareness of individuality and human limitation, there is now a new awareness of infinity and immortality, even though the physical body continues to exist and will die in the normal course of time. The initiate will live on as a "living" soul and join with Tem (individual consciousness joins Cosmic Consciousness):

"I am Tem in rising; I am the only One; I came into being with Nu. I am Ra who rose in the beginning."

The passage above is very important because it establishes the mystical transcendence of the initiate who has realized [his/her] "oneness" and union with the Divine. In other papyri, Tem is also identified with the young Harmachis (young Heru, the solar child) as the early morning sun. Thus, Kheperi-Ra-Temu are forms of the same being and are the object of every initiates spiritual goal. Being the oldest of the three theologies, the Mysteries of Anu formed a foundation for the unfoldment of the teachings of mystical spirituality which followed in the mysteries of Hetkaptah (Memphis), through Ptah, and the Mysteries of Waset (Thebes), through Amun. With each succeeding exposition, the teaching becomes more and more refined until it reaches its quintessence in the Hymns of Amun.

In the Ancient Egyptian Pyramid Texts there is a very important passage which provides insight into the role of Nefertem and the entire teachings behind the Trinity of Memphite Theology.

"I become Nefertem, the lotus-bloom which is at the nostril of Ra; I will come forth from the horizon every day and the gods and goddesses will be cleansed at the sight of me."
—Ancient Egyptian Pyramid Texts

Thus, we are to understand that Ptah is the source, the substratum from which all creation arises. Ptah is the will of the spirit, giving rise to thought itself and that thought takes form as Sekhmet, Creation itself. The same spirit, Ptah, who enlivens Creation, is the very essence which rises above Creation to complete the cycle of spirit to matter and then back to spirit. The Lotus is the quintessential symbol of completion, perfection and glory. Thus it is used in Ancient Egyptian and Hindu mythologies as the icon par excellence of spiritual enlightenment. Therefore, smelling the lotus, and acting as the lotus means moving above the muddy waters of

Creation and turning towards the sun which is the symbol of Ra, the Supreme Spirit.

In Chapter 24 of the Pert M Heru (Book of Coming Forth By Day), the role of Hetheru in the process of salvation is specified as the initiate speaks the words which will help him / her become as a lotus:

"I am the lotus, pure, coming forth out into the day. I am the guardian of the nostril of Ra and keeper of the nose of Hetheru. I make, I come, and I seek after he, that is Heru. I am pure going out from the field."

The lotus has been used since ancient times to symbolize the detachment and dispassion that a spiritual aspirant must develop. The lotus emerges everyday out of the murky waters of the pond in order to receive the rays of the sun. The spiritual aspirant, a follower of the Goddess, must rise above egoism and negativity (anger, hatred, greed, and ignorance) in life in order to gain in wisdom and spiritual enlightenment. Hetheru and Heru form a composite archetype, a savior with all of the complementary qualities of the male and female principles, inseparable, complete and androgynous.

The Detachment of the Lotus

Eventually, through continued practice, yoga discipline becomes a perpetual facet of day to day life. You will become as a Lotus flower, which lives in the pond but rises above it and is not touched by the turbulence below. In the same way, you will live in the world but at all times you will rise above the foibles of ordinary human experience as you continuously take in the aroma of the eternal flower, the Self. You have now realized that in the light of spiritual wisdom, ordinary human sentimentality is based on ignorance and is the cause of bondage for the soul. Your love cannot be limited to one person or a group, but it encompasses the entire universe which is you. You understand that ordinary human conflict experienced by the masses and by countries is also an expression of the depth of ignorance about the oneness of all creation. You will see the world from a detached point of view and you will experience the bliss of the Divine even while interacting with others. Even though you will deal with ordinary human situations that may require attention or others that require little or no attention you will remain with poise. In situations that under ordinary circumstances would cause allot of stress or situations that are not stressful at all, you will handle them all with evenhandedness (Maat) because you will no longer be shaken by the changes of life which affect the ego. You will be steadfast in your spiritual experience and this anchor will give you the endurance and energy to handle any situation with calmness and concentration because your energy will not be wasted in idle talk or in useless conflicts, imaginations, dreams or fears.

The hidden abilities of the soul will emerge as a dormant seed because you are essentially one with God and as such you have infinite potential. You will be able to help others who ask, by instructing them in your spiritual knowledge and you will provide a stable source of inspiration to others in times of crisis as well as times of prosperity. The initiate is to understand that the masses of people who are not aware of their spiritual Self are like lotus buds with the infinite potential of the soul. Initiates are blooming lotuses and Sages are lotuses in full bloom.

The Path of Divine Love

When spiritual practice is beginning to bloom or is in fool bloom, the appearance of objects in the world does not distract the aspirant because the aspirant has driven home the idea in the mind that the objects of the world are nothing but the non-dual Self (Amun-Asar). Though they appear to be displaying a multifaceted world of separate and distinct objects which arise, decay and cease to exist, the aspirant has an unshakable awareness of the fact that in reality the objects in the world, air, animals, rocks, people, stars, the sun, etc. have one essence which goes beyond the transient form. That essence is immutable and eternal and this essence is the same essence in the heart of each individual.

Knowing that the world is an expression of your heart, the innermost Self, whenever the eye catches a glimpse of the world you will be moved to a feeling of spontaneous ecstasy. This ecstasy translates to a feeling of universal love, devotion and compassion to the Self and to the world. This is the highest devotional form of worship of the divine; know it to be your innermost reality and the ultimate goal of life.

In the practice of Divine Love, a human being discovers that the petty attachments to the world are like chains holding him or her back from discovering a deeper realization of love. Many people, in the state of doubt and fear, wonder what will happen if they give up worldly attachments. The practice of Divine Love does not mean that you stop loving the people for whom you care. It does mean that you will discover a deeper basis for that love, and that your capacity to love will increase for them as well as for humanity. As the lotus turns to the sun and remains detached from the muddy waters below, even while being immersed in it, so too a spiritual aspirant should turn away from the world of human attachments, even while existing in the world of human experience, and like a blooming lotus, he or she should turn to the Divine Self who is the source of all satisfaction, peace and love. The burning fire of Divine Love burns away doubts and ignorance, and just as the Lotus turns one-pointedly towards the sun, so too the aspirant should turn to the Self with one-pointed attention in order to derive the light of eternity and immortality. True love is not motherly, fatherly, filial, spousal, etc. True love is universal, for all creation. True love is equal and holds no favorites. In other words, there is no special love for one person or group or not for others. When the light of spiritual consciousness dawns in the human heart, the understanding arises that one is united with all, every person, every planet, every galaxy, etc. Therefore, not loving one thing over another would be like loving one leg and not the other. Further, universal love is unrestricted and does not require physical contact. It operates on a higher plane of consciousness wherein a special form of bliss is experienced. This bliss is the true state of human being when there are no restrictions, from egoistic feelings. Therefore, live according to the principles of Universal Love and discover the bliss of your true Self!

Forms for the Worship of the Divine

As explained earlier, there are two forms of Divine Worship with iconography. The first is Worship of God(ess) with form and the next and higher form is worship of God(ess) without form. The following images are presented to facilitate the practice of the Path of Divine Love. Together with the divine image other items are necessary: The worship with form is seen as the lower form of worship. When perfected, this leads to the Higher form which is without images, incense, or rituals of any kind. The higher form of worship is when the personality loses contact with the ego=based reality and becomes totally aligned with the transcendental reality.

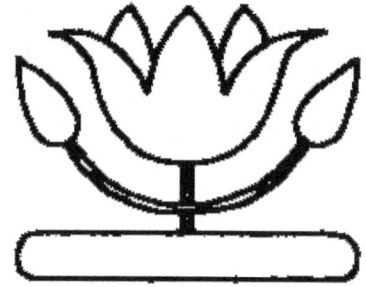

The Path of Divine Love

The God Ra

Neter Merri

The God Amun-Ra

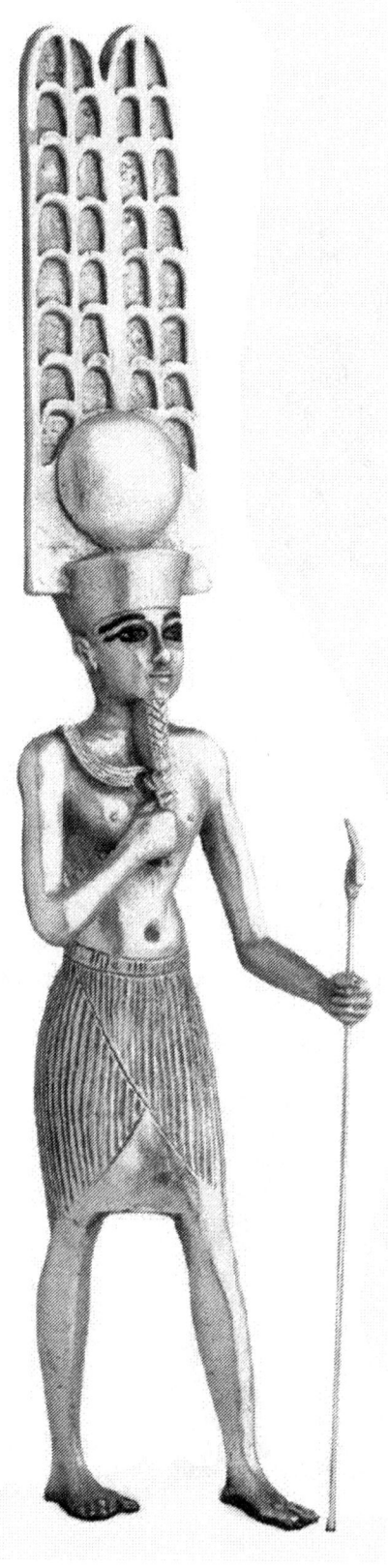

The Path of Divine Love

The God Asar

Neter Merri

The Goddess Aset

The Path of Divine Love

The God Set

Neter Merri

The Goddess Nebthet

172

The Path of Divine Love

The Goddess Hetheru

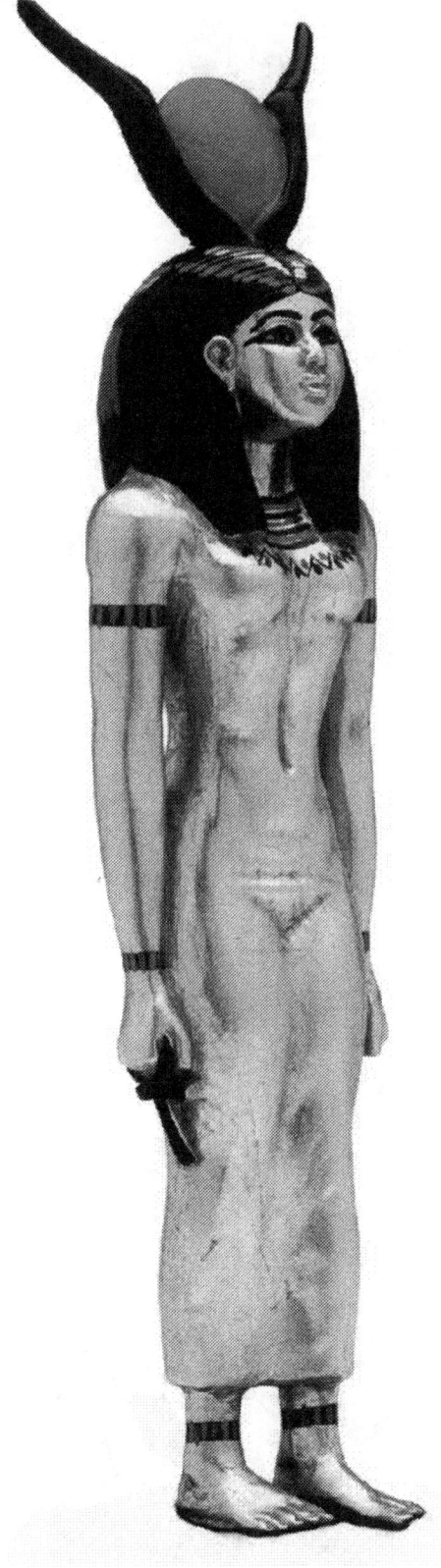

Neter Merri

The God Ptah

The Path of Divine Love

The God Djehuti

Neter Merri

The Goddess Sekhmit

The Path of Divine Love

The Goddess Maat

Neter Merri

The Divine Boat

The Daily Program of The Path fo Divine Love (Uash Neter)

PRACTICING KEMETIC DIVINE WORSHIP

Divine Worship is the process of directing the personality towards the Divine by means of the emotion and feeling capacity of the personality. This means that one's desire, one's caring capacity, one's devotion and one's love are all directed at the Divine. This has the effect of turning the personality towards what is higher that the little self, first of all. Next it has the effect of rendering the ego humble and inconsequential since loving the Divine does not lead to egoistic attachment, but rather universal admiration and reverence. Since there are not personal objects or sentimental worldly relations there can be no fluctuation or loss of the Divine Love as there is in worldly human love. Therefore, a great peace comes over the personality in the practice of Divine Worship since it quickly becomes obvious that the object of the Divine Worship, i.e. God(dess), is always there in the heart, and everywhere else and can never be lost. In this manner, Divine Worship transforms the personality, rendering it humble, peaceful and enlightened.

Tools For Divine Worship

Basic necessities for effective worship: every Shemsu should have the following items available for the daily practice of Shetaut Neter:

In order to enhance your daily spiritual practice you should set up an altar with certain basic materials which will assist you in focusing your mind on your worship disciplines (prayer, chanting, meditation). Set up the altar in the eastern or northern wall of your room so that you can make your sitting posture facing east or north.

Essentials:

- Divine image – (on paper or as sculpture (statue)) image of your tutelary divinity
- Scroll with four truths and audio cassette meditation chant tape.
- Ankh amulet
- Candle
- Incense
- Prayer mat or blanket

tu·te·lar·y (toot'l-ĕr'ē, tyoot'-) also **tu·te·lar** (toot'l-ər, -är', tyoot'-) --adj. **1.** Being or serving as a guardian or protector. **2.** Of or relating to a guardian or guardianship.

The tutelary divinity is the god or goddess that most appeals to your sensibility. It is the most fascinating and interesting to you and who you feel a connection to. The worship of this divinity (be revering its image and symbolism and studying its mythic teaching), along with the guidance of the spiritual preceptor, will guide you towards spiritual awakening and enlightenment.

Neter Merri

Daily Worship, Chanting, Devotional Practice. Recordings

Audio Cassettes-Chanting the Words of Power

501 Ushet Morning Worship: Adorations to Ra-Khepera and Hethor - approx. 30 min.
502 Ushet I Morning Worship: Adorations to Amun - - 60 min.
504 Morning Worship To Khepra and Midday worship to Ra
900 Ushet III Devotional Chanting of Hekau *Amma Su En Pa Neter* - - 60 min.
901 Ushet II Devotional Chanting of Divine Name Hekau: *Om Amun Ra Ptah* - - 60 min.
902 Ushet IV Devotional Chanting of Divine Name Hekau: *Om Asar, Aset, Heru* - - 60 min.

Audio Cassette $10.00

Audio Presentation

The Morning Worship

Begin your day with the ancient chants and meditations which will allow you to face the day with inner spiritual strength and peace.

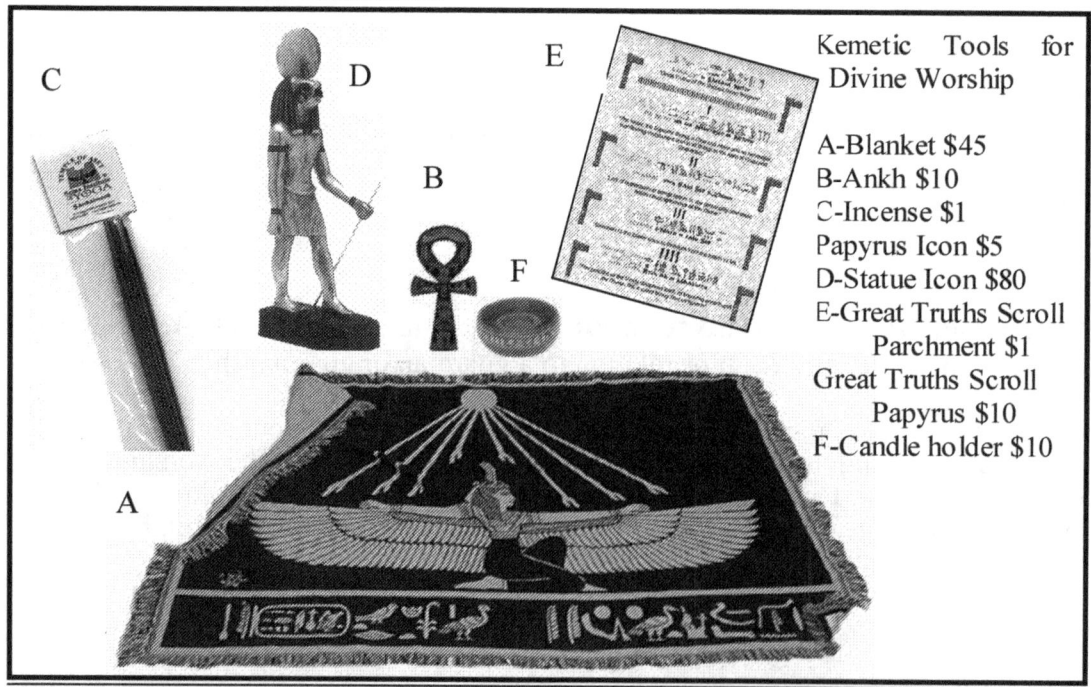

Kemetic Tools for Divine Worship

A-Blanket $45
B-Ankh $10
C-Incense $1
Papyrus Icon $5
D-Statue Icon $80
E-Great Truths Scroll
　　Parchment $1
Great Truths Scroll
　　Papyrus $10
F-Candle holder $10

The Path of Divine Love

Very Important:

- Attend Neterian class and spiritual services locally and/or online whenever possible.
- Book to read and study independently.
- Audio lecture related to the book for greater insight.
- Audio recordings of chants and divine singing to chant and sing along with if you are not part of a worship group.

Important:

- Attend Neterian seminars and workshops related to the practice and study of Shetaut Neter.
- Pilgrimages – make pilgrimages to the original Holy Land of Kamit to experience the power of Shetaut Neter – first hand, if possible with guidance from qualified Neterian teachers.

WORDS OF POWER IN MEDITATION: Khu-Hekau, Mantra Repetition:

In Neterian (Ancient Egyptian religion) terminology, "hekau" or word formulas are recited with meaning and feeling to achieve the desired end of controlling the mind and inculcating it with the vibrations of higher consciousness.

Hekau-mantra recitation or Hesi, (called Japa in India), is especially useful in changing the mental state. The sounds coupled with ideas or meditations based on a profound understanding of the meaning can have the effect of calming the mind by directing its energy toward sublime thoughts rather than toward degrading, pain filled ones. This allows the vibrations of the mind to be changed. There are three types of recitations that can be used with the words of power: 1- Mental, 2- Recitation employing a soft humming sound and 3- loud or audible reciting. The main purpose of reciting the words of power is somewhat different than prayer. Prayer involves you as a subject, "talking" to God, while words of power - hekau, are used to carry your consciousness to divine levels by changing the vibrations in your mind and allowing it to transcend the awareness of the senses, body and ordinary thought processes.

The recitation of words of power has been explored to such a degree that it constitutes an important form of yoga practice. Pupils may repeat their hekau as many as 50,000 per day. If this level of practice is maintained, it is possible to achieve specific changes in a short time. Otherwise, changes in your level of mental awareness, self-control, mental peace and spiritual realization occur according to your level of practice. You should not rush nor suppress your spiritual development, rather allow it to gradually grow into a fire which engulfs the mind as your spiritual aspiration grows in a natural way.

Hekau can be directed toward worldly attainments or toward spiritual attainment in the form of enlightenment. There are words of power for gaining wealth or control over others. We will present Egyptian, Indian and Christian words of power which are directed to self-control and mental peace leading to spiritual realization of the Higher Self. You may choose from the list according to your level of understanding and practice. If you were initiated into a particular hekau or mantra by an authentic spiritual preceptor, we recommend that you use that one as your main meditative sound formula. You may use others for singing according to your inclination in your leisure or idle time. Also you may use shortened versions for chanting or singing when not engaged in formal practice. For example, if you choose "Om Amun Ra Ptah", you may also use "Om Amun".

Reciting words of power is like making a well. If a well is made deep enough, it yields water. If the words of power are used long enough and with consistency, they yield spiritual vibrations which reach deep into the unconscious mind to cut through the distracting thoughts and then reveal the deeper you. If they are not used with consistency, they are like shallow puddles which get filled easily by rain, not having had a chance to go deeply enough to reveal what lies within. Don't forget that your movement in yoga should be balanced and integrated. Therefore, continue your practice of the other major disciplines we have described along with your practice of reciting the hekau. Mental recitation is considered to be the most powerful. However, in the beginning you may need to start with recitation aloud until you are able to control the mind's wandering. If it wanders, simply return to the words of power (hekau). Eventually the words of power will develop their own staying power. You will even hear them when you are not consciously reciting. They will begin to replace the negative thought patterns of the mind and lead the mind toward serenity and from here to spiritual realization. When this occurs you should allow yourself to feel the sweetness of reciting the divine names.

As discussed earlier, HEKAU may be used to achieve control over the mind and to develop the latent forces that are within you. Hekau or mantras are mystic formulas which an aspirant uses in a process of self-alchemy. The chosen words of power may be in the form of a letter, word or a combination of words which hold a specific mystical meaning to lead the mind to deeper levels of concentration and to deeper levels of understanding of the teaching behind the words. You may choose one for yourself or you my use one that you were initiated into by a spiritual preceptor. Also, you may have a special hekau for meditation and you may still use other hekau, prayers, hymns or songs of praise according to your devotional feeling. Once you choose a hekau, the practice involves its repetition with meaning and feeling to the point of becoming one with it. You will experience that the words of power drop from your mind and there are no thoughts but just awareness. This is the soul level where you begin to transcend thoughts and body identification. You may begin practicing it out loud (verbally) and later practice in silence (mentally). At some point your level of concentration will deepen. At that point your mind will disengage from all external exercises and take flight into the unknown, uncharted waters of the subconscious, the unconscious, and beyond. Simply remain as a detached witness and allow yourself to grow in peace. Listed below are several hekau taken from ancient Egyptian texts. They may be used in English or in ancient Kemetic according to your choice.

If you feel a certain affinity toward a particular energy expressed through a particular deity, use that inclination to your advantage by aligning yourself with that energy and then directing it toward the divine within your heart. Never forget that while you are working with a particular deity in the beginning stages, your objective is to delve into the deeper mystical implications of the symbolic form and characteristics of the deity. These always refer to the transcendental Self which is beyond all deities. According to your level of advancement you may construct your own Hekau according to your own feeling and understanding. As a rule, in meditations such as those being discussed now, the shorter the size of the hekau the more effective it will be since you will be able repeat it more often. However, the shorter the hekau, the more concentration it requires so as not to get lost in thoughts. You may wish to begin with a longer hekau and shorten it as your concentration builds. Words of power have no power in and of themselves. It is the user who gives them power through understanding and feeling.

When practicing the devout ritual identification form of meditation, the recitation of hymns, the wearing of costumes and elaborate amulets and other artifacts may be used. Ritual identification with the divine may be practiced by studying and repeatedly reading the various hymns to the divine such as those which have been provided in this volume, while gradually absorbing and becoming one with the teachings as they relate to you. When a creation hymn is being studied, you should reflect upon it as your true Self being the Creator, as your true Self being the hero(heroine), and that you (your true essence) are the one being spoken about in all the teachings. It is all about you. "You" are the Creator. "You" are the sustainer of the universe. "You" are the only one who can achieve transcendence through enlightenment according to your own will. When you feel, think and act this way, you are using the highest form of worship and meditation toward the divine by constantly bringing the mind back to the idea that all is the Self and that you essentially are that Self. This form of practice is higher than any ritual or any other kind of offering. Here you are concentrating on the idea that your limited personality is only an expression of the divine. You are laying down your ego on the offering mat.

The following outline for the frequency of possible recitations is provided as a guideline. We have included two types of words of power: short, containing one or two syllables, medium length, containing two to three and average, containing six to eight. They are presented as guidelines for practice of hekau-mantra repetition practice.

Generally, when the words of power are used over a sustained period of time, the benefits or psychic powers arise. The most important psychic powers you can attain to facilitate your spiritual program are peace, serenity of mind, and concentration of the mental vibrations. Concentration opens the door to transcendental awareness and spiritual realization. Various estimates are given as to when you may expect to feel results; these vary from 500,000 repetitions to 1,200,000 or more. The number should not be your focus. Sustained practice, understanding the teachings about the Self and practicing of the virtues and self-control in an integral, balanced fashion are the most important factors determining your eventual success.

While Om is most commonly known as a Sanskrit mantra (word of power from India), it also appears in the ancient Egyptian texts and is closely related to the Kemetic Amun. More importantly, it has the same meaning as Amun and is therefore completely compatible with the energy pattern of the entire group. According to the Egyptian Leyden papyrus, the name of the "Hidden God", referring to Amun, may be pronounced as Om, or Am.

Om is a powerful sound; it represents the primordial sound of creation. Thus it appears in ancient Egypt as Om, in modern day India as Om, and in Christianity as Amen, being derived from Amun. Om may also be used for engendering mental calm prior to beginning recitation of a longer set of words of power or it may be used alone as described above. One Indian Tantric scripture (Tattva Prakash) states that Om or AUM can be used to achieve the mental state free of physical identification and can bring union with Brahman (the Absolute transcendental Supreme Being - God) if it is repeated 300,000 times. In this sense, words of power such as Om, lead to union with the Absolute Self. Their shortness promotes greater concentration and force toward the primordial level of consciousness.

There is one more important divine name which is common to both Indian as well as ancient Egyptian mystical philosophy. The sanskrit mantra Hari* Om is composed of Om preceded by the word Hari. In Hinduism, Hari means: "He who is Tawny". The definition of tawny is: "A light golden brown". This is a reference to the dark colored skin of Vishnu and Krishna. Vishnu is usually depicted with a deep blue and Krishna is depicted with a deep blue or black hue symbolizing infinity and transcendence. Hari is one of Krishna's or Vishnu's many divine names. It also means "hail" as in "hail to the great one" or it may be used as "The Great One". In the ancient Egyptian magical texts used to promote spiritual development (words of power or HEKA - mantras) the word Haari also appears as one of the divine names. Thus, the hekau-mantra Hari Om was also known and used in ancient Egypt and constitutes a most powerful formula for mystical spiritual practice. *(the spelling may be Hari or Hare)

Simply choose a hekau which you feel comfortable with and sit quietly to recite it continuously for a set amount of time. Allow it to gradually become part of your free time when you are not concentrating on anything specific or when you are being distracted by worldly thoughts. This will serve to counteract the worldly or subconscious vibrations that may emerge from the your own unconscious mind. When you feel anger or other negative qualities, recite the hekau and visualize its energy and the deity associated with it destroying the negativity within you.

For example, you may choose Amun-Ra-Ptah. When you repeat this hekau, you are automatically including the entire system of all gods and goddesses. Amun-Ra-Ptah is known as Nebertcher, the "All-encompassing Divinity". You may begin by uttering it aloud. When you become more advanced in controlling your mind, you may begin to use shorter words. For example simply utter: Amun, Amun, Amun... always striving to get to the source of the sound. Eventually you will utter these silently and this practice will carry your consciousness to the source of the sound itself where the very mental instruction to utter is given. Hekau are also related to the spiritual energy centers of the subtle spiritual body (Uraeus-Kundalini).

The following ancient Egyptian selections come from the "Book of Coming Forth by Day" and other ancient Egyptian scriptures:

Nuk pu NETER
I am the Supreme Divinity.

Nuk pu Ast
I am ISIS

nuk neter aa kheper tchesef
I am the great God, self created,

Ba ar pet sat ar ta.
Soul is of heaven, body belongs to the earth.

Nuk uab-k uab ka-k uab ba-k uab sekhem.
My mind has pure thoughts, so my soul and life forces are pure.

Nuk ast au neheh ertai-nef tetta.
Behold I am the heir of eternity, everlastingness has been given to me.

Sekhem - a em mu ma aua Set.
I have gained power in the water as I conquered Set (greed, lust, ignorance).

Rex - a em Ab - a sekhem - a em hati - a.

The Path of Divine Love

I know my heart, I have gained power over my heart.

Un - na uat neb am pet am ta.
The power is within me to open all doors in heaven and earth.

Hekau - Words of Power - Chanting Guide						
Hekau	# of recitations per minute			# per hour		
	Low	Med	High	Low	Med	High
Om	140	250	400	8400	15000	24000
Om Asar Aset Heru	80	120	140	4800	7200	9000
Dua Ra, Dua Ra, Dua Ra Khepera	70	110	130	4200	6600	7800
amma su en pa neter sauu - k su emment en pa neter au duanu ma qedi pa haru	6	8	10	360	480	600
Dua Asar Unefer Neteraah Dua Asar Her Abdu Dua Asar Neb Djeta Dua Asar Suten Heh!	6	8	10	360	480	600
42 Precepts of Maat				2	4	6
Hymns of Amun				2	4	6
Any of the daily recitationCollections(morning, noontime or evening)				1	2	3

SCHEDULE FOR DIVINE WORSHIP
The Daily Schedule for Sema Practice

"Ra neb Aru"

(DAILY RITUAL)

<u>Daily Shedy - Threefold daily worship</u> – Basic Discipline for the morning.

1. Bathe or Wash face and hands
2. Light candle
3. Light incense
4. Worship - Divine Song
5. Sema Yoga Postures
6. Reciting of the Great Truths
7. Chant – words of scripture
8. Meditation
9. Offering

<u>Worship Ritual – Noon and Dusk</u>
1. Reciting of the Great Truths
2. Divine Chant
3. Meditation

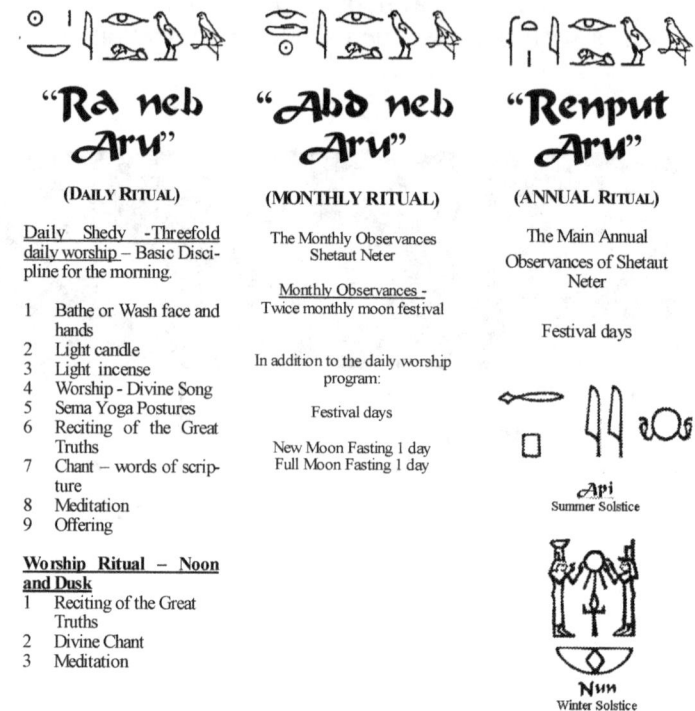

A practitioner of Sema (Yoga) must make an effort to integrate the main practices of yoga into daily life. This means that you need to begin adding small amounts of time for Prayer, Repetition of the Divine Name (Hekau), Exercise (includes proper breathing exercise), Study of the Teachings, Silence, Selfless Service, Meditation, and Daily Reflection. This also means that you will gradually reduce the practices which go against yogic movement as you gain more time for Sheti.

Below you will find an outline of a schedule for the beginning practice of Yoga. The times given here are a suggested minimum time for beginners. You may spend more time according to your capacity and personal situation, however, try to be consistent in the amount of time and location you choose to practice your discipline as well as in the time of day you choose to perform each of the different practices. This will enable your body and mind to develop a rhythm which will develop into the driving force of your day. When this occurs you will develop stamina and fortitude when dealing with any situation of life. You will have a stable center which will anchor you to a higher purpose in life whether you are experiencing prosperous times or adverse times. In the advanced stages, spiritual practice will become continuous. Try to do the best you can according to your capacity, meaning your circumstances. If your family members are not interested or do not understand what you are trying to do simply maintain your practices privately and try to keep the interruptions to a minimum. As you develop, you may feel drawn toward some forms of practice over others. The important thing to remember is to practice them all in an integrated fashion. Do not neglect any of the practices even though you may spend additional time on some versus others.

Practicing spirituality only during times of adversity is the mistake of those who are spiritually immature. Any form of spiritual practice, ritualistic or otherwise is a positive development, however, you will not derive the optimal spiritual benefits by simply becoming religious when you are in trouble. The masses of people only pray when they are in trouble...then they ask for assistance to get out of trouble. What they do not realize is that if they were to turn their minds to God at all times, not just in times of misfortune, adversity would not befall them. As you progress through your studies you will learn that adversities in life are meant to turn you toward the Divine. In this sense they are messages from the Divine to awaken spiritual aspiration. However, if you do not listen to the message and hearken to the Divine intent behind it, you will be in a position to experience more miseries of life and miseries of a more intense nature.

NOTE 1: The ritual is an important aspect of divine worship- it acts as a metaphysical conduit through which the stream of mental thought will fertilize and germinate the seed of Divine Love that is in the heart. Also, it acts to draw certain cosmic energies (Sekhem) that will be needed to make the spiritual program successful. These energies will be used in bolstering the will and resisting the inj-set or fetters of the ego or lower mind. They will be collected and purified and harnessed into a powerful force that will be used to focus the mind and forge your evolved personality through the practice of meditation. The ritual mirrors the divine act of God(dess) daily, who rises with light and warmth in order to care for all- to love all by providing sustenance and the capacity to discover all is one. Therefore it is said that God(dess) is Love, for caring is love. Therefore, an aspirant should learn to love all as an expression of God(dess) and there is no greater way to express love than through caring for all and seeing all as an expression of the Divine. All this and more is contained in the ritual and there are higher expressions (formats) of this ritual for the higher orders of clergy.

NOTE 2: In Neterian culture the morning worship program is regarded as the most important. Therefore, if it is not possible to enjoin the three-fold worship format the morning program can sustain a successful spiritual practice. The traditional time of the morning worship program is at dawn. For the purpose of personal practice the local time may be used. For the purpose of communal practice the worship timing should be attuned to the time of the rising of the sun in the eastern horizon of Kamit in Africa.

Neter Merri

Ritual of the Divine Embrace

The ritual of the Divine Embrace is integral to the practice and understanding of Uash Neter. The most important Kemetic Divinities who embody the teaching of Divine Love and the Divine Embrace are Asar and Aset. The embrace has two aspects, love and the transmittance and sublimation of sexual energy. This posture should be practiced by an aspirant with full understanding of the myth of Asar and Aset. In the first aspect the divinity embraces the aspirant.

The Goddess Aset

The Goddess Aset embracing Asar

Hept: The Aset Embrace Pose

The Path of Divine Love

Above: The goddesses Aset and Nebethet embrace Asar.

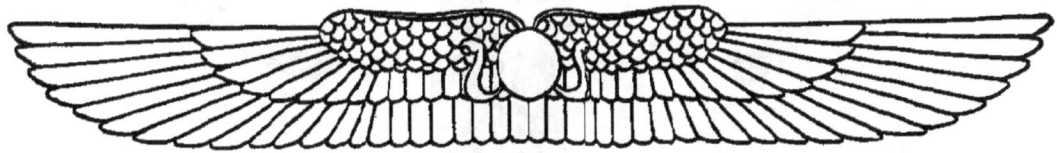

Above: The all-embracing, all-encompassing wings of Heru.

The Embrace Posture, refers to the act of hugging or embracing. The goddess Aset is the quintessential ideal of the idea behind this pose. She embraced Asar and Heru in their time of need and brought them back to life. In the same way, a spiritual aspirant should understand that the Aset quality within them is capable of encompassing their entire life in order to resurrect it from the grips of dullness, negativity and misery.

Thus, visualize yourself as a gigantic image of Aset and see yourself embracing your body, your very personality.

You are Asar and Aset has come to enfold you with the love and peace which she brings to resurrect you.

INSTRUCTION:

Wave your arms from side to side and with your eyes closed see yourself embracing the entire world. There are no good or bad things in the world, only the embrace which encompasses all. Allow Aset within you to emerge with the power of all encompassing devotion, compassion and love for all.

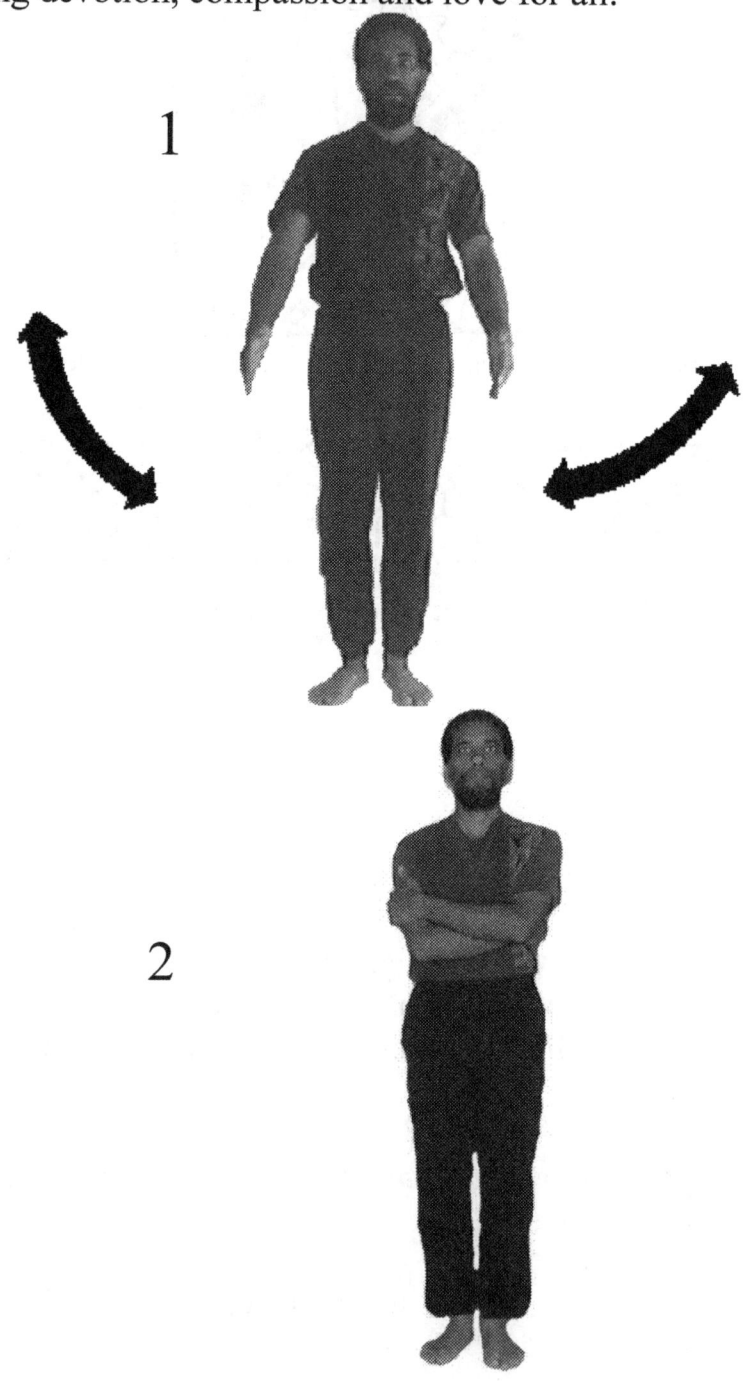

The Path of Divine Love

Above left: King Senusert and the God Ptah (Pillar from Temple of Senusert at Karnak
Above right: Goddess Hetheru embracing the king.

The Waset Temple (Karnak) is a prime example of one of the most important tantric rituals, the Divine Embrace. This ritual is to be performed by the most elevated initiates as it symbolizes the sexual union with the Divinity him/her self. No more will be said on this ritual as it is reserved for advanced practice.

The visualization is one of unity with the Divine through a loving embrace which encompasses parental, and spousal relationships. Men can see themselves with the goddess or with the god because "he" is understood to be androgynous. Women can visualize the tantric unity in the same way.

Neter Merri

Basic Daily Practice of Divine Worship (Uash) and Spiritual Disciplines (outline)

<u>POSTURE: (assume sitting posture facing the sun)</u>

Ritual step 1 Opening	*your morning worship by uncovering your altar.

Ritual step 2 Lighting Candle	*(Symbolizes the Akhu or Divine Light within that is to be awakened)

Ritual step 3 Lighting Incense	*(Symbolizes the fragrance of your personality which will exude with a divine odor that will rise up and attract as well as commune with the divine)

Ritual step 4 Libation	*Pour purified water from a container on to another receptacle. Pour continuously-silent

Ritual step 5 Offering	*Place offering (live food item-fruit or vegetable) in front of the altar. Also, a figure of Maat may be offered. Recitation of the <u>OFFERING FORMULA</u> IS ESSENTIAL. This is what starts the process of divine worship and enables the reciprocation of the divine. During the day, offer your righteousness at your work and in dealing with others, helping the needy- to the Divine

Recitation	*Great Truths (5 minutes) **Daily recitations

Chanting	5* minutes using chant book or may use the morning worship tape

Divine Singing	5*-10**- Chant *one song minutes using chant book or may use the music CDs to sing along
**Select other songs if time allows.

Listening to the philosophy	5*-15** minutes to ½ hour - *Read an Ancient Egyptian Proverb or **Follow along with the ongoing weekly class recordings from the various lecture series. Or may read from scripture or book with teachings explained.

Reflection on the Philosophy	*Silently reflect on the proverb for 5 minutes. **Or if more time is available-Keep a Spiritual Journal for writing: Answer the following questions (see below).

Meditation	5* minutes to 30* minutes – follow instructions for the GLM (Ra-Akhu, Glorious Light Meditation system) or may use the meditation tapes or – may use the morning worship tape

Closing invocation	*Chant Om Htp

<u>detailed instructions follow</u>

The Path of Divine Love

INSTRUCTIONS AND TIME FOR THE DAILY WORSHIP DISCIPLINE

*Short program - 30 minutes
**Long program - 45-60 minutes

The program can take between 30 minutes to 1 hour depending on which aspects of the program are enjoined. The abbreviated program is a shortened version of the discipline for those times when the shorter time is available. The asterisks above will clarify which elements are for the shortened* practice and which are for the extended** practice.

The suggested times given above are the minimum amount you should spend on daily spiritual practices each day. Whenever possible you should increase the times according to your capacity and ability. You should train your mind so that it rejoices in hearing about and practicing the teachings of yoga instead of the useless worldly activities. Follow this path gradually but steadily.

Once you have established a schedule of minimal time to devote to practices, even if you do 5-10 minutes of meditation time per day and nothing else, keep your schedule if at all possible. Many people feel that they do not have the time to incorporate even ordinary activities into their lives. They feel overwhelmed with life and feel they have no control. If there is no control it is because there is no discipline. If you make a schedule for all of your activities (spiritual and non-spiritual) and keep to it tenaciously, you will discover that you can control your time and your life. As you discover the glory of spiritual practice, you will find even more time to expand your spiritual program. Ultimately, you will create a lifestyle which is entirely spiritualized. This means that every act in your life will be based on the wisdom teachings (MAAT) and therefore you will not only spend a particular time of day devoted to spiritual practices, but every facet of your life will become a spontaneous worship of the divine.

Questions for discussion after listening to the tapes and readings from the books- answer these in your journal (if you are working independently) discuss with your study group.

- A- What was the message you got from this days lecture?
- B- What insight have you gained into your understanding of spirituality?
- C- How has this teaching affected you today?
- D- How have previous lessons affected your life?
- E- Describe how this lesson or any previous lesson has changed your life from your previous ways into living more in harmony with yourself, nature, humanity or God.
- F- F- How has this or any other lesson from the series given you deeper insight into the previous religion you may have practiced?

Neter Merri

THE DAILY WORSHIP PROGRAM INSTRUCTIONS
(assume sitting posture facing the sun)

1. Ritual step 1 Opening your morning worship by uncovering your altar.
2. Ritual step 2 Lighting Candle   (Symbolizes the Akhu or Divine Light within that is to be awakened)
3. Ritual step 3 Lighting Incense (Symbolizes the fragrance of your personality which will exude with a divine odor that will rise up and attract as well as commune with the divine)
4. Ritual step 4 Libation -Pour purified water from a container on to another receptacle. Pour continuously-silent
5. Offering   Place offering (live food item (fruit or vegetable) in front of the altar. Recite the Offering Formula 4 times.

Hotep di nesu Neter aah Anpu Wep wat neb ta djser per kheru cha cha-aped si Ntr ari Maa-Kheru

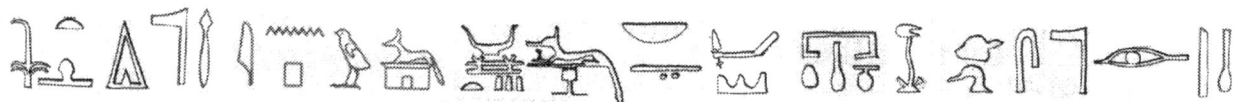

"Offering is given to the Supreme Divinity and to Anpu and Wepwat, lord of the sacred land, the spoken offering is 1000 beef (maleness) and 1000 geese (femaleness). This causes the Divine to make one True of Speech."

6. *Recitations for short program-* Great Truths of Shetaut Neter (Recite 4 times) for Morning, Noontime and Evening Worship

Four Great Principles of Shetaut Neter

Pa Neter ua ua Neberdjer m Neteru
"The Neter, the Supreme Being, is One and alone and as Neberdjer, manifesting everywhere and in all things in the form of Gods and Goddesses."

an-Maat swy Saui Set s-Khemn
"Lack of righteousness brings fetters to the personality and these fetters cause ignorance of the Divine."

s-Uashu s-Nafu n saiu Set
"Devotion to the Divine leads to freedom from the fetters of Set."

ari Shedy Rekh ab m Maakheru
"The practice of the Shedy disciplines leads to knowing oneself and the Divine. This is called being True of Speech"

6b. *Additional recitations for long program.* According to your time available If more time is available recite one or all of the prescribed readings for morning, noontime or evening worship

Recitations (Readings) for Ushet In The Morning

Opening Prayer A-from the Ancient Egyptian Book of Coming Forth By Day

Dua Ra Cheft Uben F em aket abdet ent Pet
    Adorations to Ra When he rises in horizon eastern
Anetej Ra-k iti em Khepera
    Homage to Ra, coming forth as Khepera
Khepera qemam neteru
    Khepera, Creator of the gods and goddesses
Cha – k uben – k pesd Mut – k
    Rising thee, shinning thee, lighting up thy mother
Cha ti em suten neteru
    Rising as Lord, king of the gods and goddesses
Iri – nek mut Nut aiui – em iri nini
    Your mother Nut does an act of worship to you with both arms

Neter Merri

Manu em hetep hept-tu Maat er tra
   Manu (Western Horizon) receives thee in peace, Maat embraces thee at the double season (perennially)

Adorations to Ra when He rises in the Eastern Horizon of Heaven
(From the Hymn to Ra #1 in the Pert m Hru)

Instruction: write your first name in the spaces below and recite your own name as you read.

1. Behold Asar_____ bringing divine offerings of all the gods and goddesses. Asar _____ speaks thus:
2. Homage to thee, who comes in the form of Khepri[2], Khepri the Creator of the gods and goddesses. You rise and shine, illuminating your mother, goddess Nut, the sky, crowned as king of the gods and goddesses. Your mother Nut worships you with her two arms. The western horizon receives you in peace and Maat embraces you at the double season. Give Asar _____ Glorious Spirit being[3], and spiritual strength through righteous speaking. Grant the ability to come forth as a living soul so that Asar _____ may see Heru of the two Horizons.(4) Grant this to the Ka(5) of Asar _____ who is Righteous of Speech in the presence of Asar, the Divine Self. Asar _____ says: Hail to all the gods and goddesses, weighers of the house of the soul, in heaven and on earth by means of the scales of Maat, who are givers of Life Force sustenance.
3. Tatunen(6), One, maker of men and women as well as the company of the gods and goddesses of the south, the north, the west and the east, i.e. all the neteru, grant praises to Ra, the lord of heaven, sovereign of life, vitality and health, maker of the gods and goddesses. Adorations to thee in your form as all goodness, as you rise in your boat. The beings up high praise thee. Beings in the lower realms praise thee. Djehuti and Maat(8) have written for thee, who are shining forth, every day. Your enemies are put to the fire. The fiends are put down, their arms and legs being bound securely for Ra. The children of weakness disrespect and insurrection shall not continue.
4. The great house(9) is in festival time. The voices of the participants are in the great temple. The gods and goddesses are rejoicing. They see Ra in his glorious rising, his beams of light piercing, inundating the lands. This exalted and venerable god journeys on and unites with the land of Manu, the western horizon, illuminating the land of his birth every day and at the same time he reaches the province where he was yesterday.
5. Be in peace with me! I see your beauties and I prosper upon the land; I smile and I defeat the ass fiend as well as the other fiends. Grant that I may defeat Apep(10) in his time of strength and to see the pilot fish of the Divine Boat of Ra, which is in its blessed pool.(11) I see Heru in the form as the guardian of the rudder. Djehuti and Maat are upon his two arms. Received am I in the prow(12) of the Mandet(13) Boat and in the stern of the Mesektet(14) Boat. Ra gives divine sight, to see the Aten(15), to view the moon god unceasingly, every day, and the ability of souls to come forth, to walk to every place they may desire. Proclaim my name! Find him in the wood board of offerings. There have been given to me offerings in the life-giving presence, like it is given to the followers of Heru(16). It is done for me in the divine place in the boat on the day of the sailing, the journey of The God. I am received in the presence of Asar in the land of truth speaking(17) of the Ka of Asar _____.

*******PAUSE 1 Minute for Silent Meditation*******

The Path of Divine Love

🎵 Play sistrum in pattern of three shakes three times (123-123-123) then continue

Adorations to Ra-Herakhuti
(From the Hymn to Hymn to Ated by Akhenaten)

Dua Ankh Herakhuti Ha m Akhet
Adorations to the living Horus in the two horizons, residing in the horizon
M ren-f m Shu m Aten
In his name of Shu in the form of the Sundisk
Di ankh djeta heh
Giving life forever and for eternity
In suten ankh m Maat Neb Tawi
This praise is sung by the king (Akhenaten), the living, in righteousness, Lord of the two lands (Ancient Egypt)
Nefer Kheperu Ra ua n Ra
The good king in is name Creator, one with God

Next invoke the assistance of the deity or cosmic force which removes obstacles to your success in spiritual practice. Anpu is the deity which leads souls through the narrow pathways of the Duat. Therefore, request the assistance of Anpu, who represents the discriminative intellectual ability so that you may "distinguish the real from the unreal".

"O Apuat (Anpu), opener of the ways, the roads of the North, O Anpu, opener of the ways, the roads of the South. The messenger between heaven and hell displaying alternately a face black as night, and golden as the day. He is equally watchful by day as by night."

"May Anpu make my thighs firm so that I may stand upon them".

"I have washed myself in the water wherein the god
Anpu washed when he performed the office of embalmer and bandager.
My lips are the lips of Anpu".

*******PAUSE 1 Minute for Silent Meditation*******

🎵 Play sistrum in pattern of three shakes three times (123-123-123) then continue

Next invoke the presence of Aset-Maat who is the embodiment of wisdom and inner discovery of the Divine. Aset (Aset) is the mother of the universe and she herself veils her true form, as the Supreme Transcendental Self. This "veil" of ignorance is only due to ignorance. Therefore, pray for Aset to make her presence, which bestows instant revelation of her true form. This "unveiling" is a metaphor symbolizing the intuitional revelation of the Divine or Enlightenment in your mind. Aset is in your heart and only needs to be revealed. However, she can only reveal herself to the true aspirant, one who is devoted to her (the Self) and her alone. Aset says: "I Aset, am all that has been, all that is, or shall be; and no mortal man hath ever unveiled me."

The invocatory prayer to Aset is:

"Oh benevolent Aset, who protected her brother Asar, who searched for him without wearying, who traversed the land in mourning and never rested until she had found him. She who afforded him shadow with her wings and gave him air with her feathers, who rejoiced and carried her brother home.

She who revived what was faint for the weary one, who received his seed and conceived an heir, and who nourished him in solitude while no one knew where he was. . . ."

SPEECH OF ASET. Aset saith:- I have come to be a protector unto thee. I waft unto thee air for thy nostrils, and the north wind which cometh forth from the god Tem unto thy nose. I have made whole for thee thy windpipe. I make thee to live like a god. Thine enemies have fallen under thy feet. I have made thy word to be true before Nut, and thou art mighty before the gods.

*******PAUSE 1 Minute for Silent Meditation*******

Play sistrum in pattern of three shakes three times (123-123-123) then continue

Then remember your Spiritual Preceptor, the person who taught you how to meditate, thank them for their teaching and invoke their grace for success in your meditation. "Have faith in your master's ability to lead you along the path of truth".

"The lips of the wise are as the doors of a cabinet; no sooner are they opened, but treasures are poured out before you. Like unto trees of gold arranged in beds of silver, are wise sentences uttered in due season."

Now resolve within yourself that you will stay for the prescribed period of time which you have determined and then proceed with the practice as described below. Remember the following precepts: "Have devotion of purpose", "Have faith in your own ability to accept the truth", "Have faith in your ability to act with wisdom."

Excerpts of Chapter 33(18) of the Pert M Heru From contemporary papyri(19)

1. I have lived by righteousness and truth while on earth. I live in righteousness and truth; I feed upon right and truth in my heart. I have done what is required to live in harmony in society and the gods and goddesses are also satisfied that I have worshipped rightly.
2. I have done God's will. I have given bread to the hungry, water to the thirsty, clothes to the clotheless and a boat to those who were shipwrecked. I made the prescribed offerings to the gods and goddesses and I also made offerings in the temple to the glorious spirits.
3. Therefore, protect me when I go to face The God.(20)

Closing Devotional Prayer of Aspirants:

amma su en pa neter, sauu - k su emment en pa neter
au tuanu ma qeti pa haru

*"Give thyself to GOD, keep thou thyself daily for God;
and let tomorrow be as today."*

The Path of Divine Love

Recitations (Readings) for Ushet At Noontime

Opening Prayer A-from the Ancient Egyptian Hymns of Amun*:

O Åmun, O Åmun, who art in heaven, turn thy face upon the dead body of the child, and make your child sound and strong in the Underworld.

O Åmun, O Åmun, O God, O God, O Åmun, I adore thy name, grant thou to me that I may understand thee; Grant thou that I may have peace in the Duat, and that I may possess all my members therein...

Hail, Åmun, let me make supplication unto thee, for I know thy name, and thy transformations are in my mouth, and thy skin is before my eyes. Come, I pray thee, and place thou thine heir and thine image, myself, in the everlasting underworld... let my whole body become like that of a neter, let me escape from the evil chamber and let me not be imprisoned therein; for I worship thy name..

*See the book Egyptian Yoga Vol 3 Theban Theology by Dr. Muata Ashby

Visualize that with each utterance you are being enfolded in Divine Grace and Enlightenment.

*******PAUSE 1 Minute for Silent Meditation*******

Play sistrum in pattern of three shakes three times (123-123-123) then continue

Affirmations of Innocence: The 42 Precepts of Maat from the Pert m Heru texts

(1) "I have not done what is wrong." Variant: I have not acted with falsehood.
(2) "I have not robbed with violence."
(3) "I have not done violence (to anyone or anything)." Variant: I have not been rapacious (taking by force; plundering.)
(4) "I have not committed theft." Variant: I have not coveted.
(5) "I have not murdered man or woman." Variant: I have not ordered someone else to commit murder.
(6) "I have not defrauded offerings." Variant: I have not destroyed food supplies or increased or decreased the measures to profit.
(7) "I have not acted deceitfully." Variant: I have not acted with crookedness.
(8) "I have not robbed the things that belong to God."
(9) "I have told no lies."
(10) "I have not snatched away food."
(11) "I have not uttered evil words." Variant: I have not allowed myself to become sullen, to sulk or become depressed.
(12) "I have attacked no one."
(13) "I have not slaughtered the cattle that are set apart for the Gods." Variant: I have not slaughtered the Sacred bull – (Apis)
(14) "I have not eaten my heart" (overcome with anguish and distraught). Variant: I have not committed perjury.
(15) "I have not laid waste the ploughed lands."
(16) "I have not been an eavesdropper or pried into matters to make mischief."

(17) "I have not spoken against anyone." Variant: I have not babbled, gossiped.
(18) "I have not allowed myself to become angry without cause."
(19) "I have not committed adultery." Variant: I have not committed homosexuality.
(20) "I have not committed any sin against my own purity."
(21) "I have not violated sacred times and seasons."
(22) "I have not done that which is abominable."
(23) "I have not uttered fiery words. I have not been a man or woman of anger."
(24) "I have not stopped my ears listening to the words of right and wrong (Maat)."
(25) "I have not stirred up strife (disturbance)." "I have not caused terror." "I have not struck fear into any man."
(26) "I have not caused any one to weep." Variant: I have not hoodwinked.
(27) "I have not lusted or committed fornication nor have I lain with others of my same sex." Variant: I have not molested children.
(28) "I have not avenged myself." Variant: I have not cultivated resentment.
(29) "I have not worked grief, I have not abused anyone." Variant: I have not cultivated a quarrelsome nature.
(30) "I have not acted insolently or with violence."
(31) "I have not judged hastily." Variant: I have not been impatient.
(32) "I have not transgressed or angered God."
(33) "I have not multiplied my speech overmuch (talk too much)."
(34) "I have not done harm or evil." Variant: I have not thought evil.
(35) "I have not worked treason or curses on the King."
(36) "I have never befouled the water." Variant: I have not held back the water from flowing in its season.
(37) "I have not spoken scornfully." Variant: I have not yelled unnecessarily or raised my voice.
(38) "I have not cursed The God."
(39) "I have not behaved with arrogance." Variant: I have not been boastful.(21)
(40) "I have not been overwhelmingly proud or sought for distinctions for myself(22)."
(41) "I have never magnified my condition beyond what was fitting or increased my wealth, except with such things as are (justly) mine own possessions by means of Maat." Variant: I have not disputed over possessions except when they concern my own rightful possessions. Variant: I have not desired more than what is rightfully mine.
(42) "I have never thought evil (blasphemed) or slighted The God in my native town."

Conclusion

I am pure. I am pure. I am Pure.
I have washed my front parts with the waters of libations,
I have cleansed my hinder parts with drugs which make wholly clean,
and my inward parts have been washed in the liquor of Maat

Closing Devotional Prayer of Aspirants:

>   amma su en pa neter
>   sauu - k su emment en pa neter
>   au tuanu ma qeti pa haru

> "Give thyself to GOD,
> keep thou thyself daily for God;
> and let tomorrow be as today."

The Path of Divine Love

Recitations (Readings) for Ushet at Sunset

The following is a Hymn to the Supreme Being in the form of Tem or the setting sun. In the theology surrounding the god Ra, Ra is seen as a representation of the Supreme Being (Neberdjer, Pa Neter). As such Ra is depicted as the sun and the sun has three phases which it manifests every day. These phases are the morning, the middle of the day and the setting sun. Thus we have the following quotation:

In the Myth of Ra and Aset Ra says, "I am Khepera in the morning, and Ra at noonday, and Temu in the evening.

Thus, the following hymn is effective for the evening hours, prior to practicing intense meditation and also at the time of death. In the mystical mythology of the ancient Egyptian city of Anu (Sun city) it is understood that Ra travels in barque which is itself the sun. From this barque hang cords by which those who are righteous can grab hold of in order to be lifted unto the boat. Thus through the practice of Maat (righteous living) one is able to be raised to the company of Ra who travels on the boat of millions of years (eternity) and thus attain immortality and communion with God. For more on this teaching see the books The Ausarian Resurrection: The Ancient Egyptian Bible and The Mystical Teachings of The Ausarian Resurrection: Initiation Into the Third Level of Shetaut Asar.

A HYMN TO RA-TEM
(From the papyrus of Lady Mut Hetep)

The lady Mut-Hetep says, "0 Ra-Tem, in thy splendid progress thou risest, and thou settest as a living being "in the glories of the western horizon; thou settest in thy "territory which is in the Mount of Sunset (Manu). "Thy Uraeus is behind thee, thy Uraeus is behind thee. Homage (Ushet) to thee, 0 thou -who art in peace; homage to thee, 0 thou who art in peace. Thou art joined unto the Eye of Tem, and it chooseth its powers of protection [to place] behind thy members. Thou goest forth through heaven, thou travellest over the earth, and thou journeyest onward. 0 Luminary, the northern and southern halves of heaven come to thee, and they bow low in adoration, and they do homage unto thee, day by day. The gods of Amentet rejoice in thy beauties, and the unseen places sing hymns of praise unto thee. Those who dwell in the Sektet boat go round about thee, and the Souls of the East do homage "to thee, and when they meet thy Majesty they cry: "Come, come in peace!" There is a shout of welcome to thee, 0 lord of heaven and governor of Amentet! Thou art acknowledged by Aset (Aset) who seeth her son ,Heru (Horus) in thee, the lord of fear, the mighty one of terror. Thou settest as a living being in the hidden place. Thy father [Ta-]tunen raseth thee up and he placeth both his hands behind thee; thou becomest endowed with divine attributes in [thy] members of earth; thou wakest in peace and thou settest in Manu. Grant thou that I may become a being honoured before Asar (Asar), and that I may come to thee, 0 Ra-Tem! I have adored thee, therefore do thou for me that which I wish. Grant thou that I may be victorious in the presence of the company of the gods. Thou art beautiful, 0 Ra, in thy western horizon of Amentet, thou lord of Maat, thou being who art greatly feared, and whose attributes are majestic, 0 thou who art greatly beloved by those who dwell in the Duat! Thou shinest with thy beams upon the beings that are therein perpetually, and thou sendest forth thy light upon the path of Ra-stau. Thou openest up the path of the double Lion-god (Aker), thou settest the gods upon [their] thrones, and the spirits in their abiding places. The heart of Naarerf (i.e., An-rut-f, a region of the Underworld) is glad [when] Ra setteth; the heart of Nahrerf is glad when Ra setteth. Hail, 0 ye gods of the land of Amentet who make offerings and oblations unto Ra-Tem, ascribe ye glory [unto him when] ye meet him. Grasp ye your weapons and overthrow ye the fiend Seba on behalf of Ra, and repulse the fiend Nebt on behalf of Asar. The gods of the land of Amentet rejoice and lay hold upon the cords of the Sektet boat, and they come in peace; the gods of the hidden place who dwell in Amentet triumph.

*******PAUSE 1 Minute for Silent Meditation*******

Play sistrum in pattern of three shakes three times (123-123-123) then continue

Pert M Heru CHAPTER 8(23)
A Conversation Between Asar _____ and God in the Form of Atum(24)

1. These are the words which when spoken and understood protect an aspirant from dying a second time. These words are to be spoken by Asar _____ who is Righteous of Speech.
2. Oh Djehuti! What is it that has come into being through the conflict of the children(25) of Nut?
3. They have engendered unrest, unrighteousness and have created fiends and they have slaughtered (themselves, animals and nature(26)). They have created (for themselves) fetters by their doings which render them weak.(27)
4. Give them, Oh Great Djehuti, a commandment of Atum so that their unrighteousness may not be seen, so that you will not experience that. Shorten their years; shorten their mouths because they have committed unrighteousness towards you in secret(28).
5. I am your pallet(29) and I even brought you the inkpot as well. I am not among those with hidden unrighteousness. There is no wrongdoing within me!
6. These words are spoken by me: "Oh Atum, I am Asar _____! Tell me, what place(30) is this that I have come to? There is no water here. There is no air and there is a great darkness."
7. In this plane you have no physical body, therefore, you may live here through peace of heart. Moreover, there is no sexuality here, in place of water, air, bread, beer and lovemaking, I have given you the opportunity to attain the state of Akhu(31) together with peace of heart.
8. Atum has decreed that my face should be seen and that I should not suffer the things that cause pain.
9. Every god is sending his throne to the leader of eternity. It is thy throne, given to thy son Heru. Atum, holding what was sent to him by the elder divinities commanded this. It is he who has been ruling thy throne. It is he inheriting the throne within the island of double fire.(32) Command that I may be seen, as I am his double and that my face may see the face of Lord Atum.
10. What is the duration of life?
11. It has been decreed for millions of millions of years of duration. It is given to me to send the old ones. After that period of time I am going to destroy all created things.
12. It is the earth that came forth from Nun, now coming forth into its former state.(33)
13. I am fated with Asar; done for me to become images of the serpents, not knowing they the people and not knowing the gods and goddesses the excellent beauty that I made for Asar which was greater than all the gods and goddesses. I gave to him the desert. His son Heru is his heir on his throne within the island of double fire.
14. I made, also, a divine ruling place for him in the Divine Boat of Millions of Years.
15. It is Heru, who is now established on the Serek(34) for those who are beloved and who are attaining sturdiness. Furthermore, the soul of Set, which is greater than all the gods and goddesses, was sent. It is given to me to make fettered his soul within the Divine Boat, for his desire is feared by divine body parts.

The Path of Divine Love

16. Hail father mine, Asar; do make for me what you did for thy father Ra, the achievement of long life on earth, achieving the throne, health, progeny and endurance for my tomb, and my loved ones who are on earth.
17. Grant that my enemies be destroyed, that the scorpion goddess may be on top of them, fettering them. Father mine, Ra make thee for me these things: Ankh, Udja, Seneb (**life, vitality and health**).
18. Heru is now firmly established(35) on his Serek. Give thee movement in course of time, that of advancing towards blessedness.(36)

Closing Devotional Prayer of Aspirants:

>amma su en pa neter
>sauu - k su emment en pa neter
>au tuanu ma qeti   pa haru
>
>"Give thyself to GOD,
>keep thou thyself daily for God;
>and let tomorrow be as today."

Neter Merri

7. Daily Chants of Shetaut Neter and Smai Tawi for Morning, Noontime and Evening Worship

(Chant each 4 times)

1
Om Amun Ra Ptah
(The One Divine Self manifesting and the Trinity of Witnessing Consciousness, Mind and The Physical Universe)

2
Om Asar Aset Heru
The One Divine Self manifesting and the Trinity of the Divine Father, Mother and Child

3
Om Maati Maakheru
The One Divine Self manifesting as the dual goddesses of truth of above and below (Heaven and Earth) Assist me in attaining spiritual enlightenment.

4
amma su en pa neter sauu - k su emment en
pa neter au tuanu ma qeti pa haru
Give thyself to GOD; keep thou thyself daily for God; and let tomorrow be as today.

5
HTP di si neter iri mettu wadj
An offering is made to propitiate that God may make the vascular system flourish
(An invocation of Health)

6
Dua Ra Dua Ra Dua Ra Khepera
Adorations to Ra, Adorations to Ra in the form of the Creator
Drumming Notation DD tktkt DD tktk - FAST

7
Dua Asar Unefer Neteraah (Adorations to Asar- Pure Existence, Exalted Divinity)
Dua Asar Her Abdu (Adorations to Asar- Innermost essence of Abdu City of God)
Dua Asar Neb Djeta (Adorations to Asar- Lord of Forever)
Dua Asar Suten Heh! (Adorations to Asar- King of Eternity)
Drumming Notation Beat #1 DD t DD t DD t DD t – Slow
Beat #2 DD tk D - SLOW

8
Net Net Dua Net Goddess Net, Goddess Net, Adorations to Goddess Net
Sefek Cheras Senhu – S Remove your vail so that I may see your true form (creation Unveiled-to see the Divine Self, i.e. spiritual enlightenment)
Drumming Notation D tk DD tk DD tk DD tk - FAST

The Path of Divine Love

9
Dua Hetheru Neteritaah
Adorations to Hetheru the Great Goddess.
Drumming Notation D DD D DD D DD D DD - SLOW

10
Maat Ankhu Maat Maat is the source of life
Maat neb bu ten Maat is in everywhere you are
Cha hena Maat Rise in the morning with Maat
Ankh hena Maat Live with Maat
Ha sema Maat Let every limb join with Maat
(i.e. let her guide your actions)

Dua Maat neb bu ten
Adorations to goddess Maat, who is in everywhere you are!
Drumming Notation D DDD tk - FAST

Next Steps in the Divine Worship Program

8. *Divine Singing* — *Choose one or **more song(s) (as time allows) form the song list to listen to and sing along with

9. *Listening* to the teachings- *read 1 Ancient Egyptian Proverb and/or **as time allows choose from a scripture or book which explains the scripture or listen to prerecorded tape of lecture on the teachings of the scriptures.

10. *Reflection* what you have heard and record your thoughts and notes in your journal. (5 minutes-short program)

11. *Meditation:* spend time in practice of the Glorious Light Meditation discipline allowing the mind to be at peace, realizing that what you have heard and reflected upon will lead you to expanded consciousness and enlightenment. (5 minutes-minimum for short program)

*short program, **extended program

Meditation- The Glorious Light Meditation System of Shetaut Neter*

Basic Instructions for the Glorious Light Meditation System- Given in the Tomb of Seti I.
(1350 B.C.E.)

Formal meditation consists of four basic elements: Posture, Sound (chant-words of power), Visualization, Rhythmic Breathing (calm, steady breath). The instructions, translated from the original hieroglyphic text in the Tomb of Seti I contain the basic elements for formal meditation.

(1)-Posture and Focus of Attention - facing the sun

                iuf iri-f ahau   maq   b-phr   nty   hau iu
           body do   make stand, within the Sundisk (circle of Ra)

Instruction: This means that the aspirant should remain established (sitting or lying down) as if in the center of a circle with a dot in the middle. Make your posture facing east or north.

(2)- Words of power-chant

Instruction: Utter the following hekau repeatedly during your practice

Nuk Hekau (I am the word* itself)
Nuk Ra Akhu (I am Ra's Glorious Shinning** Spirit)
Nuk Ba Ra (I am the soul of Ra)
Nuk Hekau (I am the God who creates*** through sound)
`

(3)- Visualization

                    Iuf   mi Ra   heru   mestu-f   n-shry   chet
                  "My body is like Ra's on the day of his birth

Instruction: visualize a golden white light at the base of your spine. As you breath in utter the hekau and visualize that the light rises up your spine to the point between your eyebrows. Then as you breath out utter the hekau again and visualize that the light is moving back down to the base of your spine. This is one cycle. Continue this practice for at least 15 minutes.

12. *Closing Invocation*- Chant Om-Htp, Htp, Htp,Htp, (Divine Self-Peace, Peace, Peace, Peace.)

*For more on the Glorious Light Meditation System see the book The Glorious Light by Sebai Muata Ashby Also available as recording on cassette and CD

The Path of Divine Love

DEVOTIONAL MUSIC AND THEATER OF ANCIENT EGYPT

Ritual is an important element of devotional practice. The theater of Ancient Kamit was actually the reenactment of the myth in the temple ritual practice or festival. Many people believe that the art of theater began with the ancient Greek theater. Thespis, the first actor-dramatist (About 560 B.C.E.), is considered to have been the first person to give the Greek drama its form and actors are still called "thespians." However, upon closer examination it must be noted that just as Greek philosophers such as Thales and Pythagoras learned their wisdom from the Ancient Egyptians and then set up their schools of philosophy in Greece, it is likely that the first Greek actors and playwrights learned their profession from the Ancient Egyptian Sages when they came from Greece to learn the religion and the sciences. (see the book "From Egypt to Greece") Actually, a great debt is owed to the Greek writers of ancient times because their records attest to many details which the Ancient Egyptians did not record.

There was no public theater in Ancient Egypt as the modern world knows theater at present. Theater in present day society is performed publicly for the main purpose of entertainment but in Ancient Egypt the theatrical performances were reserved for the temple exclusively. This was because the performing arts, including music, were held to be powerful and sacred endeavors which were used to impart spiritual teachings and evoke spiritual feeling and were not to be used as frivolous forms of entertainment. The Greek writer, Strabo, relates that multitudes of people would flock to festival centers (important cities and temples) where the scenes from myths related to the gods and goddesses would be acted out.

Sometimes the main episodes of the religious dramas (the most esoteric elements were performed in the interior portion of the temple for initiates, priests and priestesses only) were performed outside the temple, in the courtyard or between the pylons and were the most important attraction of the festivals. (see the temple diagram) The priests and priestesses took great care with costumes and the decorations (direction and set design). The spectators knew the myths that were being acted out but never stopped enjoying their annual performance, being a retelling of the divine stories, which bring purpose and meaning to life. Thus, the art of acting was set aside for spiritual purposes and was not to be used for mindless entertainment, which serves only to distract the mind from reality and truth. The spectators would take part by clapping, lamenting at sad parts and crying out with joy and celebrating when the ultimate triumph came. In this manner the spectators became part of the myth and the myth is essentially the life of the gods and goddesses and their lives are what not only sustains the world, but also what leads to understanding the connection between the physical, material and spiritual worlds. Further, the occasions were used as opportunities for enjoying life, though it was understood to be fleeting. Thus, the bridge between the mortal world and the eternal world was established, through mythological drama and the performing arts.

In the Ancient Egyptian view, life cannot be enjoyed without affirming the Divine, the Spirit. Further, theater, religion and mystical philosophy were considered to be aspects of the same discipline, known as "Shetaut Neter" or the "mysteries" or "Yoga Sciences." Every aspect of life in Ancient Egypt was permeated by the awareness and inclusion of spiritual philosophy. For example. lawyers and judges followed the precepts of Maat and medical doctors followed and worshipped the teachings of the god Djehuti, who was adopted by the Greeks as the god Asclapius. This idea is also evident in the Ancient Egyptian manner of saying grace before meals even by ordinary householders. Prior to consuming food, the host of an ordinary household would invite the guests to view an image of a divinity, principally Asar (Asar) the god of the afterlife, thereby reminding the guests that life is fleeting, even as they are about to enjoy a sumptuous meal. In this manner, a person is reminded of the ultimate fate of life and a reflective state of mind is engendered rather than an arrogant and egoistic state. This theme is present in every aspect of Ancient Egyptian culture at its height.

The Ancient Egyptian Sages instituted tight controls on theater and music because the indulgence in inappropriate entertainments was known to cause mental agitation and undesirable behaviors. The famous Greek Philosopher and student of the Ancient Egyptian Mysteries, Pythagoras, wrote that the Ancient Egyptians placed particular attention to the study of music. Another famous Greek Philosopher and student of the Ancient Egyptian Mysteries, Plato, states that they thought it was beneficial to the youths. Strabo confirms that music was taught to youths along with reading and writing, however, it was understood that music meant for entertainment alone was harmful to the mind, making it agitated and difficult to control oneself, and thus was strictly controlled by the state and the priests and priestesses. Like the sages of India, who instituted Nada Yoga, or the spiritual path of music, the Ancient Egyptians held that music was of Divine origin and as such was a sacred endeavor. The Greek writer, Athenaeus, informs us that the Greeks and barbarians from other countries learned music from the Ancient Egyptians. Music was so important in Ancient Egypt that professional musicians were contracted and kept on salaries at the temples. Music was considered important because it has the special power to carry the mind to either elevated (spiritual) states or (worldly) states. When there is overindulgence in music for entertainment and escapism (tendency to desire to escape from daily routine or reality by indulging in fantasy, daydreaming, or entertainment) the mind is filled with worldly impressions, cravings, lusting, and uncontrolled urges. In this state of mind, the capacity for right thinking and feeling are distorted or incapacitated. The advent of audio and visual recording technology and their combinations in movies and music videos, is more powerful because the visual element, coupled with music, and the ability to repeat with intensity of volume, acts to intoxicate the mind with illusory and fantasy thoughts. The body is also affected in this process. The vibrations of the music and the feelings contained in it through the lyrics and sentiment of the performer evokes the production of certain bio-chemical processes in the mind and body. This capacity of music is evident in movies musicals, converts, audio recordings, etc., in their capacity to change a persons mood. Any and all messages given to the mind affect it and therefore great care should be taken to fill the mind with the right kinds of messages in the form of ideas and feelings.

Those societies which produce and consume large quantities of audio and audio-visual entertainment for non-spiritual purposes will exhibit the greatest levels of mental agitation, violence, individual frustration, addiction, mental illness, physical illness, etc., no matter how materially prosperous or technologically advanced they may become. So true civilization and success of a society should not be judged by material prosperity or technological advancement but rather how successful it is in producing the inner fulfillment of its citizens. Being the creators of and foremost practitioners of Maat Philosophy (adherence to the principles of righteousness in all aspects of life*), the Ancient Egyptians created a culture which existed longer (at least 5,000 years) than any other known society. Therefore, the real measures of civilization and human evolution are to be discerned by the emphasis on and refinement of the performing and visual arts and spiritual philosophy, for these endeavors serve to bring harmony to the individual and to society. It should be clearly understood that art should not become stagnant or rigid in its expression since this is the means by which it is renewed for the understanding of new generations. Rather, the principles contained in the arts should be kept intact in the performance of the rituals, paintings, sculptures, music, etc. since these reflect transcendental truths which are effective today as they were 5,000 years ago in the Ancient Egyptian temple and will be effective until the end of time. The loss of these is the cause of disharmony in society but societal dysfunction is in reality only a reflection of disharmony in the individual human heart which has lost its connection with the higher Self within. (*See the book "The Wisdom of Maati." **The word spiritual here implies any endeavor which seeks to bring understanding about the ultimate questions of life: Who am I and What is life all about. So spirituality may or may not be related to organized religion.)

Thus, the question of whether or not music and entertainment has an effect on youth and the mind of a person was resolved in ancient times. The Ancient Egyptians observed that the people from Greece and the Asiatic countries were more aggressive and that their behavior was unstable.* They attributed these problems to their lifestyle, which was full of strife due to life in harsh geographical regions, meat eating and overindulgence in sense pleasures, or the inability to control the human urges and the consequent disconnection from the natural order of the universe as well as their spiritual inner selves. These observations of the psychology and lifestyle of the foreigners prompted the Ancient Egyptian Sages to refer to the Greeks and Asiatics (Middle Easterners) as "children" and "miserable"..."barbarians." Their observations allowed the Ancient Egyptian Sages to create a philosophy of life and a psycho-spiritual environment wherein the Egyptian people could grow and thrive in physical, mental and spiritual health. (See the books Egyptian Yoga Vol. 1 and 2 and The 42 Laws of Maat and the Wisdom Texts)

In Ancient Greece, theater became a practice which was open to the public and later on in the Christian era it deteriorated into mindless entertainment or a corrupted endeavor of con artists and in present times it is a big business wherein its participants are paid excessive and disproportionately high salaries for their entertainment skills; or otherwise said, their ability to sell merchandise. In modern times the almost unfettered creation and promotion of movies, videos, music and other forms of entertainment containing elements designed to promote sense pleasures and excitement, leads to mental agitation but with little true satisfaction of the inner need of the heart. Thus, while the entertainments may cause excitation they do not lead to abiding fulfillment and inner peace, but to more desires for more excitement in a never ending cycle which is impossible to fulfill. This process leads to mental confusion and stress which in turn lead to strife and conflict, internal frustration. Corresponding with the emergence of Western and Middle Eastern culture, with its negative lifestyle elements noted by the Ancient Egyptians, the world has also seen an increase in wars, violence against women, children, environmental destruction, enslavement and taking advantage of weaker human beings, drug abuse, crime, divorce, and overall personal dissatisfaction with life. In other words, the lack of restraints, both individuals and in societies as a whole, has led to frustration with life, a kind of cultural depression and degradation, which has led to record numbers of people suffering from mental illnesses such as depression, schizophrenia, psychosis, as well as medical disorders of all kinds which were not present in ancient times due to self-control and the direction of life being guided by spiritual pursuits as opposed to egoistic pursuits. The Ancient Egyptian Mystery theater provides the means for allowing a human being to come into harmony with the spiritual reality (mental expansion and self-discovery) while frivolous entertainment serves to dull the intellectual capacity to discover and understand anything beyond the physical world and the physical sense pleasures of life (mental contraction and hardening of the ego). This inability to go beyond sense pleasures and experiences the world of human activity is what leads a person to mental stress which in turn leads to mental illness and physical illness.

Devotional spiritual practice is closely related to singing and chanting the divine names. Its purpose is to purify the heart and to lead one to a harmony of mind and body so as to allow a spiritual awakening and a spiritual realization. Divine Singing is the science of sound and the art of playing music in such a manner as to lead the mind to transcendental forms of spiritual ecstasy and oneness with the Divine. The following musical compositions have been recorded and are available on quality Compact Disc formats. They have presented the original-traditional form as well as have successfully integrated the ancient melodies and devotional music with Jazz, Reggae, Pop and other musical forms. This collection explores this musical form but also incorporating the music and philosophy of ancient Africa, using the chants of the ancient Egyptian hieroglyphic texts. This combination of music is designed to show the complementary nature of Kamitan culture and spiritual philosophy and to uplift any student of Ancient African music and Divine Worship.

This production made use of reproductions of Ancient Egyptian musical instruments and modern musical instruments as well as modern western musical instruments.

KEMETIC DIVINE SINGING

Sebai Maa (Dr. Muata Ashby) began his research into the spiritual philosophy of ancient Egypt (Kemet or Kamit) and noticed that the teachings correlated to what is today referred to as mysticism and yoga. This was the catalyst for a successful book series on the subject called "Egyptian Yoga". Now he has created a series of musical compositions which explore this unique area of music from ancient Egypt and its connection to world music. Sebai Maa is the only exponent of Ancient Egyptian Music incorporating the ancient Hekau or Ancient Egyptian (Kemetic) words of power in a musical form for devotional spiritual practice, dancing, or pure listening pleasure.

"Devote yourself to adore God's name."

—Ancient Egyptian Proverb

Music has the capacity to bring us into balance with the cosmos and God is that same Divine essence. Music is a devotional exercise that carries our feelings up to the divine realms and thus leads us to spiritual enlightenment when it is dedicated to the Divine with a spiritual intent. Singing God's name or chanting God's name is the way prescribed by sages and saints the world over, for changing the vibrations of one's personality and the environment, achieving mental peace and coming closer to the Divine!

For more on the practice of the Kemetic Devotional Path see the *Divine Worship Manual* by Muata Ashby

HTP
(PEACE)

INDEX

Abdu, 43, 68
Abhyasa, 120, 122
Absolute, 18, 34, 64, 75, 93, 100, 143
Absolute XE "Absolute" Reality, 75
Affirmations, 152
Africa, 13, 16, 21, 22, 26, 31, 49, 50, 60, 79, 144
Akhenaton, 14, 20
Akhnaton, 44
Akhus, 48
Alexandria, 144
Allah, 108, 119
Amen, 145
Amenta, 227
Amentet, 228
Amma, 216, 218
Amun, 14, 19, 20, 22, 24, 29, 33, 38, 41, 134, 151, 163, 165, 216, 218, 222
Amun-Ra-Ptah, 218, 222
Ancient Egypt, 1, 3, 4, 8, 11, 13, 14, 16, 17, 20, 21, 22, 23, 24, 26, 31, 32, 34, 35, 49, 50, 51, 52, 55, 57, 58, 59, 60, 61, 63, 64, 68, 69, 70, 71, 76, 78, 80, 82, 88, 91, 100, 101, 106, 110, 112, 119, 120, 121, 122, 125, 127, 129, 131, 134, 136, 137, 140, 145, 146, 147, 151, 154, 159, 160, 161, 162, 163, 215, 217, 218, 219, 220, 221, 222, 223, 224, 225, 226, 227, 228, 229, 230, 231, 234, 235, 236, 237
Ancient Egyptian Book of the Dead, 134
Ancient Egyptian Mystical Philosophy, 162
Ancient Egyptian Pyramid Texts, 140, 154, 163
Ancient Egyptian Wisdom Texts, 217
Anger, 93
Ani, 119
Ankh, 58
Anu, 29, 38, 39, 228
Anu (Greek Heliopolis), 14, 29, 38, 39, 127, 152, 163, 228
Anubis, 24, 101
Anunian Theology, 33, 38, 39
Apedemak, 78
Apep serpent, 46
Apophis, 46, 109
Ari, 29
Arjuna, 120
Aryan, 221

Asar, 8, 14, 19, 21, 23, 24, 29, 33, 38, 39, 43, 49, 51, 59, 60, 61, 68, 76, 77, 78, 101, 106, 107, 108, 109, 120, 125, 128, 129, 131, 132, 133, 134, 136, 137, 138, 140, 141, 143, 144, 145, 147, 152, 154, 155, 156, 160, 161, 165, 216, 218, 229, 230, 236
Asarian Resurrection, 33, 71, 229, 230
Aset, 14, 19, 22, 24, 33, 39, 42, 43, 50, 59, 61, 63, 64, 68, 76, 101, 106, 107, 119, 125, 128, 129, 131, 132, 133, 134, 137, 141, 143, 160, 163, 215, 216, 218, 228, 229, 230, 236
Aset (Isis), 33, 39, 42, 43, 59, 61, 63, 64, 76, 215, 216, 218, 228, 229, 230
Ashoka, 78
Asia, 60, 75
Asia Minor, 20
Asians, 144
Asoka, 78
Aspirant, 215
Assyrians, 20
Astral, 72, 155, 156, 226
Astral Plane, 72, 226
Atman, 123
Aton, 14, 29, 38, 44
Atonism, 44
Attis, 144
Augustus, 21, 49
Awareness, 52, 150
Ba (also see Soul), 69, 77
Being, 11, 18, 22, 28, 30, 34, 35, 37, 38, 55, 60, 78, 100, 119, 126, 127, 128, 152, 160, 163
Bhagavad Gita, 55, 91, 92, 114, 120, 143, 146
Bhakti Yoga See also Yoga of Divine Love, 8, 120
Bible, 116, 118, 140, 145, 215, 229
Big Bang, 22, 50
Bliss, 93
Book of Coming Forth By Day, 19, 109, 141, 145, 163, 164, 215, 227
Book of Enlightenment, 69
Book of the Dead, see also Rau Nu Prt M Hru, 33, 38, 227
Brahma, 120, 122, 143
Brahman, 64, 114, 115, 119, 120, 122, 143, 145
Buddha, 77, 108, 134, 143, 145, 151
Buddhism, 78
Buddhist, 78, 113, 122, 151
Carl Jung, 151

Catholic, 140, 229
Celibacy, 97
Chakras (see energy centers of the body), 110
Chanting, 64, 100, 133, 216, 218
China, 57, 75, 129
Christ, 108, 113, 140, 143, 145
Christ Consciousness, 113
Christhood, 143, 145
Christian Yoga, 216
Christianity, 52, 61, 79, 101, 121, 123, 143, 144, 156, 219, 229
Church, 140, 216, 229
Civilization, 57
Coffin Texts, 33
Company of gods and goddesses, 127, 128
Concentration, 215, 216
Conception, 76
Consciousness, 21, 49, 56, 60, 149, 151, 163, 215
Contentment (see also Hetep), 31, 93, 98
Coptic, 32, 226
Cosmic consciousness, 55
Cosmogony, 127
Cosmos, 75
Cow, 42
Creation, 18, 31, 33, 34, 38, 39, 40, 41, 42, 43, 44, 60, 73, 75, 76, 77, 78, 127, 131, 160, 161, 163, 217, 222, 225, 228
Crete, 75
Culture, 31, 221, 225, 231
Cymbals, 235, 237
Death, 216
December, 229
Denderah, 226
Detachment, 96, 164
Dharmakaya, 78
Diet, 220
Diodorus, 21, 23, 49, 51
Discipline, 4, 63, 66, 93, 96
Divine Consciousness, 48
Djehuti, 19, 24, 59, 61, 101, 128, 129, 136, 152, 215
Dream, 149, 154
Duat, 109, 155, 156
Durga, 143
Dynastic period, 19
Earth, 155
Edfu, 43, 65, 226
Egoism, 46, 216
Egyptian Book of Coming Forth By Day, 19, 106, 109, 136, 140, 145, 152, 226
Egyptian civilization, 61
Egyptian Mysteries, 52, 61, 221

211

Egyptian Physics, 228
Egyptian proverbs, 59, 223
Egyptian religion, 21, 26, 60, 144
Egyptian Yoga, 2, 4, 21, 41, 49, 52, 54, 55, 57, 58, 59, 60, 61, 72, 78, 103, 107, 125, 133, 134, 215, 216, 218, 219, 221, 222, 225, 226, 234, 235, 236, 237
Egyptian Yoga see also Kamitan Yoga, 41, 55, 57, 58, 59, 60, 61, 72, 78, 215, 216, 218, 219, 221, 222, 225, 226
Egyptologists, 46, 60, 80
Enlightenment, 2, 21, 31, 45, 49, 52, 53, 56, 60, 61, 69, 88, 91, 92, 94, 96, 97, 101, 107, 111, 123, 125, 138, 146, 161, 216, 217, 221, 222, 224, 231
Ennead, 128, 131, 132
Equanimity, 93, 97
Essenes, 144
Ethics, 65
Ethiopia, 16, 21, 22, 23, 49, 50, 51, 79
Ethiopian priests, 21, 49
Eucharist, 140, 143, 144, 156, 227
Eudoxus, 231
Evil, 143
Exercise, 2, 216, 218, 225
Eye of Heru, 48, 143, 147, 154
Eye of Ra, 131
Fear, 121, 216
Feuerstein, Georg, 71
Geb, 24, 39, 71, 72, 76, 77, 128, 141, 161, 226
Gnosis, 92
Gnostic, 52, 115, 116, 122, 145
Gnostic Christianity, 52, 115
Gnostics, 92
God, 1, 30, 31, 34, 48, 55, 59, 60, 61, 62, 64, 66, 67, 69, 75, 76, 81, 82, 83, 89, 91, 92, 94, 101, 103, 108, 109, 110, 111, 112, 113, 114, 115, 118, 119, 120, 121, 125, 126, 131, 133, 134, 136, 137, 138, 141, 143, 151, 152, 153, 155, 156, 160, 161, 164, 218, 223, 227, 228, 237
<u>Goddess</u>, 19, 29, 33, 34, 38, 42, 76, 164, 228, 234, 237, 238
Goddesses, 28, 34, 39, 41, 42, 73, 141, 225
Gods, 21, 28, 34, 39, 41, 49, 73, 124, 141, 218
Good, 93, 101, 143, 215
Good Association, 101, 215
Gospels, 145, 229
Great Truths, 28, 29, 30
Greece, 23, 51, 57, 144, 221, 231
Greek philosophy, 219
Greeks, 20, 144, 231
Grimaldi, 22, 50

Guru, 101, 114, 119
Haari, 218
Hapi, 141
Hatha Yoga, 71, 72
Hathor, 19, 24, 101, 128, 226, 228, 231
Health, 215, 217, 219
Hearing, 145
Heart, 29, 88, 110, 230
Heart (also see Ab, mind, conscience), 29, 88, 110, 230
Heaven, 155
Hekau, 69, 93, 100, 145, 154, 216, 237
Heliopolis, 231
Hermes, 24, 101
Hermes (see also Tehuti, Thoth), 24, 101
Hermetic, 114
Herodotus, 23, 51
Heru, 14, 18, 19, 22, 24, 33, 37, 39, 43, 50, 57, 59, 61, 65, 71, 76, 77, 101, 106, 109, 110, 124, 125, 128, 129, 131, 132, 133, 137, 143, 144, 145, 146, 152, 153, 155, 160, 161, 163, 164, 215, 216, 218, 226, 227, 228, 229, 230, 236, 237
Heru (see Horus), 14, 18, 19, 22, 24, 33, 37, 39, 43, 50, 57, 59, 61, 65, 71, 76, 77, 101, 106, 109, 110, 124, 125, 128, 129, 131, 132, 133, 137, 143, 144, 145, 146, 152, 153, 155, 160, 161, 163, 164, 215, 216, 218, 226, 227, 228, 229, 230, 236, 237
Hetep, 58, 147, 155, 159
Hetheru, 14, 19, 24, 33, 37, 42, 59, 61, 71, 89, 91, 101, 128, 131, 137, 141, 164, 231, 235
Hetheru (Hetheru, Hathor), 33, 37, 42, 59, 61, 71, 231
Het-Ka-Ptah, see also Men-nefer, Memphis, 38
Hieroglyphic Writing, language, 224
Hindu, 69, 80, 120, 121, 122, 131, 134, 145, 161, 163
Hindu mythology, 161
Hinduism, 79, 121
Horus, 18, 19, 24, 33, 43, 76, 77, 101, 236
Hymns of Amun, 22, 110, 163
Ice Age, 22, 50
Identification, 56, 141, 144, 152
Ignorance, 154
Illusion, 216
India, 23, 51, 55, 57, 60, 63, 64, 68, 71, 75, 77, 80, 91, 101, 106, 110, 114, 124, 125, 129, 134, 137, 145, 151, 218, 220, 221, 224, 237

Indian Yoga, 55, 221, 237
Indus, 57, 215, 218, 221
Indus Valley, 57, 221
Initiate, 220
Intellect, 103
Isis, 19, 24, 33, 42, 43, 63, 64, 76, 77, 101, 226, 227, 228, 236
Isis, See also Aset, 42, 43, 63, 64, 76, 77, 226, 227, 228
Islam, 219
Israel, 118, 121
Jesus, 101, 114, 120, 121, 123, 134, 140, 144, 145, 227, 229
Jesus Christ, 140, 227
Jewish, 11
Jnana Yoga, 63, 64, 106
John the Baptist, 101
Joshua, 121
Joy, 31
Judaism, 219
Justice, 97
Jyotirmayananda, Swami, 69
Ka, 38
Kabbalah, 219
Kali, 77, 143
Kali XE "Kali" position, 77
Kali Position, 77
Kamit, 11, 13, 16, 24, 26, 28, 31, 34, 35, 42, 43, 129, 215, 218
Kamit (Egypt), 11, 13, 16, 24, 26, 28, 31, 34, 35, 42, 43, 129, 215, 218
Kamitan, 28, 32, 33, 34, 37, 45, 56, 66, 72, 74, 76, 77, 78, 80, 220, 229, 231
Karma, 23, 51, 56, 91, 113, 216, 224
Keeping the balance, 97
Kemetic, 18, 24, 74, 76, 77, 78, 80, 134, 147, 162, 234, 236, 237
Khepra, 216
Kingdom, 23, 51, 61, 71, 92, 114, 115, 140, 145, 156, 229
Kingdom of Heaven, 92, 114, 115, 140, 145, 156, 229
Kingdom of Heaven of Christianity, 145
Kingdom of the Father, 145
Kmt, 129
KMT (Ancient Egypt). See also Kamit, 22, 50
Know thyself, 45
Know Thyself, 58
Knowledge, 92, 113, 122, 143
Koran, 116, 119
Krishna, 120, 134, 143, 145, 146, 230
Kundalini, 4, 23, 51, 56, 77, 110, 143
Kush, 16, 215, 218
Lake Victoria, 22, 50
Liberation, 113, 145

Life Force, 23, 29, 51, 59, 93, 103, 161, 225
Lingam-Yoni, 80
Listening, 29, 38, 63, 64, 66, 88, 92, 106, 126, 216
Lotus, 2, 59, 83, 147, 162, 163, 164, 165, 216
Love, 1, 2, 3, 8, 26, 51, 55, 56, 66, 81, 82, 100, 125, 133, 138, 151, 158, 160, 165, 215, 223
Lower Egypt, 19, 57, 59, 80
Maakheru, 28
Maat, 11, 24, 28, 29, 33, 56, 65, 88, 97, 106, 108, 125, 128, 136, 147, 155, 164, 215, 217, 218, 224, 228, 230, 231
MAAT, 19, 106, 131, 223, 224
Maati, 88, 107
MAATI, 224
Mahabharata, 55
Manetho, 23, 51
Mantras, 69
Matter, 228
Matthew, 113, 118, 120, 123, 140
Meditating, 63
Meditation, 2, 29, 30, 42, 55, 56, 64, 65, 68, 70, 88, 103, 106, 125, 146, 149, 150, 215, 216, 218, 220, 223, 225, 237
Mediterranean, 75
Mehurt, 42
Memphis, 231
Memphite Theology, 19, 33, 40, 42, 163
Meskhenet, 91
Metaphysics, 228
Metu Neter, 59, 61
Middle East, 134, 219
Min, 131, 141, 226
Mind, 93, 97, 110
Mindfulness, 110, 151
Mookerjee, Ajit, 75
Moon, 22, 50
Morals, 231
Moses, 121
Music, 98, 133, 134, 236, 237
Mysteries, 42, 52, 61, 140, 143, 160, 161, 163, 229
Mysticism, 2, 60, 66, 163, 221, 226, 227, 228, 231
Mythology, 21, 49, 60, 114, 147, 226
Nature, 32, 101, 150, 160, 161, 215, 216
Neberdjer, 28, 222
Nebertcher, 108, 128, 136
Nebthet, 39
Nefer, 58, 101, 136, 235, 237
Nefertari, Queen, 71
Nefertem, 40
Nehast, 48
Neolithic, 18

Nephthys, 24
Net, goddess, 33, 42
Neter, 1, 11, 12, 13, 21, 26, 28, 29, 31, 32, 33, 34, 35, 37, 38, 44, 48, 55, 59, 60, 61, 128, 136, 154, 216, 218
Neterian, 28, 29, 38, 42, 46, 48
Neterianism, 29, 34, 79
Neters, 60, 62, 75
Neteru, 28, 30, 32, 34, 35, 37, 46, 48, 71, 75, 128, 218, 225, 236, 237
Netherworld, 1, 72, 109, 145, 155
New Kingdom, 41, 44, 71
Nile River, 31
Nirvana, 115
Non-violence, 217

North East Africa . See also Egypt Ethiopia Cush, 13

Nubia, 11, 16, 22, 23, 51
Nubian, 16, 20
Nubians, 31
Nun, 37, 73
Nun (primeval waters-unformed matter), 37, 73, 141
Nun (See also Nu), 37, 73
Nut, 24, 39, 72, 73, 76, 77, 88, 128, 161, 226
Om, 216, 218, 236, 237
Opposites, 19
Orion Star Constellation, 229
Osiris, 8, 14, 24, 33, 42, 43, 76, 77, 226, 227, 236, 237
Pa Neter, 28, 136, 216, 218
Paleolithic, 18
Papyrus of Any, 33
Patanjali, 55, 70
Paut, 71
Peace (see also Hetep), 31, 53, 93, 100, 138, 147, 159
Pert Em Heru, See also Book of the Dead, 59, 215, 227
phallus, 131
Phallus, 80
Philae, 14, 68, 160, 226
Philosophy, 2, 3, 4, 8, 11, 12, 13, 20, 21, 24, 30, 33, 49, 51, 52, 57, 58, 59, 61, 69, 75, 107, 108, 114, 125, 143, 147, 150, 151, 215, 216, 217, 221, 222, 223, 227, 228, 230
Phrygians, 140
Plato, 231
Plutarch, 144, 161, 231
Priests and Priestesses, 35, 221
Ptah, 14, 19, 24, 29, 33, 38, 40, 163, 216, 218, 228
PTAH, 228

Ptahotep, 19, 33
Purusha, 120, 122
Pyramid Texts, 14, 19, 23, 109, 141, 143, 144, 154, 155
Pythagoras, 231
Ra, 14, 18, 24, 29, 33, 38, 39, 41, 46, 69, 73, 91, 127, 128, 131, 141, 155, 156, 163, 164, 215, 216, 218, 225, 235, 237
Race, 215
Rama, 134, 143
Ray, Sudhansu Kumar, 80
Reality, 75
Realization, 30, 146
Realm of Light, 18
Red, 80
Reflecting, 63
Reflection, 64, 88, 106
Religion, 4, 11, 12, 13, 18, 21, 26, 32, 48, 49, 59, 60, 61, 106, 140, 215, 216, 226, 230, 231, 236
Renunciation, 113
Resurrection, 19, 33, 71, 126, 132, 133, 138, 160, 215, 225, 227, 229, 230
Righteous action, 29
Righteousness, 65
Ritual, 29, 33, 56, 66
Ritualism, 88
Rituals, 156
Roman, 33, 52, 140
Roman Catholic, 52, 140
Romans, 20
Rome, 144, 231
Saa (spiritual understanding faculty), 141
Sages, 52, 61, 97, 101, 123, 152, 164, 222, 226, 227, 230
Saints, 97, 123, 152, 227
Saints and Sages, 97
Sais, 231
Salvation, 59, 60, 62, 112
Salvation . See also resurrection, 59, 60, 62, 112
Salvation, See also resurrection, 59, 60, 62
Samadhi (see also KiaSatori), 114
Samkhya, 113
Samothracians, 140
Sanskrit, 57
Saraswati, 143
Satsanga, 101, 140
Sebai, 44
Seers, 52
Sekhem, 29, 152
Sekhmet, 19, 141, 163
Self (see Ba, soul, Spirit, Universal, Ba, Neter, Heru)., 29, 46, 56, 57, 58, 59, 60, 61, 62, 63, 64, 65, 72, 76, 216, 217, 221, 224, 226

Self (seeBasoulSpiritUniversal BaNeterHorus)., 2, 29, 56, 57, 58, 59, 60, 61, 62, 63, 64, 65, 72, 76, 89, 91, 92, 93, 96, 97, 100, 103, 108, 109, 110, 111, 112, 113, 114, 115, 119, 120, 122, 123, 125, 126, 137, 138, 140, 143, 152, 153, 154, 155, 156, 158, 161, 164, 165, 216, 217
Self-realization, 92
Sema, 3, 4, 28, 29, 57, 58, 59, 60, 63, 65, 66, 68, 71, 75, 101, 217
Sema XE "Sema" Paut, see also Egyptian Yoga, 29, 71
Semite, 22, 50
Serpent, 18, 55, 56, 68, 110, 143, 216, 218
Serpent Power, 18, 55, 56, 68, 110, 143, 216, 218
Serpent Power (see also Kundalini and Buto), 18, 55, 56, 68, 110, 143, 216, 218
Serpent Power see also Kundalini Yoga, 55, 56, 68, 216, 218
Set, 24, 28, 39, 46, 47, 57, 59, 61, 106, 109, 110, 128, 129, 131, 132, 133, 143, 152, 155, 216, 217
Seti I, 65, 68, 70
Seven, 215
Sex, 22, 50, 159, 226
Sexuality, 216
Shakti (see also Kundalini), 77, 161
Shetaut Neter, 31, 33, 38, 45, 55, 60, 226
Shetaut Neter See also Egyptian Religion, 11, 12, 13, 21, 26, 31, 33, 38, 45, 49, 55, 60, 120, 121, 226
Shiva, 77, 78, 114, 131, 161
Shiva XE "Shiva" and Shakti, 77
Shu (air and space), 39, 73, 128, 141, 160
Silence, 217
Sin, 89
Sirius, 19, 228
Sky, 18
Sleep, 149
Sma, 29, 57, 58
Smai, 28, 55, 57, 58, 59, 62, 72
Smai Tawi, 55, 57, 58, 62, 72
Solon, 231
Soul, 21, 49, 59, 62, 82, 93, 110, 134, 160, 161, 216
Sphinx, 11, 18, 61
Spinal twist, 73

Spirit, 11, 18, 28, 37, 59, 69, 160, 161, 164
Spiritual discipline, 220
Spiritual preceptor, 101
Study, 29, 60, 92, 116, 215, 216
Sublimation, 159, 226
Sudan, 13, 16
Sufism, 123
Sumer, 57
Sun, 153
Sundisk, 69, 72
Supreme Being, 11, 22, 28, 30, 34, 35, 37, 38, 39, 40, 41, 42, 43, 44, 50, 55, 60, 78, 97, 100, 108, 109, 127, 128, 137, 143, 152, 160, 161, 222, 228
Svetasvatara Upanishad, 115, 119
Swami, 4, 69
Swami Jyotirmayananda, 4, 69
Syria, 129
Tantra, 75, 131, 159, 226
Tantra Yoga, 68, 75, 159, 226
Tantric Yoga, 51, 55, 56
Tanzania, 22, 50
Tao, 108
Taoism, 219
Tawi, 28, 55, 57, 72
Tefnut, 39, 128
Tefnut (moisture), 39, 128
Tem, 128, 163
Temple of Aset, 43, 63, 64, 68, 215
Thales, 231
The Absolute, 222
The God, 19, 39, 42, 136, 218, 225
The Gods, 19, 39, 218, 225
The Hymns of Amun, 22, 50
The Pyramid Texts, 23, 51, 144
The Self, 82, 83, 110, 123, 127, 159
The way, 122
Theban Theology, 19, 33
Thebes, 14, 68, 163, 222, 225
Themis, 24
Third Eye, 143
Thoughts (see also Mind), 65
Tibetan Buddhism, 145
Time, 215
Tomb, 70, 71, 225
Tomb of Seti I, 70, 225, 237
Tradition, 29, 38, 39, 40, 41, 42, 43, 44
Triad, 160, 163, 222
Trilinga, 78
Trinity, 14, 19, 40, 41, 43, 125, 127, 132, 163, 218, 222, 227, 237
Truth, 30, 97, 119, 155, 217

Unas, 109, 143, 144, 147, 154, 155
Understanding, 125, 215
Universal Consciousness, 60, 226
Upanishads, 114, 227
Upper Egypt, 57, 59, 80
Ur, 39
Uraeus, 56
Vedanta, 52, 60, 61, 63, 64, 69, 106, 108, 110, 114, 134, 143, 151
Vedic, 221
Vegetarianism, 215
Veil, 107
Virtues, 215
Vishnu, 143
Waking, 149, 154
Waset, 29, 38, 68, 222
Western Culture, 46, 217
Will, 103
Wisdom, 29, 30, 33, 55, 56, 63, 64, 68, 215, 217, 222, 225
Wisdom (also see Djehuti), 1, 2, 19, 29, 30, 33, 55, 56, 63, 64, 65, 66, 68, 75, 81, 82, 83, 103, 107, 125, 154, 215, 217
Wisdom (also see Djehuti, Aset), 29, 30, 33, 55, 56, 63, 64, 68, 215, 217, 222, 225
Wisdom teachings, 63, 64
Words of power, 69
Yoga, 2, 3, 4, 8, 11, 12, 21, 49, 51, 52, 55, 56, 57, 58, 59, 60, 61, 63, 64, 68, 71, 72, 75, 78, 82, 88, 92, 97, 102, 103, 106, 109, 110, 111, 113, 114, 115, 120, 122, 123, 125, 133, 134, 137, 138, 140, 146, 150, 151, 158, 159, 215, 216, 217, 218, 219, 220, 221, 224, 225, 227, 228, 230, 234, 235, 236, 237
Yoga Exercise, 216, 218
Yoga of Action, 56
Yoga of Devotion (see Yoga of Divine Love), 51, 55, 56, 82, 102, 120, 125, 133
Yoga of Divine Love (see Yoga of Devotion), 56, 97
Yoga of Meditation, 51, 55, 56
Yoga of Selfless Action. See also Yoga of Righteous, 51, 55, 56
Yoga of Wisdom, 63
Yoga of Wisdom (see also Jnana Yoga), 51, 55, 56, 63, 65, 66, 68, 75, 92, 106, 115, 120, 125, 146
Yoga Sutra, 55
Yoga Vasistha, 114, 115, 120, 123
Yogic, 55, 71, 93, 103, 137

The Path of Divine Love

Other Books From C M Books

P.O.Box 570459
Miami, Florida, 33257
(305) 378-6253 Fax: (305) 378-6253

This book is part of a series on the study and practice of Ancient Egyptian Yoga and Mystical Spirituality based on the writings of Dr. Muata Abhaya Ashby. They are also part of the Egyptian Yoga Course provided by the Sema Institute of Yoga. Below you will find a listing of the other books in this series. For more information send for the Egyptian Yoga Book-Audio-Video Catalog or the Egyptian Yoga Course Catalog.

Now you can study the teachings of Egyptian and Indian Yoga wisdom and Spirituality with the Egyptian Yoga Mystical Spirituality Series. The Egyptian Yoga Series takes you through the Initiation process and lead you to understand the mysteries of the soul and the Divine and to attain the highest goal of life: ENLIGHTENMENT. The *Egyptian Yoga Series*, takes you on an in depth study of Ancient Egyptian mythology and their inner mystical meaning. Each Book is prepared for the serious student of the mystical sciences and provides a study of the teachings along with exercises, assignments and projects to make the teachings understood and effective in real life. The Series is part of the Egyptian Yoga course but may be purchased even if you are not taking the course. The series is ideal for study groups.

Prices subject to change.

1. EGYPTIAN YOGA: THE PHILOSOPHY OF ENLIGHTENMENT An original, fully illustrated work, including hieroglyphs, detailing the meaning of the Egyptian mysteries, tantric yoga, psycho-spiritual and physical exercises. Egyptian Yoga is a guide to the practice of the highest spiritual philosophy which leads to absolute freedom from human misery and to immortality. It is well known by scholars that Egyptian philosophy is the basis of Western and Middle Eastern religious philosophies such as *Christianity, Islam, Judaism,* the *Kabala,* and Greek philosophy, but what about Indian philosophy, Yoga and Taoism? What were the original teachings? How can they be practiced today? What is the source of pain and suffering in the world and what is the solution? Discover the deepest mysteries of the mind and universe within and outside of your self. 8.5" X 11" ISBN: 1-884564-01-1 Soft $19.95

2. EGYPTIAN YOGA II: The Supreme Wisdom of Enlightenment by Dr. Muata Ashby ISBN 1-884564-39-9 $23.95 U.S. In this long awaited sequel to *Egyptian Yoga: The Philosophy of Enlightenment* you will take a fascinating and enlightening journey back in time and discover the teachings which constituted the epitome of Ancient Egyptian spiritual wisdom. What are the disciplines which lead to the fulfillment of all desires? Delve into the three states of consciousness (waking, dream and deep sleep) and the fourth state which transcends them all, Neberdjer, "The Absolute." These teachings of the city of Waset (Thebes) were the crowning achievement of the Sages of Ancient Egypt. They establish the standard mystical keys for understanding the profound mystical symbolism of the Triad of human consciousness.

3. THE KEMETIC DIET: GUIDE TO HEALTH, DIET AND FASTING Health issues have always been important to human beings since the beginning of time. The earliest records of history show that the art of healing was held in high esteem since the time of Ancient Egypt. In the early 20th century, medical doctors had almost attained the status of sainthood by the promotion of the idea that they alone were "scientists" while other healing modalities and traditional healers who did not follow the "scientific method' were nothing but superstitious, ignorant charlatans who at best would take the money of their clients and at worst kill them with the unscientific "snake oils" and "irrational theories". In the late 20th century, the failure of the modern medical establishment's ability to lead the general public to good health, promoted the move by

many in society towards "alternative medicine". Alternative medicine disciplines are those healing modalities which do not adhere to the philosophy of allopathic medicine. Allopathic medicine is what medical doctors practice by an large. It is the theory that disease is caused by agencies outside the body such as bacteria, viruses or physical means which affect the body. These can therefore be treated by medicines and therapies The natural healing method began in the absence of extensive technologies with the idea that all the answers for health may be found in nature or rather, the deviation from nature. Therefore, the health of the body can be restored by correcting the aberration and thereby restoring balance. This is the area that will be covered in this volume. Allopathic techniques have their place in the art of healing. However, we should not forget that the body is a grand achievement of the spirit and built into it is the capacity to maintain itself and heal itself. Ashby, Muata ISBN: 1-884564-49-6 $28.95

4. INITIATION INTO EGYPTIAN YOGA Shedy: Spiritual discipline or program, to go deeply into the mysteries, to study the mystery teachings and literature profoundly, to penetrate the mysteries. You will learn about the mysteries of initiation into the teachings and practice of Yoga and how to become an Initiate of the mystical sciences. This insightful manual is the first in a series which introduces you to the goals of daily spiritual and yoga practices: Meditation, Diet, Words of Power and the ancient wisdom teachings. 8.5" X 11" ISBN 1-884564-02-X   Soft Cover $24.95 U.S.

5. *THE AFRICAN ORIGINS OF CIVILIZATION, MYSTICAL RELIGION AND YOGA PHILOSOPHY* HARD COVER EDITION ISBN: 1-884564-50-X $80.00 U.S.   81/2" X 11"   Part 1, Part 2, Part 3 in one volume 683 Pages Hard Cover First Edition Three volumes in one. Over the past several years I have been asked to put together in one volume the most important evidences showing the correlations and common teachings between Kamitan (Ancient Egyptian) culture and religion and that of India. The questions of the history of Ancient Egypt, and the latest archeological evidences showing civilization and culture in Ancient Egypt and its spread to other countries, has intrigued many scholars as well as mystics over the years. Also, the possibility that Ancient Egyptian Priests and Priestesses migrated to Greece, India and other countries to carry on the traditions of the Ancient Egyptian Mysteries, has been speculated over the years as well. In chapter 1 of the book *Egyptian Yoga The Philosophy of Enlightenment,* 1995, I first introduced the deepest comparison between Ancient Egypt and India that had been brought forth up to that time. Now, in the year 2001 this new book, *THE AFRICAN ORIGINS OF CIVILIZATION, MYSTICAL RELIGION AND YOGA PHILOSOPHY,* more fully explores the motifs, symbols and philosophical correlations between Ancient Egyptian and Indian mysticism and clearly shows not only that Ancient Egypt and India were connected culturally but also spiritually. How does this knowledge help the spiritual aspirant? This discovery has great importance for the Yogis and mystics who follow the philosophy of Ancient Egypt and the mysticism of India. It means that India has a longer history and heritage than was previously understood. It shows that the mysteries of Ancient Egypt were essentially a yoga tradition which did not die but rather developed into the modern day systems of Yoga technology of India. It further shows that African culture developed Yoga Mysticism earlier than any other civilization in history. All of this expands our understanding of the unity of culture and the deep legacy of Yoga, which stretches into the distant past, beyond the Indus Valley civilization, the earliest known high culture in India as well as the Vedic tradition of Aryan culture. Therefore, Yoga culture and mysticism is the oldest known tradition of spiritual development and Indian mysticism is an extension of the Ancient Egyptian mysticism. By understanding the legacy which Ancient Egypt gave to India the mysticism of India is better understood and by comprehending the heritage of Indian Yoga, which is rooted in Ancient Egypt the Mysticism of Ancient Egypt is also better understood. This expanded understanding allows us to prove the underlying kinship of humanity, through the common symbols, motifs and philosophies which are not disparate and confusing teachings but in reality expressions of the same study of truth through metaphysics and mystical realization of Self. (HARD COVER)

6. AFRICAN ORIGINS BOOK 1 PART 1 African Origins of African Civilization, Religion, Yoga Mysticism and Ethics Philosophy-<u>Soft Cover</u> $24.95 ISBN: 1-884564-55-0

7. AFRICAN ORIGINS BOOK 2 PART 2 African Origins of Western Civilization, Religion and Philosophy(Soft) -<u>Soft Cover</u> $24.95 ISBN: 1-884564-56-9

8. EGYPT AND INDIA (AFRICAN ORIGINS BOOK 3 PART 3) African Origins of Eastern Civilization, Religion, Yoga Mysticism and Philosophy-<u>Soft Cover</u> $29.95 (Soft) ISBN: 1-884564-57-7

The Path of Divine Love

9. **THE MYSTERIES OF ISIS: The Ancient Egyptian Philosophy of Self-Realization** - There are several paths to discover the Divine and the mysteries of the higher Self. This volume details the mystery teachings of the goddess Aset (Isis) from Ancient Egypt- the path of wisdom. It includes the teachings of her temple and the disciplines that are enjoined for the initiates of the temple of Aset as they were given in ancient times. Also, this book includes the teachings of the main myths of Aset that lead a human being to spiritual enlightenment and immortality. Through the study of ancient myth and the illumination of initiatic understanding the idea of God is expanded from the mythological comprehension to the metaphysical. Then this metaphysical understanding is related to you, the student, so as to begin understanding your true divine nature. ISBN 1-884564-24-0 $22.99

10. EGYPTIAN PROVERBS: TEMT TCHAAS *Temt Tchaas* means: collection of ——Ancient Egyptian Proverbs How to live according to MAAT Philosophy. Beginning Meditation. All proverbs are indexed for easy searches. For the first time in one volume, ——Ancient Egyptian Proverbs, wisdom teachings and meditations, fully illustrated with hieroglyphic text and symbols. EGYPTIAN PROVERBS is a unique collection of knowledge and wisdom which you can put into practice today and transform your life. 5.5"x 8.5" $14.95 U.S   ISBN: 1-884564-00-3

11. THE PATH OF DIVINE LOVE The Process of Mystical Transformation and The Path of Divine Love This Volume focuses on the ancient wisdom teachings of "Neter Merri" –the Ancient Egyptian philosophy of Divine Love and how to use them in a scientific process for self-transformation. Love is one of the most powerful human emotions. It is also the source of Divine feeling that unifies God and the individual human being. When love is fragmented and diminished by egoism the Divine connection is lost. The Ancient tradition of Neter Merri leads human beings back to their Divine connection, allowing them to discover their innate glorious self that is actually Divine and immortal. This volume will detail the process of transformation from ordinary consciousness to cosmic consciousness through the integrated practice of the teachings and the path of Devotional Love toward the Divine. 5.5"x 8.5" ISBN 1-884564-11-9 $22.99

12. INTRODUCTION TO MAAT PHILOSOPHY: Spiritual Enlightenment Through the Path of Virtue Known as Karma Yoga in India, the teachings of MAAT for living virtuously and with orderly wisdom are explained and the student is to begin practicing the precepts of Maat in daily life so as to promote the process of purification of the heart in preparation for the judgment of the soul. This judgment will be understood not as an event that will occur at the time of death but as an event that occurs continuously, at every moment in the life of the individual. The student will learn how to become allied with the forces of the Higher Self and to thereby begin cleansing the mind (heart) of impurities so as to attain a higher vision of reality. ISBN 1-884564-20-8 $22.99

13. MEDITATION The Ancient Egyptian Path to Enlightenment   Many people do not know about the rich history of meditation practice in Ancient Egypt. This volume outlines the theory of meditation and presents the Ancient Egyptian Hieroglyphic text which give instruction as to the nature of the mind and its three modes of expression. It also presents the texts which give instruction on the practice of meditation for spiritual Enlightenment and unity with the Divine. This volume allows the reader to begin practicing meditation by explaining, in easy to understand terms, the simplest form of meditation and working up to the most advanced form which was practiced in ancient times and which is still practiced by yogis around the world in modern times. ISBN 1-884564-27-7 $24.99

14. THE GLORIOUS LIGHT MEDITATION TECHNIQUE OF ANCIENT EGYPT ISBN: 1-884564-15-1$14.95 (PB) New for the year 2000. This volume is based on the earliest known instruction in history given for the practice of formal meditation. Discovered by Dr. Muata Ashby, it is inscribed on the walls of the Tomb of Seti I in Thebes Egypt. This volume details the philosophy and practice of this unique system of meditation originated in Ancient Egypt and the earliest practice of meditation known in the world which occurred in the most advanced African Culture.

15. THE SERPENT POWER: The Ancient Egyptian Mystical Wisdom of the Inner Life Force.   This Volume specifically deals with the latent life Force energy of the universe and in the human body, its control and sublimation. How to develop the Life Force energy of the subtle body. This Volume will

introduce the esoteric wisdom of the science of how virtuous living acts in a subtle and mysterious way to cleanse the latent psychic energy conduits and vortices of the spiritual body. ISBN 1-884564-19-4 $22.95

16. EGYPTIAN YOGA MEDITATION IN MOTION Thef Neteru: *The Movement of The Gods and Goddesses* Discover the physical postures and exercises practiced thousands of years ago in Ancient Egypt which are today known as Yoga exercises. This work is based on the pictures and teachings from the Creation story of Ra, The Asarian Resurrection Myth and the carvings and reliefs from various Temples in Ancient Egypt 8.5" X 11" ISBN 1-884564-10-0 Soft Cover $18.99   Exercise video $21.99

17. EGYPTIAN TANTRA YOGA: The Art of Sex Sublimation and Universal Consciousness This Volume will expand on the male and female principles within the human body and in the universe and further detail the sublimation of sexual energy into spiritual energy. The student will study the deities Min and Hathor, Asar and Aset, Geb and Nut and discover the mystical implications for a practical spiritual discipline. This Volume will also focus on the Tantric aspects of Ancient Egyptian and Indian mysticism, the purpose of sex and the mystical teachings of sexual sublimation which lead to self-knowledge and Enlightenment. 5.5"x 8.5"   ISBN 1-884564-03-8 $24.95

18. ASARIAN RELIGION: RESURRECTING OSIRIS The path of Mystical Awakening and the Keys to Immortality NEW REVISED AND EXPANDED EDITION!   The Ancient Sages created stories based on human and superhuman beings whose struggles, aspirations, needs and desires ultimately lead them to discover their true Self. The myth of Aset, Asar and Heru is no exception in this area. While there is no one source where the entire story may be found, pieces of it are inscribed in various ancient Temples walls, tombs, steles and papyri. For the first time available, the complete myth of Asar, Aset and Heru has been compiled from original Ancient Egyptian, Greek and Coptic Texts. This epic myth has been richly illustrated with reliefs from the Temple of Heru at Edfu, the Temple of Aset at Philae, the Temple of Asar at Abydos, the Temple of Hathor at Denderah and various papyri, inscriptions and reliefs.   Discover the myth which inspired the teachings of the *Shetaut Neter* (Egyptian Mystery System - Egyptian Yoga) and the Egyptian Book of Coming Forth By Day. Also, discover the three levels of Ancient Egyptian Religion, how to understand the mysteries of the Duat or Astral World and how to discover the abode of the Supreme in the Amenta, *The Other World*   The ancient religion of Asar, Aset and Heru, if properly understood, contains all of the elements necessary to lead the sincere aspirant to attain immortality through inner self-discovery. This volume presents the entire myth and explores the main mystical themes and rituals associated with the myth for understating human existence, creation and the way to achieve spiritual emancipation - *Resurrection.* The Asarian myth is so powerful that it influenced and is still having an effect on the major world religions. Discover the origins and mystical meaning of the Christian Trinity, the Eucharist ritual and the ancient origin of the birthday of Jesus Christ. Soft Cover ISBN: 1-884564-27-5 $24.95

19. THE EGYPTIAN BOOK OF THE DEAD MYSTICISM OF THE PERT EM HERU $26.95   ISBN# 1-884564-28-3 Size: 8½" X 11" I Know myself, I know myself, I am One With God!–From the Pert Em Heru "The Ru Pert em Heru" or "Ancient Egyptian Book of The Dead," or "Book of Coming Forth By Day" as it is more popularly known, has fascinated the world since the successful translation of Ancient Egyptian hieroglyphic scripture over 150 years ago. The astonishing writings in it reveal that the Ancient Egyptians believed in life after death and in an ultimate destiny to discover the Divine. The elegance and aesthetic beauty of the hieroglyphic text itself has inspired many see it as an art form in and of itself. But is there more to it than that? Did the Ancient Egyptian wisdom contain more than just aphorisms and hopes of eternal life beyond death? In this volume Dr. Muata Ashby, the author of over 25 books on Ancient Egyptian Yoga Philosophy has produced a new translation of the original texts which uncovers a mystical teaching underlying the sayings and rituals instituted by the Ancient Egyptian Sages and Saints. "Once the philosophy of Ancient Egypt is understood as a mystical tradition instead of as a religion or primitive mythology, it reveals its secrets which if practiced today will lead anyone to discover the glory of spiritual self-discovery. The Pert em Heru is in every way comparable to the Indian Upanishads or the Tibetan Book of the Dead." Muata Abhaya Ashby

The Path of Divine Love

20. **ANUNIAN THEOLOGY THE MYSTERIES OF RA** The Philosophy of Anu and The Mystical Teachings of The Ancient Egyptian Creation Myth Discover the mystical teachings contained in the Creation Myth and the gods and goddesses who brought creation and human beings into existence. The Creation Myth holds the key to understanding the universe and for attaining spiritual Enlightenment. ISBN: 1-884564-38-0 40 pages $14.95

21. **MYSTERIES OF MIND AND MEMPHITE THEOLOGY** Mysticism of Ptah, Egyptian Physics and Yoga Metaphysics and the Hidden properties of Matter This Volume will go deeper into the philosophy of God as creation and will explore the concepts of modern science and how they correlate with ancient teachings. This Volume will lay the ground work for the understanding of the philosophy of universal consciousness and the initiatic/yogic insight into who or what is God? ISBN 1-884564-07-0 $21.95

22. **THE GODDESS AND THE EGYPTIAN MYSTERIESTHE PATH OF THE GODDESS THE GODDESS PATH** The Secret Forms of the Goddess and the Rituals of Resurrection The Supreme Being may be worshipped as father or as mother. *Ushet Rekhat* or *Mother Worship*, is the spiritual process of worshipping the Divine in the form of the Divine Goddess. It celebrates the most important forms of the Goddess including *Nathor, Maat, Aset, Arat, Amentet and Hathor* and explores their mystical meaning as well as the rising of *Sirius,* the star of Aset (Aset) and the new birth of Hor (Heru). The end of the year is a time of reckoning, reflection and engendering a new or renewed positive movement toward attaining spiritual Enlightenment. The Mother Worship devotional meditation ritual, performed on five days during the month of December and on New Year's Eve, is based on the Ushet Rekhit. During the ceremony, the cosmic forces, symbolized by Sirius - and the constellation of Orion ---, are harnessed through the understanding and devotional attitude of the participant. This propitiation draws the light of wisdom and health to all those who share in the ritual, leading to prosperity and wisdom. $14.95 ISBN 1-884564-18-6

23. *THE MYSTICAL JOURNEY FROM JESUS TO CHRIST* $24.95   ISBN# 1-884564-05-4 size: 8½" X 11" Discover the ancient Egyptian origins of Christianity before the Catholic Church and learn the mystical teachings given by Jesus to assist all humanity in becoming Christlike. Discover the secret meaning of the Gospels that were discovered in Egypt. Also discover how and why so many Christian churches came into being. Discover that the Bible still holds the keys to mystical realization even though its original writings were changed by the church. Discover how to practice the original teachings of Christianity which leads to the Kingdom of Heaven.

24. **THE STORY OF ASAR, ASET AND HERU: An Ancient Egyptian Legend (For Children)**   Now for the first time, the most ancient myth of Ancient Egypt comes alive for children. Inspired by the books *The Asarian Resurrection: The Ancient Egyptian Bible* and *The Mystical Teachings of The Asarian Resurrection, The Story of Asar, Aset and Heru* is an easy to understand and thrilling tale which inspired the children of Ancient Egypt to aspire to greatness and righteousness. If you and your child have enjoyed stories like *The Lion King* and *Star Wars you* will love *The Story of Asar, Aset and Heru.* Also, if you know the story of Jesus and Krishna you will discover than Ancient Egypt had a similar myth and that this myth carries important spiritual teachings for living a fruitful and fulfilling life. This book may be used along with *The Parents Guide To The Asarian Resurrection Myth: How to Teach Yourself and Your Child the Principles of Universal Mystical Religion.* The guide provides some background to the Asarian Resurrection myth and it also gives insight into the mystical teachings contained in it which you may introduce to your child. It is designed for parents who wish to grow spiritually with their children and it serves as an introduction for those who would like to study the Asarian Resurrection Myth in depth and to practice its teachings. 41 pages   8.5" X 11"   ISBN: 1-884564-31-3 $12.95

25. THE PARENTS GUIDE TO THE AUSARIAN RESURRECTION MYTH: How to Teach Yourself and Your Child the Principles of Universal Mystical Religion.   This insightful manual brings for the timeless wisdom of the ancient through the Ancient Egyptian myth of Asar, Aset and Heru and the mystical teachings contained in it for parents who want to guide their children to understand and practice the teachings of mystical spirituality. This manual may be used with the children's storybook *The Story of Asar, Aset and Heru* by Dr. Muata Abhaya Ashby. 5.5"x 8.5"   ISBN: 1-884564-30-5 $14.95

26. HEALING THE CRIMINAL HEART BOOK 1 Introduction to Maat Philosophy, Yoga and Spiritual Redemption Through the Path of Virtue Who is a criminal? Is there such a thing as a criminal heart? What is the source of evil and sinfulness and is there any way to rise above it? Is there redemption for those who have committed sins, even the worst crimes? Ancient Egyptian mystical psychology holds important answers to these questions. Over ten thousand years ago mystical psychologists, the Sages of Ancient Egypt, studied and charted the human mind and spirit and laid out a path which will lead to spiritual redemption, prosperity and Enlightenment. This introductory volume brings forth the teachings of the Asarian Resurrection, the most important myth of Ancient Egypt, with relation to the faults of human existence: anger, hatred, greed, lust, animosity, discontent, ignorance, egoism jealousy, bitterness, and a myriad of psycho-spiritual ailments which keep a human being in a state of negativity and adversity. 5.5"x 8.5" ISBN: 1-884564-17-8 $15.95

27. THEATER & DRAMA OF THE ANCIENT EGYPTIAN MYSTERIES: Featuring the Ancient Egyptian stage play-"The Enlightenment of Hathor' Based on an Ancient Egyptian Drama, The original Theater - Mysticism of the Temple of Hetheru $14.95   By Dr. Muata Ashby

28. GUIDE TO PRINT ON DEMAND: SELF-PUBLISH FOR PROFIT, SPIRITUAL FULFILLMENT AND SERVICE TO HUMANITY Everyone asks us how we produced so many books in such a short time. Here are the secrets to writing and producing books that uplift humanity and how to get them printed for a fraction of the regular cost. Anyone can become an author even if they have limited funds. All that is necessary is the willingness to learn how the printing and book business work and the desire to follow the special instructions given here for preparing your manuscript format. Then you take your work directly to the non-traditional companies who can produce your books for less than the traditional book printer can. ISBN: 1-884564-40-2 $16.95 U. S.

29. Egyptian Mysteries: Vol. 1, Shetaut Neter ISBN: 1-884564-41-0 $19.99 What are the Mysteries? For thousands of years the spiritual tradition of Ancient Egypt, S*hetaut Neter,* "The Egyptian Mysteries," "The Secret Teachings," have fascinated, tantalized and amazed the world. At one time exalted and recognized as the highest culture of the world, by Africans, Europeans, Asiatics, Hindus, Buddhists and other cultures of the ancient world, in time it was shunned by the emerging orthodox world religions. Its temples desecrated, its philosophy maligned, its tradition spurned, its philosophy dormant in the mystical *Medu Neter*, the mysterious hieroglyphic texts which hold the secret symbolic meaning that has scarcely been discerned up to now. What are the secrets of *Nehast* {spiritual awakening and emancipation, resurrection}. More than just a literal translation, this volume is for awakening to the secret code *Shetitu* of the teaching which was not deciphered by Egyptologists, nor could be understood by ordinary spiritualists. This book is a reinstatement of the original science made available for our times, to the reincarnated followers of Ancient Egyptian culture and the prospect of spiritual freedom to break the bonds of *Khemn,* "ignorance," and slavery to evil forces: *Såaa* .

30. EGYPTIAN MYSTERIES VOL 2: Dictionary of Gods and Goddesses ISBN: 1-884564-23-2 $21.95 This book is about the mystery of neteru, the gods and goddesses of Ancient Egypt (Kamit, Kemet). Neteru means "Gods and Goddesses." But the Neterian teaching of Neteru represents more than the usual limited modern day concept of "divinities" or "spirits." The Neteru of Kamit are also metaphors, cosmic principles and vehicles for the enlightening teachings of Shetaut Neter (Ancient Egyptian-African Religion). Actually they are the elements for one of the most advanced systems of spirituality ever conceived in human history. Understanding the concept of neteru provides a firm basis for spiritual evolution and the pathway for viable culture, peace on earth and a healthy human society. Why is it important to have gods and goddesses in our lives? In order for spiritual evolution to be possible, once a human being has accepted that there is existence after death and there is a transcendental being who exists beyond time and space knowledge, human beings need a connection to that which transcends the ordinary experience of human life in time and space and a means to understand the transcendental reality beyond the mundane reality.

31. EGYPTIAN MYSTERIES VOL. 3 The Priests and Priestesses of Ancient Egypt ISBN: 1-884564-53-4 $22.95 This volume details the path of Neterian priesthood, the joys, challenges and rewards of advanced

The Path of Divine Love

Neterian life, the teachings that allowed the priests and priestesses to manage the most long lived civilization in human history and how that path can be adopted today; for those who want to tread the path of the Clergy of Shetaut Neter.

32. THE KING OF EGYPT: The Struggle of Good and Evil for Control of the World and The Human Soul ISBN 1-8840564-44-5 $18.95 Have you seen movies like The Lion King, Hamlet, The Odyssey, or The Little Buddha? These have been some of the most popular movies in modern times. The Sema Institute of Yoga is dedicated to researching and presenting the wisdom and culture of ancient Africa. The Script is designed to be produced as a motion picture but may be addapted for the theater as well. 160 pages bound or unbound (specify with your order) $19.95 copyright 1998 By Dr. Muata Ashby

33. FROM EGYPT TO GREECE: The Kamitan Origins of Greek Culture and Religion ISBN: 1-884564-47-X $22.95 U.S. FROM EGYPT TO GREECE This insightful manual is a quick reference to Ancient Egyptian mythology and philosophy and its correlation to what later became known as Greek and Rome mythology and philosophy. It outlines the basic tenets of the mythologies and shoes the ancient origins of Greek culture in Ancient Egypt. This volume also acts as a resource for Colleges students who would like to set up fraternities and sororities based on the original Ancient Egyptian principles of Sheti and Maat philosophy. ISBN: 1-884564-47-X $22.95 U.S.

34. THE FORTY TWO PRECEPTS OF MAAT, THE PHILOSOPHY OF RIGHTEOUS ACTION AND THE ANCIENT EGYPTIAN WISDOM TEXTS <u>ADVANCED STUDIES</u> This manual is designed for use with the 1998 Maat Philosophy Class conducted by Dr. Muata Ashby. This is a detailed study of Maat Philosophy. It contains a compilation of the 42 laws or precepts of Maat and the corresponding principles which they represent along with the teachings of the ancient Egyptian Sages relating to each. Maat philosophy was the basis of Ancient Egyptian society and government as well as the heart of Ancient Egyptian myth and spirituality. Maat is at once a goddess, a cosmic force and a living social doctrine, which promotes social harmony and thereby paves the way for spiritual evolution in all levels of society. ISBN: 1-884564-48-8 $16.95 U.S.

Music Based on the Prt M Hru and other Kemetic Texts

Available on Compact Disc $14.99 and Audio Cassette $9.99

Adorations to the Goddess

Music for Worship of the Goddess

Neter Merri

NEW Egyptian Yoga Music CD
by Sehu Maa
Ancient Egyptian Music CD
Instrumental Music played on reproductions of Ancient Egyptian Instruments– Ideal for <u>meditation</u> and reflection on the Divine and for the practice of spiritual programs and <u>Yoga exercise sessions.</u>

©1999 By Muata Ashby
CD $14.99 –

MERIT'S INSPIRATION
NEW Egyptian Yoga Music CD
by Sehu Maa
Ancient Egyptian Music CD
Instrumental Music played on reproductions of Ancient Egyptian Instruments– Ideal for <u>meditation</u> and reflection on the Divine and for the practice of spiritual programs and <u>Yoga exercise sessions.</u>
©1999 By
Muata Ashby
CD $14.99 –
UPC# 761527100429

ANORATIONS TO RA AND HETHERU
NEW Egyptian Yoga Music CD
By Sehu Maa (Muata Ashby)
Based on the Words of Power of Ra and HetHeru
played on reproductions of Ancient Egyptian Instruments **Ancient Egyptian Instruments used: Voice, Clapping, Nefer Lute, Tar Drum, Sistrums, Cymbals** – The Chants, Devotions, Rhythms and Festive Songs Of the Neteru – Ideal for meditation, and devotional singing and dancing.

The Path of Divine Love

©1999 By Muata Ashby
CD $14.99 –
UPC# 761527100221

SONGS TO ASAR ASET AND HERU
NEW
Egyptian Yoga Music CD
By Sehu Maa

played on reproductions of Ancient Egyptian Instruments– The Chants, Devotions, Rhythms and Festive Songs Of the Neteru - Ideal for meditation, and devotional singing and dancing.
Based on the Words of Power of Asar (Asar), Aset (Aset) and Heru (Heru) Om Asar Aset Heru is the third in a series of musical explorations of the Kemetic (Ancient Egyptian) tradition of music. Its ideas are based on the Ancient Egyptian Religion of Asar, Aset and Heru and it is designed for listening, meditation and worship. ©1999 By Muata Ashby
CD $14.99 –
UPC# 761527100122

HAARI OM: ANCIENT EGYPT MEETS INDIA IN MUSIC
NEW Music CD
By Sehu Maa

The Chants, Devotions, Rhythms and Festive Songs Of the Ancient Egypt and India, harmonized and played on reproductions of ancient instruments along with modern instruments and beats. Ideal for meditation, and devotional singing and dancing.
Haari Om is the fourth in a series of musical explorations of the Kemetic (Ancient Egyptian) and Indian traditions of music, chanting and devotional spiritual practice. Its ideas are based on the Ancient Egyptian Yoga spirituality and Indian Yoga spirituality.
©1999 By Muata Ashby
CD $14.99 –

UPC# 761527100528

RA AKHU: THE GLORIOUS LIGHT
NEW
Egyptian Yoga Music CD
By Sehu Maa

The fifth collection of original music compositions based on the Teachings and Words of The Trinity, the God Asar and the Goddess Nebethet, the Divinity Aten, the God Heru, and the Special Meditation Hekau or Words of Power of Ra from the Ancient Egyptian Tomb of Seti I and more...

played on reproductions of Ancient Egyptian Instruments and modern instruments - Ancient Egyptian Instruments used: Voice, Clapping, Nefer Lute, Tar Drum, Sistrums, Cymbals

— The Chants, Devotions, Rhythms and Festive Songs Of the Neteru – Ideal for meditation, and devotional singing and dancing.

©1999 By Muata Ashby
CD $14.99 –
UPC# 761527100825

GLORIES OF THE DIVINE MOTHER
Based on the hieroglyphic text of the worship of Goddess Net.
The Glories of The Great Mother
©2000 Muata Ashby
CD $14.99 UPC# 761527101129`

Order Form

Telephone orders: Call Toll Free: 1(305) 378-6253. Have your AMEX, Optima, Visa or MasterCard ready.

Fax orders: 1-(305) 378-6253   E-MAIL ADDRESS: Semayoga@aol.com

Postal Orders: Sema Institute of Yoga, P.O. Box 570459, Miami, Fl. 33257. USA.

Please send the following books and / or tapes.

ITEM

_____Cost $_____
_____Cost $_____
_____Cost $_____
_____Cost $_____
_____Cost $_____

Total $_____

Name:_____
Physical Address:_____
City:_____ State:_____ Zip:_____

Sales tax: Please add 6.5% for books shipped to Florida addresses

_____Shipping: $6.50 for first book and .50¢ for each additional

_____Shipping: Outside US $5.00 for first book and $3.00 for each additional

_____Payment:_____

_____Check -Include Driver License #:

    _____

_____Credit card: _____ Visa, _____ MasterCard, _____ Optima, _____ AMEX.

Card number:_____
Name on card:_____ Exp. date:_____/_____

Copyright 1995-2005 Dr. R. Muata Abhaya Ashby
Sema Institute of Yoga
P.O.Box 570459, Miami, Florida, 33257
(305) 378-6253 Fax: (305) 378-6253

www.ingramcontent.com/pod-product-compliance
Lightning Source LLC
Chambersburg PA
CBHW081107080526
44587CB00021B/3489